New York State
Regents Exam

CHEMISTRY

Second Edition

William Yu Wang, M.S.
Lower East Side Preparatory
New York, NY

Dana R. Freeman, M.Ed., M.A.
R. L. Osborne High School
Marietta, GA

Simon & Schuster

SYDNEY · LONDON · SINGAPORE · NEW YORK

Kaplan Books
Published by Simon & Schuster
1230 Avenue of the Americas
New York, New York 10020

For bulk sales to schools, colleges, and universities, please contact Vice President of Special Sales, Simon & Schuster Special Markets, 1633 Broadway, 8th Floor, New York, NY 10019.

Project Editor: Eileen Mager
Contributing Editor: Trent Anderson
Cover Design: Cheung Tai
Production Editor: Maude Spekes
Interior Production: Amparo Graf
Desktop Publishing Manager: Michael Shevlin
Managing Editor: David Chipps
Executive Editor: Del Franz

Special thanks are extended to Rich Christiano, David Headly, and Sara Pearl.

The New York State Regents exams in this book were administered in August 1988, June 1996, August 1996, June 1997, and August 1997. These exams are reprinted by permission of the University of the State of New York/State Education Department.

The study strategies in chapter 2, "Strategies for Mastering the Test," are excerpted from Learning Power by Cynthia Johnson and Drew Johnson (published by Kaplan and Simon & Schuster), and are used by permission.

Manufactured in the United States of America
Published simultaneously in Canada

Second Edition, February 2000

10 9 8 7 6 5 4 3 2 1

ISBN 0-684-87161-0
ISSN 1095-1881

CONTENTS

How to Use This Book

This book is designed to prepare students to take the New York State Regents Chemistry Exam. As a general outline to the material you are studying, it contains the most important facts you'll need to know and understand to succeed on the Regents exam. It's a powerful tool, for the student who can use it correctly. This book can also be used as supplemental or diagnostic material by teachers or tutors who are teaching the New York State Regents chemistry course.

Study Tips

The introduction is broken down into two chapters. The first chapter summarizes the New York State Regents Chemistry Syllabus and explains the contents of recent New York State Regents Chemistry Examinations. The second chapter offers expert tips for mastering the Regents exam.

Diagnostic Test

There are five actual, full-length New York State Regents exams in this book. The first practice test is a diagnostic test—by taking it and checking your answers, you will be able to identify your weak points and begin your work of shoring them up. The answer to every question will point you to the chapter in the book where problems like the one tested in the question are further explained. Consult the relevant chapter in your textbook to further solidify your understanding of each concept.

Content Review

The chapters after the diagnostic test are a comprehensive review of the material you are learning in class. Read these in the order that will help you best. For example, you can hit the chapters you identified as weak points in the diagnostic test first, and then read all of the others later. Or, if you've given yourself enough time, you can start at the beginning and read straight through to the end. There is no wrong way to read it . . . the most important thing is that you get the information you need to do well on the Chemistry Regents.

Practice Tests

As stated earlier, this book contains five real New York State Regents exams (the diagnostic test in the beginning of the book, and four others at the end). The first page of each Regents exam shows the original date the exam was administered in New York State. The Board of Regents has consistently maintained the structure and content of the Regents exams over the years, so tests that were administered more recently are in no way more "accurate" or "up-to date" than the older tests. The Regents exam to be given this year is as similar to the exams given last year as the exams given ten years ago.

If you score lower than you expect at first, don't panic: You're the only one who will see these practice scores, and you have the benefit of filling the gaps in your knowledge before taking the actual Regents exam. If you can do well on these practice tests, you're well on the road to mastering the Regents!

Part 1

An Overview of the Exam

Chapter 1

The Regents Exam:
Structure and Content

What is the Regents Chemistry Examination?

Regents curricula are an inescapable part of academic life for New York State high school students. Questions on Regents Chemistry examinations are drawn directly from the Regents Chemistry Syllabus, which was developed to provide for a course of study that "presents a modern view of chemistry suitable for students with a wide range of skills and abilities." The material presented in this syllabus is organized into 12 units:

Topic	Fundamental Unit in Syllabus	Extended Unit (*) in Syllabus
Matter and energy	1	
Atomic structure	2	
Bonding	3	
Periodic table	4	
Mathematics of chemistry	5	5*
Kinetics and equilibrium	6	6*
Acids and bases	7	
Redox and electrochemistry	8	8*
Organic chemistry	9	9*
Applications of chemical principles		10*
Nuclear chemistry		11*
Laboratory activities		12*

The Regents Chemistry Exam is divided into two parts. Part One of the Regents Chemistry examination is composed of 56 questions, the topics of which are taken from units 1 through 9, and counts for 65 percent of the examination score. Part Two of the Regents Chemistry examination consists of 12 different groups; students must choose seven of these groups and answer all five questions in each group. This part counts for 35 percent of the examination score.

In-depth knowledge of units 1 through 9 is required of all students; additionally, an understanding of a minimum of two sections each from Units 5*, 6*, 7*, 8*, 9*, 10*, 11*, and 12* is also required. The questions in units 1 through 4 of the Regents Chemistry Syllabus carry more weight on the exam than the questions in units 5 through 9 and 10 through 12. Actually, you can pass the exam with a thorough review of units 1 through 7. The table on the following page confirms what you need to know.

Questions by Topic: Regents Chemistry Exams 1992–1996						
Topics	Units In Syllabus (* = extended unit)	Percentage (%) of Questions from This Unit Asked in Examination of Indicated Year				
		1992	1993	1994	1995	1996
Matter and energy	1	14.3	12.1	11.0	12.1	12.1
Atomic structure	2	15.3	14.3	17.6	12.1	13.2
Bonding	3	11.0	13.2	12.1	14.3	12.1
Periodic table	4	13.2	12.1	10.0	13.2	14.3
Mathematics of chemistry	5	6.6	5.5	7.7	7.7	6.6
Mathematics of chemistry	5*	3.4	5.5	3.4	3.4	3.4
Total fundamental and extended units		10.0	11.0	11.0	11.0	11.0
Kinetics and equilibrium	6	7.8	8.9	8.9	8.9	9.9
Kinetics and equilibrium	6*	4.3	3.2	3.2	3.2	2.2
Total fundamental and extended units		11.0	12.1	12.1	12.1	12.1
Acids and bases	7	13.2	13.2	13.2	13.2	13.2
TOTAL		89.1	88.0	87.0	88.0	88.0

We have analyzed recent Regents Chemistry exams and have identified the 40 most tested issues. They are:

1. Definition and properties of compounds and mixtures (unit 1—matter and energy)

2. Calculation of calories (unit 1—matter and energy)

3. Chemical change and exothermic reactions (unit 1—matter and energy)

4. Solving of problems using the combined (Boyle's and Charles's) gas laws (unit 1—matter and energy)

5. Phase—and related energy—change (unit 1—matter and energy)

6. Model of atomic structure and properties of nucleons, electrons, etc. (unit 2—atomic structure)

7. Atomic number and mass, and atomic isotopes (unit 2—atomic structure)

8. Electron configuration including quanta and spectra (unit 2—atomic structure)

9. Orbital model of atoms (unit 2—atomic structure)

10. Radioactivity and half-life (unit 2—atomic structure)

11. Bonding and electronegativity values (unit 3—bonding)

12. Comparing covalent bonds with ionic bonds (unit 3—bonding)

13. Molecule-ion attraction (unit 3—bonding)

14. Naming and writing formulae of chemical compounds (unit 3—bonding)

15. Properties of groups on the periodic table (unit 4—periodic table)

16. Properties of periods on the periodic table (unit 4—periodic table)

17. How radii of ions and atoms change on the periodic table (unit 4—periodic table)

18. Chemistry of groups 1, 2, 17, and 18 (unit 4—periodic table)

19. Definition and calculation of mole (unit 5—mathematics of chemistry)

20. Percent composition of compounds (unit 5—mathematics of chemistry)

21. Differentiating between moles, grams, and molarity (unit 5 and 5*—mathematics of chemistry)

22. Effects of solute on solvent (unit 6 and 6*—kinetics and equilibrium)

23. Potential energy diagram (unit 6 and 6*—kinetics and equilibrium)

24. Factors affecting rate of reactions, especially catalysts (unit 6 and 6*—kinetics and equilibrium)

25. Law of chemical equilibrium (unit 6 and 6*—kinetics and equilibrium)

26. Entropy and free energy change of chemical reactions (unit 6 and 6*—kinetics and equilibrium)

27. Properties of acids and bases (unit 7—acids and bases)

28. Calculating neutralization concentrations (unit 7—acids and bases)

29. Identifying conjugate pairs (unit 7—acids and bases)

30. Calculating and interpreting the values of K_w and pH (unit 7—acids and bases)

31. Calculating oxidation numbers (unit 8 and 8*—redox and electrochemistry)

32. Identifying reduction or oxidation half-reactions (unit 8 and 8*—redox and electrochemistry)

33. Differentiating reducing agents from oxidizing agents (unit 8 and 8*—redox and electrochemistry)

34. Understanding isomers and structural formulas (unit 9 and 9*—organic chemistry)

35. Distinguishing between and among alkanes, alkenes, alkynes and the benzene series (unit 9 and 9*—organic chemistry)

36. Recognizing those functional groups of organic compounds, such as ketones, esters, ethers, etc. (unit 9 and 9*—organic chemistry)

37. Understanding the Haber process and fractional distillation (unit 10*—applications of chemical principles)

38. Understanding the principles of accelerators and nuclear reactors (unit 11*—nuclear chemistry)

39. Laboratory measurements, skills, and reports (unit 12*—laboratory activities)

40. Demonstrating knowledge and application of reference tables (all units)

Chapter 2

Strategies for Mastering the Test

TACTICS FOR TAKING THE REGENTS EXAM

During the exam, the following tactics should be used wherever applicable.

Following Directions

You need to pay very careful attention to directions. Read over the directions more than once, and don't proceed to the quesions until you have a grasp of what the questions require. Ask the proctor for help if you don't understand.

It helps to be thoroughly familiar with the examination format before the test. Know how the exam is scored and what questions get the most credit. This will prevent considerable anxiety and loss of time during the actual examination.

Reading Carefully

During the examination, read directions and questions very carefully; make sure that you understand what is being asked before you answer. After reading the questions thoroughly, predict an answer, and then look for the choice that best matches your prediction. If you don't know an answer, use common sense or eliminate the least likely answers.

Skipping Questions

Skip those questions that you are not sure of and move on to the next question. This way you can get the most points with the highest certainty within the least amount of time. When you have finished answering the easy questions, go back to those you skipped and try them.

When you skip a question, circle it or make a mark in the margin to remind you to return to it later. Remember to check to make sure you are answering each question in the right spot on the answer sheet.

Attacking the Difficult Questions

Tackle your difficult questions by using the tactics listed below after you finish all the easy questions:

- Rephrase a question, if necessary, to simplify.

- Identify what concepts or data are being tested. Some of the difficult questions use the reference information you obtained from the easy questions.

- Avoid any choice that is correct in itself but is not an answer to the question.

- Answer all questions, even by educated guesses, because *you are not penalized for wrong answers*. Eliminate any answers you know are wrong and then make a guess. Remember: Uncertain answers are better than no answers because they may be correct!

Reviewing Your Work

When you have extra time, review your work or the questions that you are not so sure about. Rethinking with more time and in a relaxed mood often results in finding errors and making better decisions.

Going with Your First Impression

As a general rule, your first impression about the answer to the question is usually the correct one. Therefore, do not change your first impression answer unless you determine that it is absolutely incorrect.

Summary of Test-Taking Tips

- Follow the directions for all exam questions.

- Read questions thoroughly, then predict an answer, and look for the answer that best matches your prediction.

- Skip difficult questions and do easy questions first.

- Avoid correct answers that don't actually answer the question.

- Answer all questions (or the full number your are instructed to answer) to get possible credit, even if you have to guess (eliminate answer choices you're sure are wrong).

- Review your work when you have time.

- Keep your first impression answers unchanged unless you are absolutely sure that they are incorrect.

YOUR INITIAL PREPARATION

Preparation for the Regents Chemistry Examination begins with fulfillment of the prerequisites for the course itself. Students who wish to enroll in the Regents Chemistry course must have a solid foundation in high school algebra. In order to be able to understand and use the principles of chemistry introduced in this course, students must be familiar with the use of standard notation of numbers, significant figures, metric system of units, and dimensional analysis (inclusion of units in mathematical computations) and have an understanding of direct and inverse relationships.

Regular attendance in class is crucial since the instructor will, invariably, be teaching directly *from* the Syllabus and *toward* the examination. Flexibility within—not lengthy digressions from—the curriculum is allowed: There is nothing extraneous here. *Everything* you learn is important! Of course, all the usual scholastic admonitions apply:

- Prepare for classroom work by reading ahead the night before; i.e., be at least nominally familiar with the material before your teacher formally introduces it to you.

- Take careful class notes and review them completely as soon as you can after class.

- Do all homework assignments in a timely fashion, submit them to your teacher for evaluation, and make sure you understand what you got wrong—and why.

A few words on studying chemistry: Unlike any other discipline—including physics—so much of the understanding of chemistry is predicated on comprehension of an extraordinary phenomenon: the nature of atomic structure and the interactions of atomic particles. If physics can be thought of as measuring to infinity on a ruler from 1 to far beyond a trillion, chemistry can be thought of as measuring to infinity between 0 and 1. So much of what happens in chemistry—so very much of what must be learned—cannot be seen. From the outset, students must reconcile themselves to learning by and within abstractions, and concentrate on understanding the logical progression of ideas as one concept builds on another.

The Basics of Body and Soul

To perform well on any test, the readiness of your mind and the wellness of your body are essential. Sometimes, despite your best efforts, the brain busters seize you: boredom, fatigue, and headache. Remember, the chances of you winding up numb, exhausted, and in pain at two in the morning will be minimized if you stay on top of your work. But just in case, here are some general things you can do to keep your motor running:

Watch Your Posture. When you are studying, sit in a chair that is comfortable but fairly stiff. You want to keep your back straight and your shoulders relaxed. Slouching or hunching over can cause your shoulder and neck muscles to tense up, which will give you a nasty headache.

Don't Squint. Squinting can bring on a headache. So can frowning or scowling—two expressions many students wear when they study. Try to keep your jaws and face relaxed. A good way to force your face to relax is to get up and brush your teeth. It loosens up your cheeks and jaws. And it clears up that nasty coffee breath!

Cut Down on Caffeine. Speaking of coffee breath, steer clear of the java, soda, or over-the-counter "pep" pills after dinner. Your brain can only stand so much, and sooner or later, it will demand rest. If you're too wired, you won't get much studying done and you won't get any sleep, so you'll just be tired and cranky when you face your test. Not very smart.

Go to Bed, for Heaven's Sake. Those "brains" who drag themselves in to class on test day moaning about the all-nighter they pulled should be pitied, not admired. Panic and insecurity are what really led them to stay up all night. They probably did not get anything much accomplished. If you have have been pacing your studying all along, there is no reason for you to burn the midnight oil the night before the test. The best favor you can do yourself is to get a good night's sleep so you will be ready to face a long day.

Take "Power Breaks." Don't try to study too much in one sitting. Concentrate for as long as you can—at least one hour—then take a ten-minute power break. Do not turn on the television, call a friend, or even talk to someone. Just get up, leave your study area, and do something mildly physical while letting your brain go blank. Walk briskly around the block. Do jumping jacks, sit-ups, or stretches. Punch a punching bag. Don't think about the material you are studying for those ten minutes. You are basically "resetting" your brain so you can start studying again.

The Persistence of Memory

Face it: To prepare for the Regents examination, you will have to memorize lots of facts. Flash cards are great, but there are a few more tricks you can use.

Sing Out Loud. It's pretty easy to remember music lyrics, right? Try singing some fact, formula, definition, or series to the tune of one of your favorite songs—you'll get the song stuck in your head, but with your new lyrics. Or make up a suitable tune of your own. Don't worry about rhyming—just sing the words you want to remember.

Give It Rhyme or Rhythm. This is for the tone deaf. You can get the same benefits of song writing by rephrasing an important piece of information so it has rhyme and/or rhythm. One example of this you have probably heard is, "In fourteen hundred and ninety-two/Columbus sailed the ocean blue." It is not necessary to give something both rhythm and rhyme, and your rhymes don't necessarily have to make perfect sense.

Visualize Something Weird or Funny. Try to come up with an image that reminds you of the fact you are trying to memorize. To remember Napoleon's defeat at Waterloo, for example, you might picture Napoleon going down the toilet—there is water in the toilet, some people call the toilet the "loo," and the fact that he's in a toilet will remind you that he was defeated in the Battle of Waterloo.

Find Sound-Alike Words. This works well for foreign language test, especially if combined with a visualization technique. For example, if you are trying to remember that the Spanish word *trabajar* means "to work," try to think of something *trabajar* sounds like. It is pronounced "trah-bah-HAR," which kind of (sort of) sounds like "travel far," right? If you picture a traveling salesman with a suitcase or an airline pilot, you can associate working with "travel far," which will make you remember *trabajar*.

Use Acronyms. Acronyms are words formed from the first letter or letters of a group of words—like SCUBA, which stands for *self-contained underwater breathing apparatus.* You can use acronyms to help you remember a series or set of facts. Sometimes you can't make the acronym into a real word, but as long as you can kind of pronounce it, it works. An example you probably already know is the name "Roy G. Biv." This is an acronym for the colors of the spectrum: red, orange, yellow, green, blue, indigo, violet.

If you can't make a word with the first letters of the series of words you want to remember, try making a new sentence that uses those letters. If you're trying to memorize the different levels of classification scientists use to categorize animals, you would be trying to learn: Kingdom, Phylum, Class, Order, Family, Genus, Species. That's not easy to remember, and neither is the acronym KPCOFGS. But you could easily remember the sentence "King Philip cooks omelets for good servants."

Ask Your Friends to Quiz You. If there are just a few pesky facts and figures you can't seem to memorize, ask your friends' help. Give each friend a different question and answer. Every time they see you or call you, they have to ask you that question.

Bringing the Things You Need

Be sure to bring everything needed for the exam to your test site. These include a black ballpoint pen, a pencil, a rubber eraser, a reliable watch, and your photo ID or test admission ticket. Do not rely on borrowing from others. Find out what else you will be allowed to bring and what, if anything, will be provided by the school. Finally, plan to dress comfortably, and be ready to adjust to a room that is overly warm or cool (dress in layers).

Good luck on the Regents Exam!

Part II

Diagnostic Test

Sample Regents Exam 1—August 1988
Diagnostic Test

Part I

Answer all 56 questions in this part. [65]

Directions (1–56): For *each* statement or question, select the word or expression that, of those given, best completes the statement or answers the question. Record your answer on the separate answer sheet in accordance with the directions on the front page of this booklet.

1 Energy is being added to a given sample. Compared to the Celsius temperature of the sample, the Kelvin temperature
  1 will always be 273° greater
  2 will always be 273° lower
  3 will have the same reading at 0°
  4 will have the same reading at 273°

2 At STP, which element has a definite shape and volume?
  (1) Ag   (3) Ne
  (2) Hg   (4) Xe

3 Which substance can be decomposed by a chemical change?
  1 sodium   3 sulfur
  2 argon   4 ammonia

4 What is the vapor pressure of water at 105°C?
  (1) 4.6 torr   (3) 906.1 torr
  (2) 760.0 torr   (4) 1074.6 torr

5 A sample of glass is a supercooled liquid rather than a true solid because it has
  1 a definite volume
  2 no definite volume
  3 a crystalline structure
  4 no crystalline structure

6 Which orbital notation represents an atom of beryllium in the ground state?

7 A neutral atom in the ground state contains 16 electrons. What is the total number of electrons in the $2p$ sublevel?
  (1) 6   (3) 8
  (2) 2   (4) 16

8 Which is the electron dot symbol for a chlorine atom in the ground state?

9 Which of the following 10-gram samples of radioisotope will decay to the greatest extent in 28 days?
  (1) $^{32}_{15}P$ (3) $^{220}_{87}Fr$
  (2) $^{85}_{36}Kr$ (4) $^{131}_{53}I$

10 A neutral atom with 6 electrons and 8 neutrons is an isotope of
  1 carbon   3 nitrogen
  2 silicon   4 oxygen

11 Which element has a completely filled third principal energy level?
  (1) Ar   (3) Fe
  (2) N   (4) Zn

12 Which of the following compounds has the highest normal boiling point?
  (1) $H_2O(\ell)$ (3) $H_2Se(\ell)$
  (2) $H_2S(\ell)$ (4) $H_2Te(\ell)$

13 What is the empirical formula of a compound with the molecular formula $C_6H_{12}O_6$?
  (1) $C_4H_8O_4$ (3) $C_2H_4O_2$
  (2) $C_3H_6O_3$ (4) CH_2O

14 Based on Reference Table C, which element exhibits the strongest van der Waals force of attraction between molecules?

1 chlorine   3 nitrogen
2 hydrogen   4 oxygen

15 Which molecule is nonpolar due to a symmetrical distribution of charge?

(1) $O=C=O$

(3) $H-N-H$ with H below

(2) H—O—H (bent)

(4) $H-Cl$

16 In a sample of solid $Ba(NO_3)_2$, the ratio of barium ions to nitrate ions is

(1) 1:1   (3) 1:3
(2) 1:2   (4) 1:6

17 Which substance is a good conductor of electricity in both the solid and liquid phases?

1 a metallic substance
2 an ionic substance
3 a network substance
4 a molecular substance

18 The formula for nitrogen (IV) oxide is

(1) N_4O (3) N_2O
(2) NO_4 (4) NO_2

19 All isotopes of which element in Group 16 (VIA) are naturally radioactive?

(1) S   (3) Po
(2) Se   (4) Te

20 Which elements contain atoms that form colored ions and have more than one positive oxidation state?

1 alkali metals   3 noble gases
2 alkaline earths   4 transition elements

21 Low ionization energies are most characteristic of atoms that are

1 metals   3 metalloids
2 nonmetals   4 noble gases

22 Which of the following elements has the most pronounced metallic properties?

(1) C   (3) Co
(2) Al   (4) Rb

23 The halogen with the highest electronegativity is

1 fluorine   3 bromine
2 chlorine   4 iodine

24 Which element has an atomic radius that is greater than its ionic radius?

(1) S   (3) F
(2) K   (4) O

25 What is the total number of moles of solute contained in 0.50 liter of 3.0 M HCl?

(1) 1.0   (3) 3.0
(2) 1.5   (4) 3.5

26 A compound has the empirical formula CH and a molecular mass of 78. What is the molecular formula of the compound?

(1) C_2H_2 (3) C_4H_4
(2) C_3H_3 (4) C_6H_6

27 The percent by mass of nitrogen in N_2O is

(1) 8.0   (3) 32
(2) 16   (4) 64

28 A solution containing 55 grams of NH_4Cl in 100. grams of water is saturated at a temperature of

(1) 47°C   (3) 67°C
(2) 57°C   (4) 77°C

29 Given the equation:

$$C_3H_8(g) + 5O_2(g) \rightarrow 3CO_2(g) + 4H_2O(g)$$

At STP, how many liters of $O_2(g)$ are needed to completely burn 5.0 liters of $C_3H_8(g)$?

(1) 5.0   (3) 15
(2) 10.   (4) 25

30 Which change results in an increase in entropy?

(1) $H_2O(g) \rightarrow H_2O(\ell)$ (3) $H_2O(s) \rightarrow H_2O(\ell)$
(2) $H_2O(\ell) \rightarrow H_2O(s)$ (4) $H_2O(g) \rightarrow H_2O(s)$

31 Based on Reference Table *I*, which reaction is endothermic?

(1) $NaOH(s) \xrightarrow{H_2O} Na^+(aq) + OH^-(aq)$

(2) $NH_4Cl(s) \xrightarrow{H_2O} NH_4^+(aq) + Cl^-(aq)$

(3) $CO(g) + \frac{1}{2}O_2(g) \rightarrow CO_2(g)$

(4) $CH_4(g) + 2O_2(g) \rightarrow CO_2(g) + 2H_2O(\ell)$

32 In the potential energy diagram below, which arrow represents the potential energy of the activated complex?

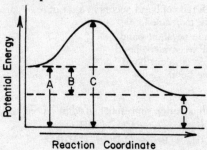

(1) *A*   (3) *C*
(2) *B*   (4) *D*

33 The reaction $A(g) + B(g) \rightarrow C(g)$ is occurring in the apparatus shown below.

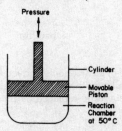

The rate of reaction can be decreased by increasing the

1 pressure on the reactants
2 temperature of the reactants
3 concentration of reactant $A(g)$
4 volume of the reaction chamber

34 Based on Reference Table *L*, which compound is the weakest electrolyte?

(1) HI   (3) HCl
(2) HF   (4) HBr

35 Which potential energy diagram indicates a reaction that must occur spontaneously?

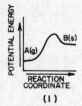

(1)

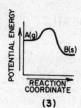

(3)

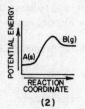

(2)

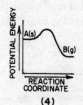

(4)

36 According to the Arrhenius theory, a substance that is classified as an acid will always yield

(1) $H^+(aq)$ (3) $F^-(aq)$
(2) $K^+(aq)$ (4) $I^-(aq)$

37 If the $[OH^-]$ equals 1×10^{-10} at 298 K for a given solution, the $[H^+]$ of the solution equals

(1) 1×10^{-4} (3) 1×10^{-10}
(2) 1×10^{-7} (4) 1×10^{-14}

38 If 100. milliliters of 0.75 M HCl is required to exactly neutralize 50. milliliters of KOH, what is the concentration of the base?

(1) 1.0 M   (3) 0.75 M
(2) 1.5 M   (4) 0.25 M

39 Which equation correctly represents the K_w for water?

(1) $K_w = \dfrac{[H^+]}{[OH^-]}$

(2) $K_w = [H^+][OH^-]$

(3) $K_w = \dfrac{[OH^-]}{[H^+]}$

(4) $K_w = [H^+] - [OH^-]$

40 In the reaction $H_2S + NH_3 \rightleftharpoons NH_4^+ + HS^-$, the two Brönsted bases are

(1) NH_3 and HS^-　　(3) H_2S and NH_3
(2) NH_3 and NH_4^+　(4) H_2S and HS^-

41 In which compound does chlorine have an oxidation number of +5?
(1) $HClO$　　(3) $HClO_3$
(2) $HClO_2$　(4) $HClO_4$

42 Elements that readily gain electrons tend to have
1 high ionization energy and high electronegativity
2 high ionization energy and low electronegativity
3 low ionization energy and low electronegativity
4 low ionization energy and high electronegativity

43 Which half-reaction correctly represents reduction?
(1) $Ca^{2+} \rightarrow Ca + 2e^-$
(2) $Ca^{2+} + 2e^- \rightarrow Ca$
(3) $2F^- + 2e^- \rightarrow F_2$
(4) $2F^- \rightarrow F_2 + 2e^-$

44 Which equation represents a redox reaction?
(1) $NaCl + AgNO_3 \rightarrow NaNO_3 + AgCl$
(2) $HCl + KOH \rightarrow KCl + H_2O$
(3) $2KClO_3 \rightarrow 2KCl + 3O_2$
(4) $H_2CO_3 \rightarrow H_2O + CO_2$

45 An electrolytic cell differs from an electrochemical cell in that the electrolytic cell
1 involves redox
2 is exothermic
3 produces an electric current
4 uses an applied electric current

46 Given the unbalanced equation:
　$\_Mg(s) + \_Fe^{3+} \rightarrow \_Mg^{2+} + \_Fe(s)$
When the equation is completely balanced using smallest whole numbers, the coefficient of Mg(s) will be
(1) 1　　(3) 3
(2) 2　　(4) 4

47 Which functional group is found in all organic acids?

(1) $-\overset{\overset{\textstyle H}{|}}{\underset{\underset{\textstyle H}{|}}{C}}-H$　　(3) $-\overset{\overset{\textstyle H}{|}}{C}=O$

(2) $-\overset{\overset{\textstyle H}{|}}{\underset{\underset{\textstyle H}{|}}{C}}-OH$　(4) $-\overset{\overset{\textstyle O}{\|}}{C}-OH$

48 Which type of bond occurs in a saturated hydrocarbon molecule?
1 single covalent bond
2 double covalent bond
3 triple covalent bond
4 ionic bond

49 Which equation represents an addition reaction?
(1) $CH_4 + 2O_2 \rightarrow CO_2 + 2H_2O$
(2) $C_2H_6 + Br_2 \rightarrow C_2H_5Br + HBr$
(3) $C_3H_6 + Cl_2 \rightarrow C_3H_6Cl_2$
(4) $C_4H_{10} + Cl_2 \rightarrow C_4H_9Cl + HCl$

50 To which series does the hydrocarbon with the structure shown at the right belong?

1 acetylene　　　3 benzene
2 olefin　　　　4 paraffin

51 When the name of an alcohol is derived from the corresponding alkane, the final "-e" of the name of the alkane should be replaced by the suffix
(1) "-al"　　(3) "-one"
(2) "-ol"　　(4) "-ole"

　Note that questions 52 through 56 have only three choices.

52 As the elements in Period 3 of the Periodic Table are considered from left to right, the degree of nonmetallic character of each successive element tends to
1 decrease
2 increase
3 remain the same

53 Given the reaction at equilibrium:
$$H_2(g) + Cl_2(g) \rightleftharpoons 2HCl(g)$$
As the pressure increases at constant temperature, the number of moles of HCl
1 decreases
2 increases
3 remains the same

54 As a radioactive element emits gamma radiation only, the atomic number of the element
1 decreases
2 increases
3 remains the same

55 As the pressure on a liquid is changed from 700 torr to 800 torr, the temperature at which the liquid will boil
1 decreases
2 increases
3 remains the same

56 As sodium phosphate dissolves in 100 milliliters of pure water, the pH of the resulting solution
1 decreases
2 increases
3 remains the same

Part II

This part consists of twelve groups, each containing five questions. Each group tests a major area of the course. Choose seven of these twelve groups. Be sure that you answer all five questions in each group chosen. Record the answers to these questions on the separate answer sheet in accordance with the directions on the front page of this booklet.   [35]

Group 1 — Matter and Energy

If you choose this group, be sure to answer questions 57 – 61.

57 The diagrams below represent four 500-milliliter flasks. Each flask contains the gas represented by its symbol. All gas samples are at STP.

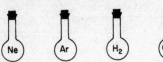

Each flask contains the same number of
1 atoms, only
2 molecules, only
3 atoms and molecules
4 atoms, but different numbers of molecules

58 An ideal gas is made up of gas particles that
1 have volume
2 can be liquefied
3 attract each other
4 are in random motion

59 A pressure of 1140 millimeters of mercury is equal to how many atmospheres of pressure?
(1) 1.00   (3) 0.670
(2) 2.00   (4) 1.50

60 In substances that sublime, the intermolecular forces of attraction are
1 weak and the vapor pressure is low
2 weak and the vapor pressure is high
3 strong and the vapor pressure is low
4 strong and the vapor pressure is high

61 At standard pressure, the steam-water equilibrium temperature occurs at
(1) 0 K   (3) 273 K
(2) 100 K   (4) 373 K

Group 2 — Atomic Structure

If you choose this group, be sure to answer questions 62–66.

62 The nuclides $^{14}_{6}C$ and $^{14}_{7}N$ are similar in that they both have the same
1 mass number   3 number of neutrons
2 atomic number   4 nuclear charge

63 Which principal energy level of an atom contains an electron with the *lowest* energy?
(1) $n = 1$ (3) $n = 3$
(2) $n = 2$ (4) $n = 4$

64 An alpha particle has the same composition as a
1 hydrogen nucleus   3 beryllium nucleus
2 deuterium nucleus   4 helium nucleus

65 What is the nuclear charge of an atom with a mass of 23 and an atomic number of 11?
(1) 11 +   (3) 23 +
(2) 12 +   (4) 34 +

66 In the diagram below, the radiation from a radioactive source is being separated as it passes between electrically charged plates. What are the three types of radiation observed on the detector?

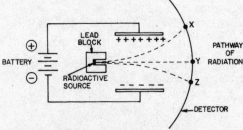

(1) X = alpha, Y = beta, Z = gamma
(2) X = gamma, Y = beta, Z = alpha
(3) X = beta, Y = gamma, Z = alpha
(4) X = gamma, Y = alpha, Z = beta

Group 3 — Bonding

If you choose this group, be sure to answer questions 67–71.

67 When the equation __Al(s) + __O_2(g) → __Al_2O_3(s) is correctly balanced using smallest whole numbers, the sum of the coefficients will be

(1) 9   (3) 3
(2) 7   (4) 12

68 Which type of bonds are formed when calcium atoms react with oxygen atoms?

1 polar covalent   3 ionic
2 coordinate covalent   4 hydrogen

69 Which is a nonpolar molecule containing a non-polar covalent bond?

(1) CO_2 (3) I_2
(2) H_2O (4) NH_3

70 A proton (H^+) could form a coordinate covalent bond with

(1) H:H

(3)
$$H:\overset{\displaystyle H}{\underset{\displaystyle H}{\ddot{C}}}:H$$

(2) $\left[\text{H:} \right]^-$

(4)
$$\left[H:\overset{\displaystyle \ddot{H}}{\underset{\displaystyle H}{\ddot{N}}}:H \right]^+$$

71 A crystalline solid has a high melting point and is a good conductor of electricity in the liquid state. This solid could be

(1) CO_2 (3) $C_6H_{12}O_6$
(2) Hg   (4) KCl

Group 4 — Periodic Table

If you choose this group, be sure to answer questions 72–76.

72 In the modern Periodic Table, the elements are arranged according to

1 atomic mass   3 oxidation number
2 atomic number   4 mass number

73 How many halogens are in Period 3 of the Periodic Table?

(1) 1   (3) 3
(2) 2   (4) 4

74 An atom of an element contains 20 protons, 20 neutrons, and 20 electrons. This element is

1 an alkali metal
2 an alkaline earth metal
3 a halogen
4 a noble gas

75 Given the reaction:
$$M + 2H_2O → M(OH)_2 + H_2$$
The metal represented by M is most likely a metal from Group

(1) 1 (IA)   (3) 11 (IB)
(2) 2 (IIA)   (4) 13 (IIIA)

76 Which element in Period 3 has the greatest tendency to gain electrons?

(1) Na   (3) Cl
(2) Si   (4) Ar

Group 5 — Mathematics of Chemistry

If you choose this group, be sure to answer questions 77–81.

77 Given the reaction:

$$3Cu + 8HNO_3 \rightarrow 3Cu(NO_3)_2 + 2NO + 4H_2O$$

The total number of grams of Cu needed to produce 1.0 mole of $Cu(NO_3)_2$ is

(1) 32   (3) 128
(2) 64   (4) 192

78 Which of the following gases will diffuse most rapidly at STP?

(1) He   (3) O_2
(2) Ne   (4) N_2

79 What is the total number of molecules of SO_2 in a 0.10-mole sample of SO_2?

(1) 6.0×10^{21} (3) 6.0×10^{23}
(2) 6.0×10^{22} (4) 6.0×10^{24}

80 Which of the following solutions, each containing a nonvolatile solute, will boil at the highest temperature?

(1) 1 mole of electrolyte dissolved in 1000 g of H_2O
(2) 2 moles of electrolyte dissolved in 1000 g of H_2O
(3) 1 mole of nonelectrolyte dissolved in 1000 g of H_2O
(4) 2 moles of nonelectrolyte dissolved in 1000 g of H_2O

81 What is the volume occupied by 11.0 grams of a gas at STP if the molecular mass of the gas is 44.0?

(1) 5.60 L   (3) 22.4 L
(2) 11.2 L   (4) 89.6 L

Group 6 — Kinetics and Equilibrium

If you choose this group, be sure to answer questions 82–86.

82 According to Reference Table G, which compound is formed spontaneously from its elements?

(1) $NO(g)$ (3) $HI(g)$
(2) $NO_2(g)$ (4) $HF(g)$

83 Which K_{sp} value indicates a salt with the greatest solubility in water?

(1) 1.0×10^{-4} (3) 3.0×10^{-8}
(2) 2.0×10^{-6} (4) 4.0×10^{-10}

84 The free energy change $(\triangle G)$ that occurs during a chemical reaction is equal to

(1) $\triangle S - T\triangle H$ (3) $\triangle H - T\triangle S$
(2) $\triangle S + T\triangle H$ (4) $\triangle H + T\triangle S$

85 The reaction $A(g) + B(g) \rightleftarrows C(g)$ is at equilibrium, $K = 1$, at 25°C. Which relationship is correct for this reaction at equilibrium at 25°C?

(1) $[C] = [A][B]$ (3) $[C] < [A][B]$
(2) $[C][A] = [B]$ (4) $[C] > [A][B]$

86 A saturated solution is represented by the equation $AgCl(s) + heat \rightleftarrows Ag^+(aq) + Cl^-(aq)$.
Which change will cause an increase in the amount of $AgCl(s)$?

1 a decrease in pressure
2 an increase in temperature
3 a decrease in the concentration of $Ag^+(aq)$
4 an increase in the concentration of $Cl^-(aq)$

☞ GO RIGHT ON TO THE NEXT PAGE.

Group 7 — Acids and Bases

If you choose this group, be sure to answer questions 87–91.

87 Which 0.1 M solution contains the highest concentration of OH^- ions?

  (1) H_2SO_4 (3) KNO_3
  (2) NH_4Cl (4) NaOH

88 According to Reference Table N, which metal will react spontaneously with hydrochloric acid?

  1 gold   3 copper
  2 silver   4 zinc

89 One sample of a solution with a pH of 10 is tested with phenolphthalein and another sample of this solution is tested with litmus. In this solution the color of the litmus is

  1 blue and the phenolphthalein is pink
  2 red and the phenolphthalein is pink
  3 blue and the phenolphthalein is colorless
  4 red and the phenolphthalein is colorless

90 An acid solution exactly neutralized a base solution according to the equation acid + base → salt + water. If the neutralized mixture contained the salt KCl, the pH of the aqueous mixture would be closest to

  (1) 9   (3) 3
  (2) 7   (4) 11

91 Which equation illustrates the amphiprotic properties of a reactant species?

  (1) $NH_3(aq) + H_2O(\ell) \rightarrow NH_4^+(aq) + OH^-(aq)$
  (2) $H_2O(\ell) + H_2O(\ell) \rightarrow H_3O^+(aq) + OH^-(aq)$
  (3) $HCl(aq) + H_2O(\ell) \rightarrow H_3O^+(aq) + Cl^-(aq)$
  (4) $2H_2(g) + O_2(g) \rightarrow 2H_2O(\ell)$

Group 8 — Redox and Electrochemistry

If you choose this group, be sure to answer questions 92–96.

Base your answers to questions 92 and 93 on the diagram of the chemical cell below which is at 298 K and 1 atmosphere.

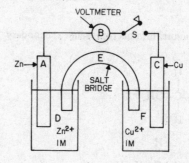

92 When switch S is closed, which series of letters shows the path and direction of the Zn^{2+} ion flow?

  (1) ABC (3) DEF
  (2) CBA (4) FED

93 When switch S is closed, which series of letters shows the path and direction of the electron flow?

  (1) ABC (3) DEF
  (2) CBA (4) FED

94 When the reaction __Cu + __H_2SO_4 → __$CuSO_4$ + __SO_2 + __H_2O is completely balanced using smallest whole numbers, the coefficient of H_2O will be

  (1) 1   (3) 3
  (2) 2   (4) 4

95 Which of the following elements is the *poorest* reducing agent?

  (1) Al   (3) Zn
  (2) H_2 (4) Ba

96 The half-reaction $2H^+(aq) + 2e^- \rightarrow H_2(g)$ will occur when $H^+(aq)$ reacts with

  (1) Pb(s)   (3) $Hg(\ell)$
  (2) Cu(s)   (4) Ag(s)

Group 9 — Organic Chemistry

If you choose this group, be sure to answer questions 97–101.

97 One of the products of condensation polymerization is
1 water
2 an acid
3 a monomer
4 a ketone

98 Which structural formula represents a secondary alcohol?

(1) 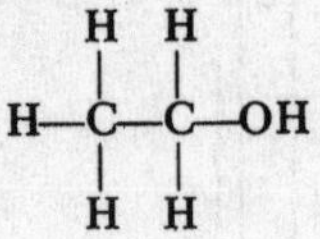
```
    H  H
    |  |
H—C—C—OH
    |  |
    H  H
```

(2) 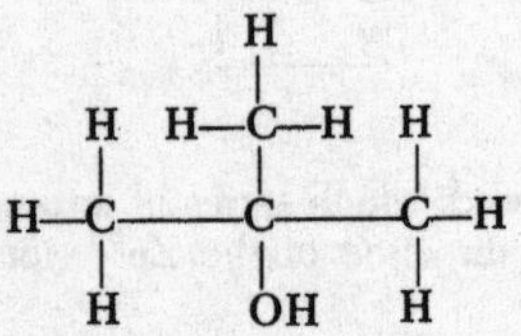
```
         H
         |
    H  H—C—H  H
    |    |    |
H—C————C————C—H
    |    |    |
    H   OH    H
```

(3) 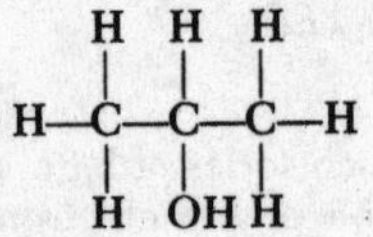
```
    H  H  H
    |  |  |
H—C—C—C—H
    |  |  |
    H OH H
```

(4) 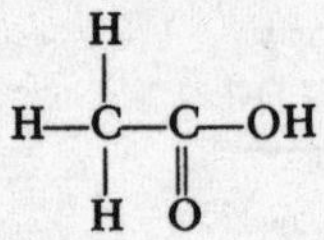
```
    H
    |
H—C—C—OH
    |  ‖
    H  O
```

99 Which compound has the formula shown below?

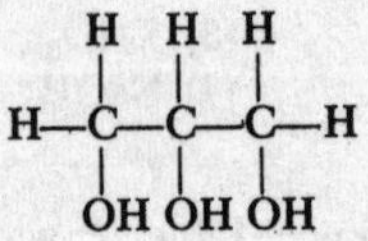

```
    H  H  H
    |  |  |
H—C—C—C—H
    |  |  |
   OH OH OH
```

(1) ethylene glycol
(2) propylene glycol
(3) 1,2-ethanediol
(4) 1,2,3-propanetriol

100 Methanal is the IUPAC name for an
1 aldehyde
2 alcohol
3 acid
4 ether

101 Which general formula represents a ketone?

(1) 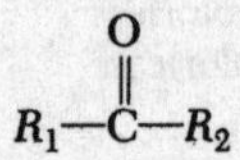
```
      O
      ‖
R₁—C—R₂
```

(2) 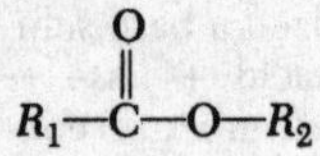
```
      O
      ‖
R₁—C—O—R₂
```

(3) R—OH

(4) 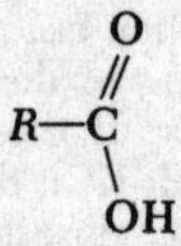
```
      O
      ‖
  R—C
      |
      OH
```

Group 10 — Applications of Chemical Principles

If you choose this group, be sure to answer questions 102–106.

102 In a rechargeable battery system, the discharging reaction is
1 exothermic and the charging reaction is exothermic
2 exothermic and the charging reaction is endothermic
3 endothermic and the charging reaction is exothermic
4 endothermic and the charging reaction is endothermic

103 Which process is used to break down a complex petroleum mixture into simpler mixtures?
1 condensation
2 addition
3 fractional crystallization
4 fractional distillation

104 Which product is produced commercially by the Haber process?
1 sulfuric acid
2 ammonia
3 propane
4 calcium

105 When aluminum exposed to air forms a protective layer, which change occurs?
(1) Al is reduced.
(2) Al is oxidized.
(3) Al^{3+} is reduced.
(4) Al^{3+} is oxidized.

106 The metals in Group 1 (IA) are obtained commercially from their fused salts by
1 decomposing with electricity
2 decomposing with heat
3 reduction with carbon
4 reduction with aluminum

Group 11 — Nuclear Chemistry

If you choose this group, be sure to answer questions 107–111.

107 Which particle can *not* gain kinetic energy in an accelerator?
1 alpha particle
2 beta particle
3 proton
4 neutron

108 Which radioisotope can be used to check for thyroid gland disorders?
1 iodine-131
2 technetium-99
3 strontium-90
4 radon-222

109 In the reaction $^{14}_{7}N + ^{4}_{2}He \rightarrow ^{17}_{8}O + ^{1}_{1}X$, the X represents a
1 triton
2 deuteron
3 proton
4 neutron

110 Which component of the nuclear reactor is used to slow down neutrons?
1 control rods
2 moderator
3 internal shield
4 external shield

111 When a nucleus with a high mass undergoes fission, the resulting nuclei are more stable than the original nucleus because they have a
1 higher binding energy per nucleon
2 lower binding energy per nucleon
3 higher number of electrons
4 lower number of electrons

Group 12 – Laboratory Activities

If you choose this group, be sure to answer questions 112–116.

112 When NH_4NO_3 is dissolved in water, the temperature of the water decreases. When NaOH is dissolved in a separate water sample, the temperature of the water increases. Based on these observations, it can be concluded that the dissolving of

(1) both salts is endothermic
(2) both salts is exothermic
(3) NH_4NO_3 is endothermic and the dissolving of NaOH is exothermic
(4) NH_4NO_3 is exothermic and the dissolving of NaOH is endothermic

113 The graph below represents the uniform cooling of a substance, starting as a gas at 160°C. At which temperature does a phase change occur for this substance?

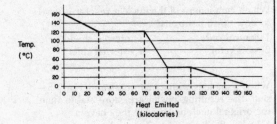

(1) 0°C (3) 80°C
(2) 40°C (4) 140°C

114 Which of the following statements contained in a student's laboratory report is a conclusion?

1 A gas is evolved.
2 The gas is insoluble in water.
3 The gas is hydrogen.
4 The gas burns in air.

115 A student determined the mass, in grams, of compound X that would saturate 30. grams of water over a temperature range of 40°C in 10.-degree intervals. The results are tabulated below.

Grams of Dissolved Compound X	Temperature of 30. grams of H_2O
2.0 g	10.°C
4.0 g	20.°C
8.0 g	30.°C
16 g	40.°C
32 g	50.°C

If this solubility trend continues, what is the total number of grams of compound X that will dissolve in 30. grams of water at 60.°C?

(1) 16 (3) 48
(2) 32 (4) 64

116 The diagram below represents the meniscus on an acid and a base buret at the endpoint of a titration in which 0.10 M NaOH was used to neutralize an unknown concentration of HCl.

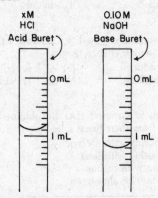

If the solution level in each buret was 0.00 milliliter at the start of the titration, what is the molarity of the unknown HCl solution?

(1) 1.2 M (3) 0.30 M
(2) 0.13 M (4) 0.090 M

Sample Regents Exam 1

Answers

1. The correct answer is 1. The relationship between the Celsius scale and the Kelvin scale amounts to a difference of 273 degrees. 0° C is the freezing point of water but not the lowest temperature possible. That would be 0 K, which has been found to be 273 degrees lower than 0° C. Therefore, the Kelvin temperature will always be the Celsius temperature plus 273 degrees. For more information on this topic, see part III, section C in chapter 3, "Matter, Energy, and Measurement."

2. The correct answer is 1. At Standard Temperature (0° C) and Pressure (1 atm), only silver, of the four choices listed, is a solid. The definition of a solid is that it has a definite shape and volume. For more information on this topic, see part II in chapter 3, "Matter, Energy, and Measurement."

3. The correct answer is 4. Of the choices listed, only ammonia is a compound made up of more than one element. This means it can be decomposed further by chemical (also known as "ordinary") means or change. The other choices are elements and are already "decomposed" as far as they can be by chemical change. For more information on this topic, see part II of chapter 2, "Matter, Energy, and Measurement," and part I of chapter 4, "Atomic Structure."

4. The correct answer is 3. When water reaches the boiling point, its vapor pressure equals atmospheric pressure; under standard conditions, this is 1 atmosphere. In order for water to have a vapor pressure at 105° C, it must still be in the liquid state, and this implies a pressure > 760 torr since boiling point increases as pressure does. Table O tells us the answer directly! For more information on this topic, see part II of chapter 3, "Matter, Energy, and Measurement," and Table O.

5. The correct answer is 4. Seeing no crystalline structure in a sample of glass, we cannot designate it as a solid. The lack of a crystalline structure would make us consider it a special liquid—in particular, one that is the result of supercooling the substance that composes it. For more information on this topic, consult the discussion of glasses in your chemistry textbook.

6. The correct answer is 3. Each arrow in the diagrams presented stands for an electron. In the ground state, all electrons should be as close to the nucleus as they can be, which would follow the Aufbau principle. Diagram 3 has all of the arrows in the lowest energy levels possible, closest to the nucleus. For more information on this topic, see section E of chapter 4, "Atomic Structure."

7. The correct answer is 1. A neutral atom in the ground state with sixteen electrons would have the following configuration: $1s^2\, 2s^2\, 2p^6\, 3s^2\, 3p^4$. Therefore, in the 2p subshell, this atom would have six electrons. Each s-sublevel would have two (choice 2), but we were asked about the 2p. For more information on this topic, see section E of chapter 4, "Atomic Structure."

8. The correct answer is 3. In the ground state, chlorine, which is element number 17, has seven electrons in the outer or third energy level. Choice 3 indicates this with seven dots. Choice 1 would be an ion of chlorine, not a ground state condition, and choices 2 and 4 show the incorrect designation of only part of the third energy level, 3s and 3p respectively. For more information on this topic, see chapter 5, "Bonding."

9. The correct answer is 3. From Table H, Fr-220 with a half-life of 27.4 seconds would exhibit the most amount of decay within twenty-eight days because it would pass through the most half-lives. The others have the following half-lives: P-32—14.28 days; Kr-85—10.76 years; I-131—8.07 days. For more information on this topic, see part II, section D in chapter 4, "Atomic Structure."

10. The correct answer is 1. If this is a neutral atom with six electrons then it must also have six protons. This indicates atomic number 6, which is carbon. Having six protons and eight neutrons makes this the isotope C-14. For more information on this topic, see part I, section C in chapter 3, "Matter, Energy, and Measurement."

11. The correct answer is 4. The tricky part to this question is the inclusion of argon as a possible answer. As an inert gas and being in the third period, one might decide all too soon that all of this might mean its third energy level is full. This is true for its 3s and 3p, but the third energy level has one more level—a "d" sublevel—to fill. There are six electrons in the 3d of iron but this does not fill the 3rd energy level. Only zinc fills up the entire third energy level with ten electrons, the maximum a "d" suborbital can hold. For more information on this topic, see part I, section E in chapter 3, "Matter, Energy, and Measurement."

12. The correct answer is 1. Water is the only compound of those listed that has hydrogen bonding between molecules in the liquid state. This attractive force requires the most energy to overcome in order to boil. The heavier weight of H_2Te does make it harder to boil than H_2S or H_2Se, but hydrogen bonding is even more important than weight to consider. For more information on this topic, see part IV, section B in chapter 3, "Matter, Energy, and Measurement," and section III, part B in chapter 5, "Bonding."

13. The correct answer is 4. The empirical formula of a compound is its molecular formula in the lowest whole-number terms.

Taking $C_6H_{12}O_6$, one notices that each element subscript can be divided by 6, with the result being the whole-number subscripts for each element as seen in choice 4. For more information on this topic, see part III, section A in chapter 6, "The Mathematics of Chemistry," and part V in chapter 5, "Bonding."

14. The correct answer is 1. With the largest number of electrons and largest size among the substances listed, we would expect chlorine to have the greatest van der Waals forces among the four listed. This is confirmed (a) by the highest boiling point among the four—the energy needed to separate the molecules from each other into a vapor; and (b) by the highest density among the four—more substance within the same volume. None of the other four have sufficiently high dipole interactions to have stronger van der Waals forces than any of the others. For more information on this topic, see part III, section C in chapter 5, "Bonding."

15. The correct answer is 1. Choice 1, which is carbon dioxide, positions oxygen atoms on opposite sides of the molecule making for a symmetrical distribution of charge and the only nonpolar molecule of the choices indicated. The other three choices all have a clear separation of charge through a nonsymmetrical distribution of that charge in this molecule. For more information on this topic, see part II, section B in chapter 5, "Bonding."

16. The correct answer is 2. The parentheses in the formula of barium nitrate indicate that there is two of everything inside the parentheses. Overall that would give one barium to every two nitrates or choice 2. For more information on this topic, see parts V and VI in chapter 5, "Bonding."

17. The correct answer is 1. Only metals will be good conductors in both the liquid state (like mercury) and the solid state (like iron, copper, aluminum, etcetera). Ionic substances are nonconductors in the solid phase. For more information on this topic, see section II in chapter 5, "Bonding."

18. The correct answer is 4. Nitrogen (IV) has an oxidation number of +4 (the meaning of the roman numeral IV). To form a compound with nitrogen, the element oxygen, with an oxidation number of –2, must be present in double the amount of the nitrogen; thus choice 4 is correct. For more information on this topic, see part VI, section F in chapter 5, "Bonding."

19. The correct answer is 3. All of the isotopes of polonium are naturally radioactive, which is indicated as such on the periodic table with parentheses around the symbol of the element. For more information on this topic, see part II, section D in chapter 12, "Nuclear Chemistry."

20. The correct answer is 4. The transition elements contain the loosest network of electrons in the outer shells and thus usually have more than one oxidation

number. When excited, this phenomenon results in the most variety of color
given off among a group of elements as
the various electrons drop back to their
ground state. For more information on
this topic, see part III in chapter 6, "The
Periodic Table."

21. The correct answer is 1. Metals give up
their sole outer electrons easiest and thus
have the lowest energy requirement
(called ionization energy because when
they lose electrons, they become ions) to
do so. The inert gases have the highest,
followed by the nonmetals, then the metalloids, and finally the metals, choice 1,
being the lowest. For more information
on this topic, see part II, section C in
chapter 6, "The Periodic Table."

22. The correct answer is 4. For at least two
reasons, Rb is the correct answer to this
question. First of all, it is in Group 1, the
metals. Second, it has a large atomic number, meaning the atom is large. This places
the lone outer electron farther from the
nucleus than any of the others listed,
which is another metallic property. For
more information on this topic, see section III in chapter 6, "The Periodic Table."

23. The correct answer is 1. Fluorine is the
smallest atom on the list—the electrons
will all be held quite closely and, therefore,
quite vigorously to the nucleus—and
would therefore, grab available electrons
most strongly, making it the most electronegative halogen listed (choice 1). For

more information on this topic, see part
IV in chapter 6, "The Periodic Table."

24. The correct answer is 2. When potassium
loses its lone outer electron, it loses an
entire energy level making the ionic radius
smaller than the atomic radius. The other
three all gain electrons making their ions
nearly the same size or larger than the
atomic form. For more information on
this topic, see part II, section B in chapter
6, "The Periodic Table."

25. The correct answer is 2. Using the formula
for Molarity = # of moles of solute/L of
solution and the figures given, we get 3.0M
= # of moles of solute/.5 L of solution.
Solving for the number of moles of solute,
we get 1.5 moles of solute (choice 2). For
more information on this topic, see part
IV in chapter 7, "The Mathematics of
Chemistry."

26. The correct answer is 4. With an empirical formula that has a ratio of 1:1, we
need to look for that ratio of
carbon:hydrogen atoms in a molecule
that gives us a total molecular mass of 78.
The mass of carbon is 12 and the mass of
hydrogen is 1. Choice 4 provides just the
right mass. Six carbons equal a mass of
72, and the six hydrogens equal a mass of
6. The two combined equal a molecular
mass of 78. For more information on this
topic, see part III, section A in chapter 7,
"The Mathematics of Chemistry."

27. The correct answer is 4. The total mass of the molecule is 44 amu. Of that, nitrogen is 28 amu. Dividing 28 by 44 gives us the percentage of nitrogen by mass which is 64 percent. For more information on this topic, see part III, section A in chapter 7, "The Mathematics of Chemistry."

28. The correct answer is 2. According to graph D, 55 grams of NH_4Cl in 100 grams of water would be considered saturated at 57° C (choice 2). For more information on this topic, see part II, section B in chapter 8, "Kinetics and Equilibrium," and Graph D.

29. The correct answer is 4. The equation indicates a 1:5 molar ratio between C_3H_8 and O_2, and because for gases moles and volume are directly proportional, this means a 1:5 volume ratio as well. In order to preserve that ratio while burning 5 liters of C_3H_8, we would need five times that amount of oxygen or 25 liters. For more information on this topic, see part III, section B, in chapter 7, "The Mathematics of Chemistry."

30. The correct answer is 3. An increase in disorder will be evidenced in equation 3 only. It is going from a low-energy state to a higher one meaning the amount of disorder has increased. For more information on this topic, see part II, section D, in chapter 8, "Kinetics and Equilibrium."

31. The correct answer is 2. Endothermic reactions absorb energy as is evidenced by a ΔH that is positive. Choice 2 is the only answer that, on Reference Table I, has a ΔH that is positive. The negative ΔH of the other three indicates a release of energy, which is typical of an exothermic—*exo-* indicating a release of energy reaction. The negative sign indicates that, in its completion, this reaction ends up taking energy from itself and giving it to the environment. For more information on this topic, see part I, section A in chapter 8, "Kinetics and Equilibrium."

32. The correct answer is 3. The activated complex resides on the curve in the region to the left of the peak of potential energy between the tops of regions A and C. Therefore, the activated complex reaches its maximum potential energy at the peak indicated by arrow C. On the right of the curve—from the peak, downward—is the release of energy in the kinetic form. For more information on this topic, see part I, section A in chapter 8, "Kinetics and Equilibrium."

33. The correct answer is 4. Rates of reactions in general increase with increasing temperature or concentration of reactants. Using this knowledge you can eliminate choices 2 and 3. For gas phase reactions, choices 1 and 4 produce the opposite effect of each other (Boyle's Law)—increasing pressure is the same as decreasing container volume. As pressure decreases the number of collisions per second between reactants will decrease, and this means that the chance for reactions to

occur per unit time—the rate—must go down. For more information on your topic, consult the discussions of Boyle's Law and kinetics and equilibrium in your chemistry textbook.

34. The correct answer is 2. Choices 1, 3, and 4 have very high acid dissociation constants (K_a), indicating a large number of ions in solution. Choice 1, HF, has the smallest K_a of the four and therefore will not have available a large number of ions with which to conduct electricity, a characteristic of a weak electrolyte. For more information on this topic, see parts I and IV in chapter 9, "Acids and Bases."

35. The correct answer is 4. Spontaneity means that deltaG < 0, and this will always be true if deltaH < 0 (exothermic, products lying below reactants on the graph) and at the same time deltaS > 0, the latter of which is always true for a solid gas transition. Choice 4 is the only one with these two criteria met—the word *must* in the question was important. For more information on this topic, see part II, section D in chapter 8, "Kinetics and Equilibrium."

36. The correct answer is 1. By definition, an Arrhenius acid in aqueous solution donates hydrogen ions, or protons. For more information on this topic, see part II, section A in chapter 9, "Acids and Bases."

37. The correct answer is 1. At 25° C, the sum of the H^+ and OH^- ions in any given aqueous solution equals 1×10^{-14} which is known as the ion product. Since the OH^- is given as 1×10^{-10}, the H^+ ion concentration in this solution must be 1×10^{-4}, choice 1. For more information on this topic, see part IV, section C in chapter 10, "Redox and Electrochemistry."

38. The correct answer is 2. Using the relationship $M_1V_1 = M_2V_2$, where M = molarity and V = volume, we find the molarity of the base to be 1.5M or double the concentration of the acid. This would be expected since the volume of KOH we have is half the volume of the HCl.

39. The correct answer is 2. K_w, the ionization constant for water, is correctly indicated by multiplying the concentrations of the H^+ (or H_3O^+) and the OH^- ions. Choices 1 and 3 bear a similarity to the way we calculate other concentrations but leave out the product—in this case, it would be water—and choice 4 indicates a subtraction of the concentrations, which has little, if any, meaning in chemistry. For more information on this topic, see part IV, section B in chapter 9, "Acids and Bases."

40. The correct answer is 1. Brönsted bases are defined as receiving H^+ ions or protons. Going to the right, NH^3 does this to become NH^4 and going to the left, HS– also does this to become H_2S. Choices 2 and 4 are misleading, and choice 3 is half right—as well as misleading—by indicating H_2S as having received, not donated, a proton. For more information on this topic, see part III, section B in chapter 9, "Acids and Bases."

41. The correct answer is 3. If hydrogen can be counted on to almost always have an oxidation number of +1, then the polyatomic ion opposite it must have an oxidation number of −1 in order to form a compound. That means if oxygen can equally be counted on to most often have an oxidation number of −2, and applying this reasoning to each choice, only the polyatomic ion $ClO3^{-1}$ requires Cl to have an oxidation number of +5. The answer is choice 3. For more information on this topic, see part I, section C in chapter 10, "Redox and Electrochemistry."

42. The correct answer is 1. Low ionization energy, as one might expect, means that an atom easily loses electrons. If it does this so readily, then it would also tend to have a low electronegativity (the tendency of an atom to attract an electron to form a covalent bond). Elements like F that readily gain electrons also have high electronegativity. For more information on this topic, see part II in chapter 5, "Bonding."

43. The correct answer is 2. Reduction is represented by a gain of electrons in the substance being reduced, which will change its oxidation number in a more negative direction. Reaction 2 satisfies that condition since the equation indicates that not only does the oxidation number for calcium go from +2 on the left side to 0 on the right, the left side clearly indicates that two electrons are being added to the calcium. For more information on this topic, see part II in chapter 10, "Redox and Electrochemistry."

44. The correct answer is 3. A redox reaction involves two changes in oxidation numbers; one substances loses electrons, is oxidized, and so becomes more (+) and the other substance gains those electrons and so becomes more (−) or is reduced. In reaction three, chlorine goes from +5 oxidation number on the left to −1 oxidation number on the right, indicating reduction. Oxygen, on the other hand, goes from −2 oxidation number to 0 oxidation number, indicating oxidation. In none of the other reactions do any of the substances change their oxidation numbers. For more information on this topic, see chapter 10, "Redox and Electrochemistry."

45. The correct answer is 4. An electrolytic cell involves electrolysis, which requires an applied electric current to decompose compounds. An electrochemical cell can use a current or produce a current and is exothermic. Both reactions involve redox, which removes it as an answer to support one or the other. For more information on this topic, see part II, sections C and D in chapter 10, "Redox and Electrochemistry."

46. The correct answer is 3. The total number of electrons transferred from Fe^{+3} on the left side of the equation to Mg^{+2} on the right side is six. The coefficient of Mg(s) will have to be 3; likewise, the coefficient for Fe(s) will have to be 2. For more information on this topic, see part III in chapter 10, "Redox and Electrochemistry," and the relevant chapter in your chemistry textbook.

47. The correct answer is 4. The –COOH complex is the functional group that is common to all organic acids and, in fact, defines them as carboxylic, or organic, acids. For more information on this topic, see part IV, section B in chapter 11, "Organic Chemistry."

48. The correct answer is 1. Hydrocarbon molecules only contain covalent bonds, and, by definition (or convention) single bonds are referred to as saturated bonds. Saturated hydrocarbons contain single covalent bonds—choice 1. For more information on this topic, see part III, section A in chapter 11, "Organic Chemistry."

49. The correct answer is 3. Addition—also known as synthesis—reactions, involve the making of something from two or more simpler components. Choice 3 clearly, and uniquely, satisfies that definition among the choices offered. For more information on this topic, see chapter 11, "Organic Chemistry."

50. The correct answer is 3. The core indication—minus the CH_3—of a six-sided figure is the classic benzene ring. Therefore, what we see represented is clearly an example of choice 3. For more information on this topic, see part III, section A in chapter 11, "Organic Chemistry."

51. The correct answer is 2. Alcohols derive their names from adding -ol to the corresponding alkane from which they are derived, e.g., methane can be used to pro-duce the alcohol methanol. For more information on this topic, see part IV, section A in chapter 11, "Organic Chemistry."

52. The correct answer is 2. Traveling from left to right along any period—row—of the periodic table produces a trend toward more and more nonmetallic (by definition) properties, marked by the tendency to gain electrons. For more information on this topic, see part IV in chapter 6, "The Periodic Table."

53. The correct answer is 3. If pressure is applied to this reaction at equilibrium and involving only gases, by Le Châtelier's principle the position of equilibrium will shift to relieve the stress. This can only be done by reducing the total number of gas particles present—i.e., the side of the reaction with fewer moles of gas will be favored, no matter what kind of gas it is. But in this reaction the number of product moles equals the number of reactant moles, so pressure has no effect. For more information on this topic, see part II, section C in chapter 8, "Kinetics and Equilibrium."

54. The correct answer is 3. Gamma radiation involves pure energy and not particles, which means it has no charge or mass. Therefore, it will have no effect on the atomic number, which remains the same (choice 3). For more information on this topic, see part II, section A in chapter 4, "Atomic Structure."

55. The correct answer is 2. Increasing the pressure on a liquid means that in order to boil, the vapor pressure of the liquid will need to be raised to match that increase in pressure. In order to do that, we will have to provide more energy to the liquid particles by raising the temperature. For more information on this topic, see part IV, section B in chapter 3, "Matter, Energy, and Measurement."

56. The correct answer is 2. The phosphate ion is the conjugate base of a weak acid (HPO_4^{2-})and hence the phosphate will generate OH^- in water:

$$PO_4^{3-} + H_2O = OH^- + HPO_4^{2-}$$

The presence of OH^- raises the pH. For more information on this topic, see part III, section A in chapter 9, "Acids and Bases."

57. The correct answer is 3. Following Avogadro's principle, equal volumes of gases under equal conditions contain equal numbers of particles, whether they be atoms, as in flasks 1 and 2, or molecules, as in flasks 3 and 4. Choice 3 is the best representation of this concept. For more information on this topic, see part IV, section A in chapter 3, "Matter, Energy, and Measurement."

58. The correct answer is 4. The individual gas particles in an ideal gas are defined as NOT having any of the characteristics indicated by choices 1 through 3: They have no volume, remain always as gases, and are not attracted to each other. The particles are, however, thought to be in constant random motion. For more information on this topic, see part IV, section A in chapter 3, "Matter, Energy, and Measurement."

59. The correct answer is 4. One atmosphere of pressure is equivalent to 760 mm Hg. Dividing this into 1140 mm Hg yields an atmospheric pressure of 1.5, choice 4. For more information on this topic, see part IV, section A in chapter 3, "Matter, Energy, and Measurement."

60. The correct answer is 2. So weak are the intermolecular forces of attraction in substances that sublime, that they go from solid to gas directly with no intermediate liquid stage. This, of course, is our definition of sublimation. As one would assume, these weak intermolecular forces result in conditions where the vapor pressure is quite high. For more information on this topic, see part IV, section C in chapter 3, "Matter, Energy, and Measurement," and parts II and III in chapter 5, "Bonding."

61. The correct answer is 4. The phrase *steam-water equilibrium* simply means we are at the boiling point of water, which occurs at 100° C or 373 K. For more information on this topic, see part IV, section B in chapter 3, "Matter, Energy, and Measurement."

62. The correct answer is 1. The top number in the symbols given indicates the mass number of the nuclide represented. Therefore C–14 and N–14 both have the same mass number. The bottom number is the atomic number, which is different between the two, making the nuclear charges different. Subtracting the bottom number—the atomic number and the number of protons—from the top number also gives the neutrons for each. These numbers are also different. For more information on this topic, see part I, section C in chapter 4, "Atomic Structure."

63. The correct answer is 1. The farther out from the nucleus one travels, the higher in electric potential energy one goes (just as the farther up in the atmosphere one goes, the higher in gravitational potential energy one reaches). Electrons in principal energy level 1 would have the lowest energy. For more information on this topic, see part I, section E in chapter 4, "Atomic Structure."

64. The correct answer is 4. An alpha particle of radiation is composed of two protons and two neutrons, the exact composition of a helium nucleus. For more information on this topic, see part II, section A in chapter 4, "Atomic Structure."

65. The correct answer is 1. The atomic number of 11 tells us that the nucleus has eleven protons. These are positively charged and so this makes the nuclear charge on the sodium atom 11+. For more

information on this topic, see part I, section C in chapter 4, "Atomic Structure."

66. The correct answer is 3. Pathway X radiation is attracted to a (+) plate so they are (–), which makes them beta particles. Pathway Y radiation is unchanged by the electrically charged plates which makes it neutral gamma radiation. Pathway Z radiation is attracted to the (–) plate, making it (+), and, therefore, alpha particles. Remember that normally *beta* refers to beta minus. For more information on this topic, see part II, section A in chapter 4, "Atomic Structure."

67. The correct answer is 1. When balancing this reaction, the coefficients will, in order, be 4 for Al, 3 for O_2, and 2 for Al_2O_3, totaling 9. For more information on this topic, see parts VI and VII in chapter 5, "Bonding."

68. The correct answer is 3. Calcium atoms will give up electrons to the oxygen atoms, which will create bonds known as ionic bonds. There is no hydrogen involved, and the bonds will not be covalent. For more information on this topic, see part II in chapter 5, "Bonding."

69. The correct answer is 3. Carbon dioxide, with its symmetrical bonding between the C and the two Os, results in a nonpolar molecule but with a polar covalent bond between the C and each O. For more information on this topic, see part II in chapter 5, "Bonding."

70. The correct answer is 2. A coordinate covalent bond means the electrons in the bond will be supplied by one of the reactants. The H^+ ion will clearly do this with the diagram indicated in choice 2. For more information on this topic, see part II in chapter 5, "Bonding."

71. The correct answer is 4. Mercury is already a liquid at room temperature, not a very high melting point. At room temperature, CO_2 is a gas, well beyond any melting point (which it does not have since at $-40°$ C, it undergoes sublimation). Glucose, choice 3, has a fairly low melting point and does not conduct electricity in any state. KCl is the one that satisfies all conditions. For more information on this topic, see part II in chapter 5, "Bonding."

72. The correct answer is 2. Atomic number is the correct answer; the atoms reveal their periodicity best when arranged this way. For more information on this topic, see part I, section B in chapter 6, "The Periodic Table."

73. The correct answer is 1. There is only one halogen in each period (row) on the periodic table, just as there is one inert gas family member in each period. For more information on this topic, see part II in chapter 6, "The Periodic Table."

74. The correct answer is 2. This atom has two valence electrons placing it in Group (IIA), or the alkaline earth metals. For more information on this topic, see part II,

section A in chapter 6, "The Periodic Table."

75. The correct answer is 2. If this metal forms a compound with a 1:2 ratio with OH^-, then it must have an oxidation number of +2, which would place it in Group (IIA)— see previous question. For more information on this topic, see part III in chapter 6, "The Periodic Table."

76. The correct answer is 3. Sodium will have the greatest tendency to give electrons. Sulfur will gain slightly less than chlorine, which is the one that will tend to gain them the most, and argon is an inert gas, not having any tendency to gain electrons. For more information on this topic, see part III in chapter 6, "The Periodic Table."

77. The correct answer is 2. The molar ratio of copper to copper(II) nitrate is 1:1. Therefore, 1 mole, or approximately 64 grams of copper, will produce 1 mole of the nitrate. For more information on this topic, see part III, section B, in chapter 7, "The Mathematics of Chemistry."

78. The correct answer is 1. The lightest gas, at STP, will diffuse the fastest, which is known as Graham's Law. Each of the gases given, being observed under the same conditions, will have access to the same amount of energy to move them. The lightest, helium, will exhibit the biggest change—motion—due to this or any other level of energy that all four

experience. For more information on this topic, see part IX in chapter 7, "The Mathematics of Chemistry."

79. The correct answer is 2. One tenth of a mole of any substance will have one tenth of the Avogadro number of particles. The tricky part to this question is which exponent to use? Since one tenth will make the amount smaller, and the exponent is (+), we select 10^{22} as the exponent, a smaller number than 10^{23}. For more information on this topic, see part I in chapter 7, "The Mathematics of Chemistry."

80. The correct answer is 2. Two moles of an electrolyte, which will dissociate into at least two particles, the (–) and the (+) ions, will produce a total of at least 4 moles of charged particles. All of the others will produce only 2 or less, assuming the same electrolyte in choices 1 and 2. This was a tricky question. For more information on this topic, see part VI in chapter 7, "The Mathematics of Chemistry."

81. The correct answer is 1. If the molecular mass of the gas is 44 g, then 11 g is one fourth of that amount. At STP, it will occupy one fourth of a molar volume (22.4 L) or 5.60 L. For more information on this topic, see part B in chapter 7, "The Mathematics of Chemistry."

82. The correct answer is 4. When the free energy of formation is greater than 0 (> 0), the reaction will always be non-spontaneous. The other choices—1, 2, and 3—all have free energies of formation (ΔG) > 0. In the equation $\Delta G = \Delta H - T\Delta S$, where the ΔS (entropy) is positive and sufficiently higher than ΔH, the ΔG will always be < 0, the earmark of a spontaneous reaction. For more information on this topic, see part II, section D in chapter 8, "Kinetics and Equilibrium."

83. The correct answer is 1. If no other information is given in a question, then the largest K_{sp} is to be taken as an indication of the highest solubility. However, this problem is too ambiguous because the *only* way to decide maximum solubility based solely on the magnitude of the solubility product is if all ionic compounds that are being compared dissolve to liberate the same numbers of cations and ions per formula unit of the compound—i.e., either one cation and one anion per formula unit, or one cation and two anions per, etcetera. If the compounds are of different ratios of cations to anions, then a calculation must be done to solve for the concentration of one of the ions. For more information on this topic, consult the relevant chapter in your chemistry textbook.

84. The correct answer is 3. Choice 3 is a simple statement of the formula for calculating the amount of Gibb's free energy from a chemical reaction. For more information on this topic, see part II, section D in chapter 8, "Kinetics and Equilibrium."

85. The correct answer is 1. If $K = 1$ then the correct relationship is choice 1. Choices 3 and 4 cannot apply since we are given $K = 1$, not <1 nor >1. Choice 2 incorrectly relates C with A. For more information on this topic, see part II, section C in chapter 8, "Kinetics and Equilibrium."

86. The correct answer is 4. An increase in the amount of one of the products will favor the reactant side, which will produce more AgCl. Choice 4 gives that option; all others are incorrect. Of course, this is a physical change, not a chemical reaction, but the reasoning is similar. For more information on this topic, see part I, section C in chapter 8, "Kinetics and Equilibrium."

87. The correct answer is 4. NaOH is the only compound with OH^- available to donate. For more information on this topic, see part II in chapter 8, "Kinetics and Equilibrium."

88. The correct answer is 4. According to Reference Table N, zinc has the lowest reduction potential (E^o), meaning that among the four choices, it has the strongest potential of being oxidized. The aqueous hydrogen ions from the HCl, therefore, have the highest potential for being reduced by the zinc. The other three choices all have an $E^o > 0$, which means they have the greater potential for being reduced than the H^+ given from HCl. For more information on this topic, see chapter 10, "Redox and Electrochemistry."

89. The correct answer is 1. A pH of 10 indicates we are testing a base, which turns litmus from red to blue and makes the phenolphthalein indicator turn pink. For more information on this topic, see chapter 9, "Acids and Bases."

90. The correct answer is 2. We have a mixture of a strong base and a strong acid, which always yields a neutral (pH 7) solution—the question stem even said "neutralized mixture." For more information on this topic, see part III in chapter 9, "Acids and Bases."

91. The correct answer is 2. Only in reaction 2 does the reactant display the ability to form both a conjugate acid and base. For more information on this topic, see part II in chapter 9, "Acids and Bases."

92. The correct answer is 3. In order to be oxidized, since copper is the stronger oxidizer, zinc ions will move opposite to the flow of electrons. The Zn electrode becomes the anode (oxidation) with electrons leaving through the wire and Zn ions through the salt bridge. For more information on this topic, consult the relevant chapter in your chemistry textbook.

93. The correct answer is 1. Electrons will flow from the electrode that produces positive ions (labeled A) toward the copper electrode. For more information on this topic, consult the relevant chapter in your chemistry textbook.

94. The correct answer is 2. The coefficients, in order, will be: Cu – 4; H_2SO_4 – 2; $CuSO_4$ – 1; SO_2 –1; and H_2O –2. For more information on this topic, see part I, section C in chapter 8, "Kinetics and Equilibrium."

95. The correct answer is 2. Reduction is the gain of electrons for a particular substance; the reducing agent being the source of those electrons. We must first search for a candidate that gives electrons poorly. The poorest among those listed is the hydrogen molecule. Al, Zn, and Ba all have positive reduction potentials, meaning they give electrons readily. For more information on this topic, consult the relevant chapter in your chemistry textbook.

96. The correct answer is 1. Lead is above all of the other elements listed, including hydrogen in the activity series. Its half reaction will be favored. In other words, H^+ will be reduced to H_2 by any species below it on table N. For more information on this topic, consult the relevant chapter in your chemistry textbook.

97. The correct answer is 1. The word *condensation* refers to the removal of water from the molecules being polymerized. For more information on this topic, consult the relevant chapter in your chemistry textbook.

98. The correct answer is 3. A secondary alcohol is one in which the –OH complex is attached to carbon in the hydrocarbon chain, which in turn is connected to two other carbons, and choice 3 does just that. For more information on this topic, see part IV, section A in chapter 11, "Organic Chemistry."

99. The correct answer is 4. Use of the suffix *-triol* indicates the addition of three –OH complexes. Choice 3 requires two, but the compound indicated has three. Neither choices 1 nor 2 qualify since all the bonds are saturated. For more information on this topic, see part IV, section A in chapter 11, "Organic Chemistry."

100. The correct answer is 1. The *-al* suffix in methanal indicates we are naming an aldehyde (choice 1). For more information on this topic, see part IV, section C in chapter 11, "Organic Chemistry."

101. The correct answer is 1. Ketones have a double-bonded oxygen attached to the core carbon. For more information on this topic, see part IV, section D in chapter 11, "Organic Chemistry."

102. The correct answer is 2. In a rechargeable battery, as in any battery, the discharging would be exothermic and this process must be reversed in order to recharge the batteries. Choice 2 identifies the reactions in their proper place. For more information on this topic, consult the relevant chapter in your chemistry textbook.

103. The correct answer is 4. To break down any complex mixture, we might use distillation.

In doing this with a petroleum mixture, under very carefully controlled conditions, we regulate the temperature fractionally. For more information on this topic, consult the relevant chapter in your chemistry textbook.

104. The correct answer is 2. The Haber process is the name given to the modern day process for the production of ammonia. For more information on this topic, consult the relevant chapter in your chemistry textbook.

105. The correct answer is 2. In the presence of atmospheric oxygen, the aluminum "rusts" or is oxidized to form Al_2O_3. For more information on this topic, consult the relevant chapter in your chemistry textbook.

106. The correct answer is 1. The alkali metal salts are melted and then decomposed in this state through the use of electrolysis. Obviously, no water or aqueous solutions can be involved as these metals react strongly with water. For more information on this topic, see part III, section A in chapter 6, "The Periodic Table."

107. The correct answer is 4. The neutron cannot gain kinetic energy in a particle accelerator. Since it has no charge, it will not respond to an electric field such as the kind that drives a particle accelerator. For more information on this topic, see part I, section B in chapter 4, "Atomic Structure."

108. The correct answer is 1. An essential element for the production of thyroxin in the thyroid gland is iodine. Thus I–131 can be traced radioactively to aid in the diagnosis of thyroid gland disorders. For more information on this topic, consult the relevant chapter in your chemistry textbook.

109. The correct answer is 3. The X can only be a hydrogen nucleus because its atomic number (lower left number) is one. For more information on this topic, see chapter 4, "Atomic Structure."

110. The correct answer is 2. The control rods, which often contain the element boron, are used to regulate the release of neutrons from the fuel rods by absorbing the neutrons, not slowing them down. Shielding is for protection, not moderation. For more information on this topic, see part II, section A in chapter 12, "Nuclear Chemistry."

111. The correct answer is 1. Binding energy per nucleon peaks in the region of iron, decreasing as atomic number increases or decreases. Fission of the large mass increases the binding energy per nucleon of the resulting smaller-mass atoms. "Large" masses refer to A ≳ 150. For more information on this topic, consult the relevant chapter in your chemistry textbook.

112. The correct answer is 3. Given the temperature changes indicated, choice 3 is the only conclusion one can arrive at: Lowering of temperature is endothermic and

raising the temperature is exothermic. For more information on this topic, see part I, section A in chapter 8, "Kinetics and Equilibrium."

113. The correct answer is 2. It is at 40° C that the phase change occurs since the temperature change is constant while heat is being emitted. The rearrangement of the particles internally is causing energy to be released while the average amount of energy in the substance—the temperature—stays the same. Note that 120° C is also a phase change. For more information on this topic, see part IV in chapter 3, "Matter, Energy, and Measurement."

114. The correct answer is 3. Choices 1, 2, and 4 are all directly observable events. Choice 3 would have to be a conclusion achieved by comparing the behavior of the gas with the behavior of a gas known to be hydrogen. For information on this topic, see chapter 3, "Matter, Energy, and Measurement."

115. The correct answer is 4. Simply graphing the results and plotting a line for these data causes an intersection of grams dissolved in 30 grams of water at 60° C to be at 64 g of the compound. Even a casual inspection of the data indicates a doubling of the amount dissolved every 10° C, which also leads to the conclusion that at 60° C, we will dissolve 64g of the solute. For information on this topic, consult the relevant chapter in your chemistry textbook.

116. The correct answer is 2. Using the relationship $M_1V_1 = M_2V_2$ in this titration that reached equilibrium with the figures given and where M = Molarity and V = Volume needed to titrate to equilibrium, we get 0.13M for the acid. Subscript 1 = the acid figures and Subscript 2 = the figures given for the base. For information on this topic, see part III, section A in chapter 9, "Acids and Bases."

Part III

Chemistry Review

Chapter 3

Matter, Energy, and Measurement

I. Chemistry

    A. Definition—Chemistry is the study of (a) the composition, structure, and properties of matter, (b) the changes it undergoes, and (c) the energy involved in those changes.

    B. Application—Among the items explored in the study of chemistry, (a) would be thought of by most people as the embodiment of the subject. One of the first areas to be studied in chemistry is the makeup of the individual parts of matter, how they are put together and, in the final analysis, how these parts act. The study of the elements and their constituent parts—protons, electrons, and neutrons—is critical. Following this, one would become involved in the interactions between these pieces of matter. Are there any patterns, any consistencies in the way the elements act and react? The study of the periodic table, the definition of chemical change involving many examples and approaches would be included here. Finally, the study of energy changes, or thermodynamics, provides critical information for a better understanding of the universe: It's all chemistry.

II. Matter

    A. Forms

        1. Homogeneous forms of matter in which all specimens have the same properties and composition are studied in detail, with emphasis, first, on the simplest form of matter (from a chemistry point of view) known as an element. Then combinations of elements (that are the result of chemical reactions) called *compounds* would be studied.

           a. *Elements* are substances that cannot be further decomposed by chemical change. An atom of a particular element cannot be broken down any further and still have the properties of that element. Examples include: helium, oxygen, hydrogen, iron, copper, carbon, and nitrogen.

b. *Compounds* are substances that CAN be decomposed by chemical changes—ordinary means available in an ordinary lab, such as heating, cooling, reacting with other chemicals, etcetera—and are composed of two or more elements combined chemically in a definite ratio. Example include: water, table salt (or sodium chloride), baking soda, and carbon dioxide.

2. Heterogeneous forms of matter known as *mixtures* occur when two or more distinct substances that differ in properties and composition comingle. A mixture has the properties of the substances of which it is composed, is not uniform, and may have two or more phases. Examples would be ice cream, coffee with sugar and cream, cough medicine, and oil and water.

B. Properties—Matter is generally agreed to have two properties: chemical and physical.

1. Chemical properties are observed solely during chemical reactions and involve chemical changes wherein chemical bonds are broken or formed and new substances result. Reactivity is an example of a chemical property.

2. Physical properties are generally those that we observe with our senses and that do not involve chemical bonds or the formation of a new substance. If we dissolve sugar in water, let the water evaporate and retrieve the sugar with no further effort, this dissolving of sugar is a physical property.

III. Energy

A. Forms—Energy may be converted from one form to another but is never destroyed in the conversion. This is a statement of the *Law of Conservation of Matter and Energy*. Energy appears in at least six forms: heat, light, electrical, mechanical, nuclear and, of course, chemical. Energy is generally classified as either *potential* or *kinetic*, the latter being a condition where energy is being actively observed in one of the six forms.

B. Role in chemical change—Energy is either absorbed or given off in a chemical reaction, resulting in two basic kinds of energy, *exothermic* and *endothermic*—exchanging reactions. Some physical changes exchange energy also but usually on a much smaller scale than in chemical reactions.

    1. Exothermic—the release of energy in a chemical reaction; an example is the burning of matches.

    2. Endothermic—the absorption of energy in a chemical reaction; an example is the electrolysis of water.

C. Measurement—The chemist uses units for measuring everything from the length of a piece of copper wire to the energies involved in chemical reactions.

    1. Units commonly used:

        a. Calorie (heat or energy)

        b. Degrees Kelvin (temperature)

        c. Meter (linearity)

        d. Cubic centimeter (cm^3) or liter (volume)

        e. Kilogram (mass)

        f. Derived units such as density (mass/volume)

        g. Seconds (time)

    2. Significant figures—These designed to ensure that the result of any measurement, and any mathematical operation performed on it, does not convey more accurate results than the least precisely known factor in that calculation. Significant figures are meant to convey some idea as to the accuracy of the measuring device as well. All nonzero digits are significant as are zeroes to the right of the decimal (unless those zeroes are place-holding zeroes). Place-holding zeroes are not significant.

    3. Scientific notation—This is the system of expressing both large and small numbers, using powers of ten. It makes use of positive and negative exponents. For example:

        $163\ 000\ 000\ 000\ 000 = 1.63 \times 10^{14}$

        whereas $.00014 = 1.4 \times 10^{-4}$.

IV. Phases of Matter—*Phase* is used to refer to the form of matter: gas, liquid, or solid, wherein a change from one state to the other is accompanied by the absorption or release of heat.

A. Gases

    1.   General properties—Gases have no definite shape or volume; they take the shape and volume of the container. The *Kinetic Molecular Theory* states that a gas is composed of individual particles that are in continuous, random, straight-line motion. Collisions between gas particles may result in a transfer of energy between particles, but the net total energy in the system remains constant after such collisions. The volume of the gas particles themselves is ignored compared to the volume of the space they occupy. Finally, gas particles are considered to have no attraction for each other. *Standard Temperature and Pressure (STP)* is defined as 0° C (273K) and 760 mm of mercury (760 torr) or 1 atmosphere of pressure on a gas.

    2.   Laws governing their behavior—*Boyle's Law* states that at constant temperature, the volume of a given mass of gas varies inversely with the pressure exerted on it. Stated as an equation:

$$[\frac{V_1}{V_2} = \frac{P_2}{P_1}].$$

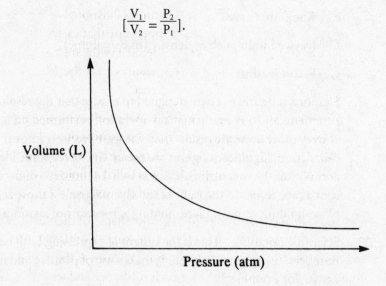

Volume (L)

Pressure (atm)

Fig. 1

A plot of volume versus pressure is shown in Fig. 1.

Charles's Law states that at constant pressure, the volume of a gas varies directly with the absolute temperature of the gas. The equation is:

$$\left[\frac{V_1}{V_2} = \frac{T_1}{T_2}\right].$$

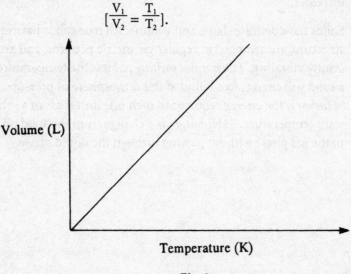

Fig. 2

A plot of volume versus temperature is illustrated in Fig. 2. *Dalton's Law of Partial Pressures* states that the pressure that each gas exerts in a mixture of gases is equivalent to the percent of the mixture that gas contributes. Adding up the partial pressures gives the total pressure that the mixture of gases exert, and vice versa.

Avogadro's Hypothesis states that equal volumes of all gases under the same conditions of temperature and pressure contain equal numbers of particles. The number of particles in 22.4 L at STP is 6.02×10^{23} particles (molecules, atoms, ions, etc.); this is called a mole and contains as many particles as there are atoms in 12g of the isotope ^{12}C.

B. Liquids have definite volume but take the shapes of their containers. *Vapor pressure* is the pressure a gas exerts on the surface of the liquid, in a closed system when the liquid changes to a gas. It increases as the temperature of the liquid increases and is unique for each substance and temperature. The *boiling point* is the temperature at which the vapor pressure of the liquid equals the external pressure. (When the external pressure is one atmosphere, the boiling point is called the "normal" boiling point.)

The *heat of vaporization* is the energy required to vaporize one unit mass of a liquid at constant temperature. As the external pressure increases on a liquid, the temperature at which the liquid boils increases.

C. Solids have definite shape and volume. All true solids have crystalline structure, are arranged in regular geometric patterns, and are constantly vibrating. The *normal melting point* is the temperature at which a solid will change to a liquid at one atmosphere of pressure. The *heat of fusion* is the energy required to melt one unit mass of a solid at constant temperature. *Sublimation* is a change from the solid phase directly to the gas phase without passing through the liquid phase.

Questions

1. Energy flows spontaneously from areas of higher temperature to
   1. areas of equilibrium.
   2. areas of lower pressure.
   3. amounts of lower mass.
   4. areas of lower temperature.

2. Iodine, when heated, passes from the solid phase directly to the gaseous phase. This is an example of
   1. Charles's Law.
   2. Sublimation.
   3. Vapor pressure.
   4. Heat of Fusion.

3. An ideal gas behaves according to
   1. Avagradro's Hypothesis.
   2. Charles's Law.
   3. The Kinetic Molecular Theory.
   4. All of the above.

4. The study of chemistry does NOT include which one of the following?
   1. the composition of particles
   2. the mechanics of particle motion
   3. the structure of particles
   4. the properties of particles

5. Charles's Law involves which relationship in gases?
   1. volume/temperature
   2. volume/pressure
   3. pressure/temperature
   4. STP

6. Boyle's Law involves which relationship in gases?
   1. volume/temperature
   2. volume/pressure
   3. pressure/temperature
   4. STP

7. Elements
   1. can be decomposed by chemical means.
   2. cannot be decomposed by chemical means.
   3. contain two or more atoms chemically combined.
   4. comingle two or more substances.

8. In any exothermic chemical change, energy is
   1. lost.
   2. gained.
   3. absorbed.
   4. increased.

9. The amount of heat required to change 1 kilogram of water by 1 degree Kelvin at 1 atmosphere is known as
   1. a kilocalorie.
   2. heat of fusion.
   3. heat of vaporization.
   4. sublimation.

10. Which of the following represents an element?
    1. Cl^{1-}
    2. OH^{1-}
    3. Ag
    4. Li_2O

11. Which of the following represents a compound?

1. Cl^{1-}
2. OH^{1-}
3. Ag
4. Li_2O

12. Which of the following is NOT true of solids?

1. True solids have a crystalline structure.
2. They take the shape of the container.
3. The particles vibrate.
4. They have a definite volume.

13. Which of the following is NOT true of liquids?

1. They have no definite shape or volume.
2. They have no definite shape.
3. They have a boiling point.
4. Their heat of vaporization can be measured.

14. Which of the following is NOT true of an ideal gas?

1. It has a definite shape and volume.
2. It is composed of individual particles that are in constant motion.
3. The volume of individual gas particles is ignored.
4. Gas particles have no attraction for each other.

15. The composition of a mixture

1. may vary.
2. remains constant.
3. has a definite ratio throughout.
4. is easily calculated.

16. The intrinsic energy in the particles of any pure substance is highest in the

1. solid phase.
2. liquid phase.
3. gaseous phase.
4. gel phase.

17. The form of energy in sunlight is

1. chemical.
2. mechanical.
3. nuclear.
4. radiant.

18. Which of the following is not a pure substance?

1. water.
2. hydrogen.
3. milk.
4. oxygen.

19. A(n) _____ is always composed of the same elements combined in a definite proportion by mass.

1. isotope
2. compound
3. ion
4. allotrope

Answers

1. The correct answer is 4. Energy spontaneously flows from areas of higher temperature to lower temperature. The result might be an equilibrium, but heat does not flow to it. Lower pressure and mass do not apply here, since we are talking about temperature.

2. The correct answer is 2. This is the definition of sublimation: change from solid to gas with no apparent liquid phase, under normal conditions. Charles's Law describes gas behavior, and vapor pressure and Heat of Fusion have little to do with the physical change we are observing here.

3. The correct answer is 4. The Kinetic Molecular Theory outlines the properties of an ideal gas. Both Charles's Law and Avogadro's principle describe particular aspects of a gas under normal conditions.

4. The correct answer is 2. Mechanics falls strictly under the realm of Physics. All the others are areas covered in Chemistry.

5. The correct answer is 1. With pressure held constant, Charles's Law investigates the direct relationship between Volume and Temperature. Boyle's Law involves pressure and volume, while pressure and temperature are dealt with in Gay-Lussac's Law. STP simply means standard temperature and pressure.

6. The correct answer is 2. With temperature held constant, Boyle's Law investigates the inverse relationship between volume and pressure. See answer to question 6 for the explanation of the other components in this question.

7. The correct answer is 2. Elements are defined as indivisible by chemical (i.e., "ordinary") means. Therefore, they are one substance, the simplest form and answers 1, 3, and 4, which refer to more than one substance, cannot apply here.

8. The correct answer is 1. Exothermic reactions lose energy to the environment. Answers 2, 3 and 4 all refer to increases in energy in some way in the substances involved. These are examples of endothermic reactions.

9. The correct answer is 1. This is the definition of the calorie multiplied by 1,000 since we are heating 1,000 grams. Therefore the energy would be known as a kilocalorie. The other choices describe particular points in the changes of state that a substance might experience. The heat of fusion is the amount of energy required to change one gram of a solid to one gram of a liquid at a constant temperature. Likewise with the heat of vaporization, the amount of energy required to change on gram of a liquid to one gram of a gas at a constant temperature. Sublimation occurs when a solid changes directly into a gas.

10. The correct answer is 3. Ag is the only one on the list that fits the definition of an element. 1 and 2 are ions since they are showing an electric charge and 4 is the compound lithium oxide.

11. The correct answer is 4. It is the only substance that fits the definition of a compound. See the answer to question 11.

12. The correct answer is 2. Solids have a definite shape and therefore do not take the shape of any container. They have a definite volume, they primarily vibrate in position as the only evidence of movement, and they have a crystalline structure.

13. The correct answer is 1. Liquids have no definite shape, but they do have a definite volume. Their Heat of Vaporization can be measured, making use of their boiling point and they also take the shape of their container.

14. The correct answer is 1. Gases have no definite shape or volume. The other three statements are major parts of the Kinetic Molecular Theory with respect to gases and are true.

15. The correct answer is 1. Mixtures vary in composition and structure. One can never really say a mixture has an exact composition at any one point in the mixture compared to any other point in the mixture. Therefore the composition is not constant nor does it have a definite ratio throughout which means it cannot be easily calculated.

16. The correct answer is 3. When dealing with the same substance, the gaseous particles contain the most energy. In descending order among the choices given, it would be gas, liquid, and solid. If a substance had a gel phase, it might go in between liquid and solid.

17. The correct answer is 4. The definition of radiant energy best fits sunlight. Nuclear energy would be at the source, but it would not be the sunlight coming from that source. Chemical energy involves electron bond energy and mechanical energy involves only the motion of particles. These could not apply to the solar environment.

18. The correct answer is 3. Milk is a mixture since some of its components can be separated by physical means, e.g., homogenization. Therefore it is not a pure substance. Water, hydrogen, and oxygen are all substances wherein each particle in that substnace compared to any other particle in that substance has the same ratio of the materials that make up that substance.

19. The correct answer is 2. A compound is defined as having two or more elements chemically combined in a particular ratio. An isotope is another form of an element and an ion is a charged atom or group of atoms. The charge means that the chemical combination is not yet completely satisfied.

Chapter 4

Atomic Structure

I. Atoms

   A. Introduction to atomic structure.

      Our concept of the nature of the atom has changed over time and will likely continue to do so. Characteristic of the history of science from the time of Aristotle to the present day, the wave-particle theory of the atom finds pure science and technology almost leap-frogging each other as new discoveries in pure science are made possible by technological improvements, and new information discovered through pure science enables improvements in technology. Our present day view of the atom includes some past views, all of which help us visualize this small particle that makes up a large portion of matter in the universe.

   B. Important subatomic particles.

      1. *Nucleons* are particles found in the nucleus and include the proton and neutron. The historical record reveals how these particles were discovered, named and then utilized in understanding the nature of matter in the universe.

         a. Protons—The proton's mass is designated as one atomic mass unit and it has a unit positive charge. The number of protons in an atom has been arbitrarily designated as its atomic number. Atoms were eventually aligned in order of their atomic number, which corrected several anomalies on the periodic chart that occurred previously when atoms were aligned by their mass. The number of protons is not easily changed in the nucleus.

         b. Neutrons—The neutron has a mass of slightly more than one atomic mass unit and a zero charge. Comparisons of the atomic number and the mass number of an atom reveal a discrepancy that can be accounted for only by the presence of a particle that is approximately the mass of a proton but with no charge. The neutron and our present understanding of its structure successfully account for this discrepancy. The number of neutrons is not easily changed in the nucleus.

2. Electrons—Electrons have a mass that is 1/1836 of a proton and a unit negative charge. They are much smaller than protons yet their charge is equal and opposite to the proton. The exact nature and location of the electron has fueled most of the debate over the nature of the atom itself. The nature of chemical activity in an atom is the result of the number and placement of its electrons. Compared with the nucleons, electrons are more easily removed or added to atoms.

C. Structure of atoms—Atoms differ in the number of protons and neutrons and in the configuration of electrons surrounding the nucleus. This fact leads to the following understandings as to the structure of the atom and is fundamental to all chemistry.

1. "Empty space" concept—Most of the atom consists of empty space. The space between the placement of the electrons and the nucleus on a universal scale would be enormous, which gives you an idea as to the size of the particles we are dealing with in the atom. Early discoveries with cathode ray tubes and the like revealed the potential for the empty space concept.

2. Nucleus—the mass of the atom is concentrated in the nucleus. The nucleons are very compacted and sit very close to each other. The proposal of a particle known as the gluon accounts for how—with the number of neutrons matching or exceeding the number of protons—the closely associated positive particles, the protons, can remain so close to each other and not fly apart, thus destroying the nucleus. It seems unlikely that the neutrons would be able to keep the protons together in the nucleus by themselves.

a. Atomic number—The atomic number is arbitrarily set as the number of protons in the nucleus. Aligning the elements by atomic number allows us to predict certain properties of the present elements and the existence of future elements and their theoretical properties.

b. Mass number—Mass number is the total number of protons and neutrons in an atom and accounts for almost the entire mass (the mass of electrons is for all practical purposes ignored). For example, the mass number of one isotope of oxygen is 16: It has eight protons and eight neutrons. For any one form of an atom, also called an isotope (see *d* below), the mass number is a whole number.

c. Atomic mass—Atomic mass is the weighted average mass of all the naturally occurring isotopes of an element and is a decimal number. The mass number listed on the periodic table, also called the atomic mass, is calculated by taking the percent occurrence of each isotope times its mass and adding up all the resulting numbers. For example, if element X had two isotopes, one weighing 33 AMU and 75 percent abundant and one weighing 35 AMU and 25 percent abundant, the atomic mass would be listed as

$$(33 \times .75) + (35 \times .25) \text{ or } 33.50.$$

d. Isotopes—Isotopes are defined as atoms with the same atomic number but different masses due to the differing numbers of neutrons in each form. For example, deuterium is an isotope of hydrogen with one proton and one neutron in the nucleus, thus its atomic number is number 1, but its mass number is 2.

3. Electrons—Electrons are located outside the nucleus, and in a neutral atom, the number of electrons is equal to the number of protons inside the nucleus. The activity of the electrons is the driving force behind chemical reactions and defines the reactivity of each element, chemically, with respect to every other element. "Chemically combined" means something has occurred with respect to the electrons. Certain elements do not chemically combine under normal conditions and these are thought to be chemically unreactive.

Subatomic Particle	Symbol	Relative Mass	Charge	Location
Proton	$^1_1 H$	1	+1	Nucleus
Neutron	$^1_0 n$	1	0	Nucleus
Electron	e^-	0	-1	Electron Orbitals

D. The Bohr atom—Models that represent the structure of the atom have passed through many stages of development. In the Bohr atom, electrons were considered to revolve around the nucleus in one of several concentric circular orbits. While we use this model to create a "freeze-frame" of the atom in order to understand chemical reactions and the structure of atoms and compounds, the atom is, in fact, in a dynamic state as the following examples will suggest. Different models allow us to understand different aspects of atomic structure.

1. Principal energy levels—are denoted by the numbers 1, 2, 3 . . . up to infinity. Electrons near the nucleus are in the lower energy levels and can jump to higher levels with the addition of energy to the atom and fall back to the energy level from which they originated when that energy is removed. See "spectral lines" below.

2. Quanta—are the discrete amounts of energy the electrons can absorb and the amount of energy that the electrons emit when they return to a lower energy level.

3. Spectral lines—are produced when radiant energy of a specific frequency is emitted as the electrons, in an excited state, return (or fall back) to lower levels. These characteristic lines can be used to identify specific elements, using spectroscopes designed to reveal the lines to an observer.

E. Orbital Model of the Atom—also known as the Electron Cloud Model, it refers to the average region of most probable electron location. Electron orbitals may differ in size, shape or axis of orientation and may contain varying numbers of electrons, depending on the element. All isotopes of any element will have the same number of protons as well as electrons in the ground state.

1. Energy levels—are represented by quantum numbers similar to those in the Bohr atom.

a. Principal quantum numbers—Designated as n, they represent the principal energy levels in an atom. The first is $n = 1$, which stands for the innermost level of electrons.

b. Sublevels—The principal energy levels are divided into sublevels. The total number of sublevels for each principal energy level is equal to the number of that principal energy level, with the sublevels designated as s, p, d, f, g, etcetera. For example, energy level number 3 has three sublevels—s, p, and d.

c. Orbitals—Each sublevel consists of one or more orbitals. Each of these orbitals holds no more than two electrons as stated in the Pauli Exclusion Principle. The "s" sublevels consist of one orbital, which means the "s" sublevel in any one principal energy level can only hold two electrons. The "p" sublevels, which consist of three orbitals, will always hold a maximum of six electrons. The "d" sublevels consist of five orbitals, the "f" sublevels consist of seven orbitals, etcetera.

2. Electron configurations—Starting with hydrogen, the configurations of electrons in an atom are built up by adding one electron at a time according to the following rules: (a) No more than two electrons can be accommodated in any orbital, (b) The added electron is placed in the unfilled orbital of lowest energy (the Aufbau principle), (c) In a given sublevel, a second electron is not added to an orbital until each orbital in the sublevel contains one electron (Hund's rule), and (d) No more than four orbitals are occupied in the outermost principal energy level of any atom.

3. Valence electrons—Valence electrons are the electrons in the outermost principal energy level of the atom. These are the electrons available for allowing the atom to take part in a chemical reaction. The inert gases, with eight electrons in their outermost orbit, satisfy the "octet rule" and are nonreactive under ordinary conditions.

4. Ion—An ion is an electrically charged atom by virtue of a gain or loss in the number of electrons. In an ionic reaction, electrons first move from one atom to another, causing the atoms to become charged; then ions respond to each other's electrical nature.

For example, O^{2-} is the most common oxygen ion. The charge and the number together indicate that an oxygen atom can gain two electrons, whereas aluminum becomes a positive aluminum ion Al^{3+} by having an aluminum atom lose three electrons. The loss of three electrons can be viewed as being similar to the operation involving signed numbers, e.g., loss would be a subtraction and involves negative particles, so it would be written: $-(3-) = 3+$.

F. Ionization energy—Ionization energy is the amount of energy required to remove the most loosely bound electron from an atom or ion in the gaseous phase. This is the basis for predicting the nature of chemical reactions, including accounting for energy released or absorbed in those chemical reactions.

II. Natural Radioactivity

Natural radioactivity is the spontaneous disintegration of the nucleus of an atom with the subsequent emission of particles and/or radiation, such as high speed electrons or gamma rays. Some naturally occurring elements are radioactive, such as uranium, polonium, and radon. Despite the fact that we talk about radiation in this section, this form of energy is most often referred to as nuclear. Radiant energy refers to waves of energy without respect to medium and includes in this section, gamma- and x-rays. Outside the realm of the nuclear discussion, radiant energy classically includes UV rays, solar energy, infrared light, etcetera.

A. Types of radiation—differ from each other in mass, charge, penetrating power, and ionizing power.

1. Alpha decay—occurs when an alpha particle (a helium nucleus) is given off as the result of nuclear disintegration. This particle has the least penetrating power; pieces of paper will stop it. The atom from which an alpha particle is removed changes to an atom that is reduced by two atomic numbers and four mass numbers. Thus, if barium-139, atomic number 56, loses an alpha particle, it becomes Xe-135, atomic number 54.

2. Beta decay—occurs when a beta particle (a high-speed electron) is given off as the result of nuclear disintegration. This particle can sometimes penetrate a sheet of paper but not something like a sheet of aluminum foil. Beta decay here refers to beta minus (B–) decay, the more common of the two forms of beta decay, in which a neutron in the nucleus decays into a proton and electron with the latter ejected from the nucleus. However, the electron was not there in the nucleus before the decay (the actual mechanism is not necessary to understand). This decay actually increases the atomic number by one, as a neutral particle is turned into a positive particle in the nucleus. Therefore, a beta decay of atomic number 14 (the parent) will yield a beta particle and element with atomic number 15 (the daughter) and of the same mass number as the parent, before the decay. Therefore, a beta decay of element number 14

will yield a beta particle and element number 15 of the same mass as the mass of element number 14 before the decay.

3. Gamma radiation—is similar to high energy x-rays and will penetrate through most materials. Gamma rays are by definition any radiant energy emitted during a nuclear process, regardless of energy, although most gamma rays are higher in energy than any other form of light. Gamma rays constantly bombard our atmosphere from outer space. Gamma rays have no mass or charge.

B. Separating types of radiation—can be done for those types with mass (not radiant energy like gamma rays) with an electric or a magnetic field. Both will separate positive particles (alpha) from negative (beta) and, therefore, the neutral particles from the positive/negative particles.

C. Detection of radioactivity—is done by its ionizing, fluorescent and photographic effects. Different forms of radiation will ionize certain materials, thereby revealing their presence. In a like manner, different forms of radiation will cause certain materials to fluoresce while others will affect unexposed photographic plates, making them appear exposed.

D. Half-life—is the time required for one half of the nuclei of a given sample of a radioactive isotope to decay. Radioactive elements go through a number of half-lives until the material has been completely converted to the next element in the decay series which may or may not also be radioactive. For example, if we start with a kilogram of a substance, there will be 0.5 kilograms left in one half-life, 0.25 kg left after two, 0.125 left after three, etcetera.

Basic Concept

Fraction of original nuclei remaining after
$$n \text{ half-lives} = \left(\frac{1}{2}\right)^n$$

Fraction of nuclei that has decayed away after
$$n \text{ half-lives} = 1 - \left(\frac{1}{2}\right)^n$$

Questions

1. Which of the following is true of our understanding of the nature of the atom?
   1. It has undergone little, but significant change and is now complete.
   2. It has undergone change and will likely continue to do so.
   3. It is just as the ancients originally described it.
   4. It has undergone such major changes it is returning to the ancient model.

2. Particles in the nucleus are known as
   1. isotopes
   2. neutrons
   3. nucleons
   4. electrons

Use the following information for questions 3 through 6.

The element Beryllium [Be] has an isotope with five neutrons and four protons.

3. The atomic number of Be is
   1. 5.
   2. 4.
   3. 9.
   4. not given.

4. The mass number of this isotope of Be is
   1. 5.
   2. 4.
   3. 9.
   4. not given.

5. The number of electrons in the element Be is
   1. 5.
   2. 4.
   3. 9.
   4. not given.

6. The atomic mass of Beryllium is
   1. 5.
   2. 4.
   3. 9.
   4. not given.

7. Zinc with 30 protons, 30 electrons, and 35 neutrons, is atomic number
   1. 30.
   2. 35.
   3. 60.
   4. 65.

8. Zinc with 30 protons, 28 electrons, and 35 neutrons, is a zinc
   1. atom that is neutral.
   2. ion that is charged −2.
   3. ion that is charged +2.
   4. isotope with a mass number of 63.

9. Which of the following is not an isotope of hydrogen?
   1. uranium
   2. deuterium
   3. hydrogen
   4. tritium

10. Energy level 5 has
    1. s, p, and d sublevels only.
    2. s, p, d, and f sublevels only.
    3. s, p, d, f, and g sublevels only.
    4. a number of sublevels not yet determined.

11. The maximum number of electrons that could fit in the "p" sublevel is
    1. 9.
    2. 6.
    3. 3.
    4. 2.

12. Element number 13 has ____ valence electrons.
    1. 13
    2. 10
    3. 8
    4. 3

13. Which of the following is the energy configuration for element number 13?
    1. $1s^2 2s^2 2p^6 3s^2 3p^1$
    2. $1s^2 2s^2 2p^6 3s^1 3p^1 3d^1$
    3. $1s^2 2s^2 2p^6 3s^3$
    4. $1s^2 2s^2 2p^6 3p^3$

14. The octet rule allows for a maximum of ____ outermost electrons in any one atom.
    1. 2
    2. 8
    3. 16
    4. There is no limit.

15. Which of the following would not come from a radioactive source?
    1. gamma rays
    2. laser beam
    3. alpha particles
    4. high-speed electrons from nuclear decay

16. Starting with 1 kg of a radioactive substance, after four half-lives, there will be approximately _____ grams left.
    1. 63
    2. 125
    3. 250
    4. 500

17. Which of the following types of radiation will be stopped by a piece of paper?
    1. alpha
    2. neutron
    3. Gamma ray
    4. x-ray

18. Whose rule or principle delineates the placement of additional electrons in the unfilled orbital of lowest energy?
    1. Avogadro
    2. Aufbau
    3. Hund
    4. Pauli

19. Spectral lines are produced
    1. when electrons are knocked out of their energy level.
    2. when electrons interact with protons.
    3. when electrons move up to higher energy levels.
    4. when electrons return to their energy level.

Answers

1. The correct answer is 2. Choice 2 more accurately describes the current status of our understanding of the atom, while choice 3 is grossly inaccurate or misleading. Our understanding is NOT complete, and it bears little resemblance to what the ancients felt.

2. The correct answer is 3. An isotope is a form of an entire atom; in addition to neutrons, the nucleus contains protons, and electrons orbit outside the nucleus. The correct name for the particles in the nucleus is nucleons.

3. The correct answer is 2. This is given directly from the periodic table and reflects the presence of four protons in beryllium.

4. The correct answer is 3. The mass number is simply the number of neutrons plus the number of protons in the nucleus.

5. The correct answer is 2. The number of electrons is equal to the number of protons since the question designates the substance Beryllium as an element, not an ion. As such, the number of protons equals the number of electrons. Of course 5 is the number of neutrons, and 9 is the protons and neutrons added together.

6. The correct answer is 4. This is always a decimal number as it is the weighted average of all of the naturally occurring isotopes of the element in question. Technically then, the atomic mass, as it would appear on the periodic chart, is not given since it is 9.012 AMU.

7. The correct answer is 1. The atomic number equals the number of protons, which is choice 1. Choice 2 is the number of neutrons. Choice 3 is the protons and electrons added together, something we never see done for any good reason, and choice 4 is the mass number.

8. The correct answer is 3. Since the number of electrons indicates a loss of two from the element Zn, this means the one we are given here is an ion of Zn. It is not neutral, given the number of protons and electrons. It also has not gained two electrons as choice 2 suggests and its mass number is 65, the sum of the protons and neutrons, not electrons and neutrons.

9. The correct answer is 1. All of the names listed are forms of hydrogen except uranium. Uranium is element number 92. Deuterium has one proton and one neutron, and tritium has one proton and two neutrons.

10. The correct answer is 3. Energy levels have the number of sublevels equal to their energy level number, therefore energy level 5 has five sublevels—s, p, d, f, and g.

11. The correct answer is 2. The "p" sublevel has 3 orbitals, and the Pauli Exclusion Principle allows for only two electrons per orbital, giving 6 as the maximum in any "p" sublevel. There is no sublevel that holds either three or nine as a maximum, and it is the "s" orbital that holds a maximum of two.

12. The correct answer is 4. Filling in the energy levels and sublevels according to standard electron configuration understanding, three electrons are placed in the outermost energy, or valence, level. Two electrons go in the first energy level, then eight, satisfying the octet rule and the maximum number in the second energy level. The total so far is ten leaving three for the outermost energy level.

13. The correct answer is 1. This is the correct placement of thirteen electrons. First the 1s fills with two electrons, leaving eleven left to be placed. The 2s fills with two, leaving nine to go. The 2p fills with six, two for each of the three sublevels, leaving three to go. The 3s fills with two leaving one electron for the 3p sublevel.

14. The correct answer is 2. "No more than four orbitals are occupied in the outermost principal energy level of the atom" is the basis for the octet rule. Two applies to the first energy level only as its maximum, sixteen does not apply for any energy level, and, yes, there is a limit—namely eight.

15. The correct answer is 2. Lasers come from stimulating atoms, not from a radioactive source. The other three are three of the major forms of radiation known to science.

16. The correct answer is 1. Four half-lives would reduce the mass to 500 in the first; half of that would be another half-life, bringing it to 250, then 125 and then 62.5 or approximately 63 in four half-lives.

17. The correct answer is 1. The weakest radiation listed in the question (regarding penetrating power) is alpha particles. Neutrons, gamma- and x-rays have an enormous amount of penetrating power in most substances.

18. The correct answer is 2. This is a statement of Aufbau's principle. Choice 1 is a series of descriptions of the number of particles in a specified amount of an element as well as its volume and mass. Choice 3 comments on Hund's rule governing the addition of a second electron to an orbital, and choice 4 tells us that each orbital can hold no more than two electrons.

19. The correct answer is 4. When an electron is excited out of its energy level, it enters a higher level by virtue of that additional energy. When it drops back, after the source of the additional energy is no longer there, it gives off the absorbed energy as light. Each element is special in the type of light each electron releases.

Chapter 5

Bonding

I. The Nature of the Chemical Bond

    A. Chemical Energy—is potential energy that substances possess due to their composition and structure. The atoms that will compose or are composing compounds will, by virtue of their composition, dictate the amount of energy available in their bonds. Some atoms are more reactive or less reactive than others. In addition, the structure of an atom, due in part to its composition as well as the laws of nature, will dictate the energy available in bonds. An atom with nine electrons is in a different state of potential energy than an atom with ten electrons.

    B. Energy changes in bonding

        1. Bond broken—In order for a bond to be broken, some energy must be invested into the bond to break it. A higher state of energy than is normal then exists for that bond in that compound, and the bond breaks. This may then release that energy and more to the surroundings.

        2. Bond formed—When a bond is formed, there is a release of any extra energy not needed to maintain the bond; thus the opposite event to when a bond is broken occurs, and excess energy not needed to maintain the bond is released to the environment.

    C. Bonding and stability

        1. Systems at low energy levels are more stable than systems at high energy levels. Recalling the statements immediately above, a bond will always be most stable at its lowest level; add energy and the bond is broken, take away energy from the potential constituents and the bond forms. All of this means that with a knowledge of ionization energies, we can predict the activity of bonds.

2. Chemical changes will occur if they lead to a lower energy condition, resulting in a more stable structure. This will be the basis behind the prediction of bond formation/destruction. Noting the individual energies for the electrons involved, the existence of a net gain or loss will allow us to predict what will happen with respect to any bond.

D. Electronegativity—is the measure of the ability of an atom to attract the electrons that form a bond between it and another atom. These figures are well known, published in tables and are used in the calculations involving bonds. This increases from lower left to upper right on the periodic table.

II. Bonds between Atoms

A. Formation—occurs when electrons involved in bond formation are either transferred from one atom to another or shared equally (or unequally) between two atoms. The ionic or covalent character of the bond can be approximated from differences in the electronegativity of the reacting species.

B. Types—There are essentially only two types of bonds or situations where atoms will reside close to each other in a particular way. Atoms transfer electrons, also called give or take—one gives, the other takes. The atoms may also share electrons, which can occur in a variety of ways.

1. Ionic—formed by the transfer of one or more electrons from metals to nonmetals or between two ions in a previous reaction. This transfer makes an ion positive (by losing electrons) or negative (by gaining electrons). In doing so, the atoms become charged atoms, or ions. One such atom will be positive and the other will be negative, thus becoming attracted to each other. Ionic solids have high melting points and do not conduct electricity, except in aqueous solution or once melted to form molten salts. The term ionization refers not only to the atoms that transfer electrons but also to atoms that share electrons as if they transferred that number of electrons. An example would be the formation of sodium chloride from its elements: $Na\ Cl \rightarrow Na^+\ Cl^-$ (An electron was transferred from Na to Cl).

2. Covalent—formed when two or more atoms share electrons. Despite the fact that they share electrons, the individual atoms will still be assigned an oxidation number to help identify how many electrons will be shared— and in what way—with other atoms. Covalent materials have a variety of properties as is evident by the variety of bonds possible.

a. Nonpolar—when electrons are shared equally between atoms of the same element. Examples would be the bond between fluorine atoms in the F_2 molecule, or between two carbon atoms in acetylene, H_2CCH_2.

b. Polar—when electrons are shared unequally between atoms of different elements. An example would be the hydrogen chloride molecule, where the shared electron from hydrogen resides in between the hydrogen and the chlorine making the molecule on the side of the outward-facing hydrogen, completely nonnegative.

c. Coordinate—when the two shared electrons are both donated by one of the atoms. An example would be the bond often formed in polyatomic molecules, where the distribution of electrons does not always involve equal sharing; rather; an empty sublevel of one of the elements is positioned to overlap a full sublevel of the other.

d. Molecular substances—discrete particles formed by covalently bonded atoms and generally soft, electrical insulators, and poor heat conductors with low melting points. Examples would be H_2, NH_3, HCl, and $C_6H_{12}O_6$.

e. Network solids—covalently bonded atoms linked in a network that extends throughout the sample in which there is an absence of simple discrete particles, i.e., the network is a complex interlinkage of parts. They are generally hard, electrical insulators, poor conductors of heat, and have high melting points. Examples would be diamonds, SiC, and SiO_2.

3. Metallic—formed between the atoms of metals that have vacant valence orbitals and low ionization energies. An excess of electrons roam the latticework making metals excellent conductors of electricity. Examples would be copper, iron, zinc, and nickel.

III. Molecular Attraction.

Molecular Attraction—Covalently bonded molecules may be attracted to similar molecules or to ions. In this way, we find a variety of ways compounds can be formed and the nature of the forces that bind them.

A. Dipoles—the asymmetrical distribution of electrical charge gives rise to this type of polar molecule. An example would be water molecules wherein the electron shared resides mainly between the two hydrogens and the oxygen. This makes the oxygen side negative and the hydrogen side positive, thus setting the stage for hydrogen bonds.

B. Hydrogen bonds—formed when hydrogen is covalently bonded to an element of small atomic radius and high electronegativity (F, O, or N) and is a special case of a dipole-dipole attraction. The positive side of one of the molecules—for example, the hydrogen in water—attracts to the negative side—for example the oxygen side of water—to form a weak attraction between molecules. Another example would be HF.

C. Van der Waals forces—the weak attraction between molecules in the absence of dipole attraction and hydrogen bonding that becomes greater with increases in size and with decreases in distance between molecules. Examples would be liquid helium, oxygen, etcetera. These are very weak forces and often require low temperatures and high pressures in order to take effect.

D. Molecule-ion attraction—occurs when polar solvents, as they interact with ionic compounds, attract ions from these compounds and form a solution. For example when water dissolves table salt, this is evidence of a molecule-ion attraction.

IV. Directional Nature of Covalent Bonds

Directional Nature of Covalent Bonds—Generally, the geometric structure of covalent substances, which results from the directional nature of the covalent bond, helps to explain the properties of the resulting molecule. It is the interactions among the various electron energy levels and the shape of the orbitals that dictate the resulting properties of the molecules formed in these interactions.

V. Chemical Formula

Chemical formula—both a qualitative and quantitative expression of the composition of an element or a compound. The attempt is to communicate as much information as possible without extra clutter. Some things will have to be memorized—or used so often as to become well known.

A. Symbol—may represent one atom or one mole of atoms of an element. A mole, as will be seen later, can represent a certain number of particles (in this case, atoms), or the volume of that number of particles, or the mass of that number of particles. The symbol is a designated one- or two-letter entity and is agreed upon by the scientific community. It is often used to honor a place or person. Some symbols have historical meaning and some retain a Latin or Greek origin. For example, C is carbon and N is nitrogen.

B. Formula—a statement in chemical symbols that represents the composition of a substance, most often two or more elements indicating a chemical combination that has occurred between them. There are several kinds of formulas including:

1. Molecular—indicates the total number of atoms of each element needed to form the molecule, examples being H_2O and Na_2HCO_3.

2. Empirical—the simplest ratio in which atoms combine to form a compound. For example, if our calculations found the ratio of sodium to chlorine in table salt to be 4:4 (i.e., Na_4Cl_4), we would reduce that to NaCl. Some substances, however, structurally contain a set number of atoms, and therefore we do not reduce these (for example, sulfur is S_8).

VI. Naming and Writing Formulas

A. The chemical name of a compound generally indicates the chemical composition of the substance. For example CS_2 is carbon disulfide.

B. Binary compounds—composed only of one metallic element and one non-metallic element. The metallic element is usually named and written first. An example would be magnesium chloride—$MgCl_2$. Note that while there are two chlorines, it is still only one element. Note also that binaries always end in -*ide*.

C. When a compound is composed of two nonmetals, the less electronegative element is usually written first as in NO or P_2O_5.

D. Prefixes are used to indicate the number of atoms of each nonmetal in the compound as in carbon disulfide and silicon dioxide. Water should be named dihydrogen oxide, but tradition prevails.

E. In a polyatomic compound, the metal is usually named first, followed by the polyatomic, negative ion as in sodium bicarbonate or lithium sulfate.

F. Roman numerals in parentheses after an element symbol refer to the oxidation number of that element in the compound.

VII. Chemical Equations

Chemical Equations—represent the qualitative and quantitative changes in bonding and energy that take place in a chemical reaction and that must conform to the laws of conservation of mass and energy.

Equations include reactants on the left side of the arrow and products on the right side. Any pertinent additional information is written above or below the arrow; for example the Greek symbol for delta (Δ) is the triangle and it stands for "addition of heat."

Example: $2H_2 + O_2 \xrightarrow{\Delta} 2H_2O + \text{heat}$

Questions

1. Which of the following is not a source of the potential energy a substance has in a chemical reaction?
   1. composition
   2. mass number
   3. structure
   4. bond type

2. When a chemical bond is broken,
   1. energy is absorbed.
   2. energy is released.
   3. there is no energy change.
   4. an exothermic reaction has occurred.

3. Chemical changes will occur if they lead to
   1. bond formation.
   2. endothermia.
   3. exothermia.
   4. lower energy conditions.

4. The transfer of electrons from one atom to another forms
   1. isotopes.
   2. allotropes.
   3. ions.
   4. molecules.

5. Which of the following is not a type of covalent bond?
   1. polar
   2. nonpolar
   3. coordinate
   4. metallic

6. When electrons are shared unequally between atoms of different elements, a _____ covalent bond occurs.
   1. polar
   2. nonpolar
   3. coordinate
   4. molecular

7. This covalent bond is most often formed in polyatomic molecules.
   1. polar
   2. nonpolar
   3. coordinate
   4. molecular

8. Which of the following is true of ionic compounds?
   1. high melting point
   2. poor conductors in aqueous solutions
   3. generally soft
   4. share electrons

9. An example of an ionic compound would be
   1. H_2O.
   2. HCl.
   3. NH_3.
   4. NaCl.

10. Which of the following would be a covalent compound?
    1. SiO_2
    2. NaCl
    3. LiF
    4. KBr

11. Which of the following is not an example of a type of molecular attraction?
    1. coordinate bond
    2. hydrogen bonds
    3. Van der Waals forces
    4. molecule-ion attraction

12. Which of the following is not a way to express the formula of a compound?
    1. structural
    2. molecular
    3. empirical
    4. metallic

13. Which of the following compounds always end in -ide?
    1. binary
    2. polyatomic
    3. covalent
    4. ionic

14. Van der Waals forces account for the formation of
    1. water molecules
    2. ionic solids
    3. conjugate bases
    4. liquid helium

15. In writing formulas, the _____ usually goes first.
    1. nonmetal
    2. metal
    3. polyatomic
    4. halide

16. Which of the following is not an atomic symbol?
    1. CO
    2. Na
    3. U
    4. Pb

17. The chemical name of a compound indicates
    1. mass.
    2. volume.
    3. composition.
    4. structure.

18. Expressing water as H_2O, despite the fact that certain of our calculations indicate a ratio of 8:4, means we are expressing its _____ formula.
    1. structural
    2. molecular
    3. empirical
    4. metallic

19. Carbon disulfide contains _____ sulfurs.
    1. 1
    2. 2
    3. 4
    4. cannot determine

20. Equal sharing of electrons in a compound tends to make the molecule
    1. polar.
    2. nonpolar.
    3. coordinate.
    4. metallic.

Answers

1. The correct answer is 2. Mass number has little to do with lowering the potential energy that may occur during a chemical change as composition, structure, and bond type will.

2. The correct answer is 1. Energy is always absorbed when a chemical bond is broken; 2 and 4 are the same thing (releasing energy) and choice 3 is incorrect.

3. The correct answer is 4. The tendency is always toward a lower energy state in a chemical change since this results in a more stable structure. Chemical changes are bond changes, and endothermia and exothermia do not directly apply here but may be the result of bond formation.

4. The correct answer is 3. The exchange of electrons forms charged particles called ions. Isotopes are different forms of the same element, allotropes refer to a different form of the same element with a different bonding pattern, and molecules are too general.

5. The correct answer is 4. A metallic bond with excesses of electrons roaming the network is not characteristic of the sharing that occurs during covalent bonding; all the others are characteristic.

6. The correct answer is 1. The unequal sharing of electrons will always lead to a definite polarity in the compound. Nonpolarity results from an equal distribution of elec-

trons, thereby preventing any one area from becoming more positive or negative than any other. The other two choices are too general.

7. The correct answer is 3. This is most often characteristic of the coordinate bond where shared electrons often come from one of the atoms.

8. The correct answer is 1. Some covalent compounds have high melting points, but ionic compounds, due to the strong attraction between ions, all have high melting points. In addition, they are good conductors in aqueous solution, do not share electrons, and are not soft.

9. The correct answer is 4. Choices 1, 2, and 3 all represent compounds where the sharing, or covalent bonding, of electrons occurs. Choice 4 is the ionic compound in which electrons have been transferred.

10. The correct answer is 1. Choices 2, 3, and 4 are all examples of transfer of electrons whereas in 1, electrons are shared, which is the reverse of question 9.

11. The correct answer is 1. Choice 1 represents a bond within a molecule whereas 2, 3, and 4 represent attractions, or bonds, between particles.

12. The correct answer is 4. The word *metallic* represents a kind of attraction or bond within a network of metallic ions; the other

three choices are ways to express the formula of a substance, whether it is an element or a compound.

13. The correct answer is 1. Binary compounds always end in -*ide* by changing the ending of the nonmetal so that it contains the -*ide*. For example, an oxide is a metal and oxygen chemically combined. Choices 2, 3, and 4 have some compounds ending in -*ide*, but not always.

14. The correct answer is 4. Van der Waals forces account for the weak attractions between particles, which, at very low forces—temperature and pressure—allow the liquid form of some substances such as liquid helium, oxygen and hydrogen to form. The other choices represent larger forces or, in the case of the conjugate bases, a different subject altogether.

15. The correct answer is 2. Metals, the positive part of the compound, are generally designated first in the naming of a compound. The second part represents the nonmetal, whether one element or several as in a polyatomic.

16. The correct answer is 1. CO is the formula for carbon monoxide, which is actually two elements chemically combined as a compound. The others are representations of atoms; Na is sodium, U is uranium, and Pb is lead.

17. The correct answer is 3. Mass, volume, and structure are all characteristics of a compound that require further interpretation. The chemical name readily indicates what the substance is made of.

18. The correct answer is 3. The empirical formula is expressing the composition of the substance as a formula in its lowest form, much like the lowest common denominator in math. The molecular formula tells us the composition but not necessarily in the simplest form, and the structural formula shows us how atoms are oriented in space. The word *metallic* refers to a bond type.

19. The correct answer is 2. The *di*- in disulfide indicates that carbon disulfide contains two sulfurs and that its formula is probably CS_2. All the other numbers are incorrect, and the formula is designed to help us determine the formula from the words.

20. The correct answer is 2. The equal sharing of electrons distributes the charge and, therefore, makes it so that no one area is charged more than others—creating a nonpolar substance. Unequal distribution makes the molecule more positive or negative in one area compared with others, which will be oppositely charged, creating polarity. Coordinate refers to a sharing bond in which one element donates both electrons to the bond, and metallic, as we have seen, involves an excess of electrons that roam a network of atoms.

Chapter 6

The Periodic Table

I.   Development of the Periodic Table

   A.   The periodic table has passed through many stages of development up to its
        present form. Historically, we first encounter Newland's "triads" wherein
        predictions can be made of the existence of an element squarely between two
        others in the same group by averaging the two known atomic masses.
        Mendeleev arranged elements by their atomic masses and produced the first
        periodic table by rearranging cards with the name of the atoms and their
        atomic masses for his graduate students. Mendeleev's chart, however, had
        gaps in it. Finally, Moseley suggested arrangement by atomic number, which
        cleared up the anomalies on Mendeleev's chart.

   B.   The present-day arrangement is based on atomic number. Such an arrange-
        ment reveals the true periodic nature of the elements. The atomic number is
        derived from the number of protons in the nucleus, or, put another way, the
        charge on the nucleus.

   C.   The properties of the elements depend on the structure of the atom. Aligning
        the elements by atomic number also increases them by one electron as they
        increase by one proton. These changes in structure account for the chemical
        properties, or the activity of the atom based on electron configuration, which
        generally repeat every eight protons, following an observation by Dobereiner
        of the so-called octave rule.

   D.   The properties vary with the atomic number in a systematic way. The nature
        of the electron configurations vary as we progress across the periodic table. It
        is this variation, which is then repeated in the next row for the atoms directly
        below the previous ones, that accounts for the periodicity of chemical proper-
        ties. Lithium combines with oxygen in a 2:1 ratio as does sodium, the element
        directly below lithium.

II. Properties of the Elements in the Periodic Table

A. Arrangement of the elements—There are several characteristics of the elements that emerge as we travel across the rows or down the columns of the periodic table. It is these changes and their periodic nature that gives the table its name. The properties are different, depending which way we travel on the table.

   1. Periods

      a. The horizontal rows of the periodic table are called periods. The name most likely comes from the fact that the properties change as we progress across a row. The repeating nature of those properties can best be described as periodic—thus the name.

      b. The properties of elements change systematically throughout a period. The properties in consideration here, of course, are the chemical properties, and we will find some physical properties such as atomic size and the number of electrons also changing, as well as where the electrons are located. Lithium, for instance, has one outer electron as does the element directly below it, sodium.

   2. Columns

      a. The vertical columns of the periodic table are called groups or families. Their chemical properties do not change as we progress through the column. Traversing the periods reveals a constant change in chemical properties, whereas going down a column reveals remarkably similar properties. Fluorine, for instance, combines with hydrogen on a 1:1 ratio, as do chlorine, bromine, and iodine.

      b. The elements of a group exhibit similar or related chemical properties since they all have the same number of electrons in their outermost principal energy levels. Their physical properties vary, but their chemical properties are the same.

B. Atomic radii—varies within the covalent and ionic nature of the atoms.

   1. Covalent atomic radius—designated as one half the measured internuclear distance in the solid phase, it is a periodic property of the elements. Within a single period on the table, the covalent atomic radius generally decreases as the atomic number increases. Adding more protons and corresponding electrons within any group in the periodic table causes an increase in the covalent atomic radius.

2. Ionic radius—A loss or gain of electrons by an atom causes a corresponding change in size of the atom. (Cations are smaller than the neutral atoms from which they came, while anions are larger.) Since we are adding or subtracting electrons, we are adding or subtracting energy levels and sublevels. Coupled with the changes in the nucleus, this brings about the changes listed above.

C. Types of elements found on the table

1. Metals—Another periodic characteristic to emerge on the table, these elements possess relatively low ionization energies. They tend to lose electrons to form positive ions when combining with other elements and usually possess the properties of high thermal and electrical conductivity, metallic luster, malleability, and ductility.

2. Nonmetals—found on the right side of the table, these elements possess high ionization energies. They also have relatively high electronegativities, tend to gain electrons when combined with metals or share electrons when combined with other elements, and in the solid phase, tend to be brittle, have low thermal and electrical conductivities, and lack metallic luster.

3. Metalloids—are elements that have some properties characteristic of metals and other properties characteristic of nonmetals. They reside between the two on the periodic table: B, Si, Ge, As, Sb, Te.

III. Chemistry of a Group (Family)

A. Groups, general

The elements in the periodic table are divided into Groups A and B except for Groups VIII and O. (More recently the groups are numbered 1 through 18, from left to right.) Elements in each group exhibit related chemical properties and are associated with similarity in the number of valence electrons. The properties of elements in a group change progressively as the atomic number increases. In the "A" groups, as the atomic number increases, the radius of the atom increases, the ionization energy and the electronegativity of the element generally decrease, and the elements tend to have more metallic properties.

B. Groups IA and IIA—are the most reactive metals. Elements in both groups have relatively low ionization energies and electronegativities. They lose electrons readily to form ionic compounds that are relatively stable. Reactivity within both groups tends to increase with an increase in the atomic number. In the same period, each Group IA metal is more reactive than the corresponding Group IIA metal. The elements in both groups are usually reduced to their free state by the electrolysis of their fused compounds. Group IA elements are called the alkali metals, and Group IIA are called alkaline earth metals.

C. Groups VA and VIA—These elements show distinct progression from non-metallic to metallic properties with an increase in atomic number. Nitrogen is relatively inactive at room temperature and its compounds are essential constituents of all living matter. Nitrogen compounds are relatively unstable. Phosphorus is more reactive than nitrogen at room temperature, and its compounds are also essential constituents of all living matter. Oxygen is an active nonmetal. Sulfur is less reactive than oxygen. Selenium and tellurium are rare elements. Polonium is a radioactive element.

D. Group VIIA—are typical nonmetals known as the halogens and have relatively high electronegativities. The physical form of the free element at room temperature varies with increasing atomic number and is usually prepared from the corresponding halide ion by removing one of the electrons from the ion.

E. Group O—are monatomic gases known as the "noble" or "inert" gases. Their outer electron configuration is stable, each holding eight electrons in the outer principal energy level (except for He, with two) They are for the most part unreactive under normal circumstances.

F. Transition elements—those elements where electrons from the two outermost sublevels may be involved in a chemical reaction. Transition elements generally exhibit multiple positive oxidation states. Their ions tend to exhibit color both in solid compounds and in solution.

IV. Chemistry of a Period

Chemistry of a period—In each period, as the atomic number increases, several things occur. The radius of the atom decreases. The ionization energy of the element generally increases. The electronegativity of the element generally increases. The elements generally change from very active metals to less active nonmetals to very active nonmetals and usually to an inert gas. There is a transition from positive to negative oxidation states. The metallic characteristics of the "A" group elements decrease.

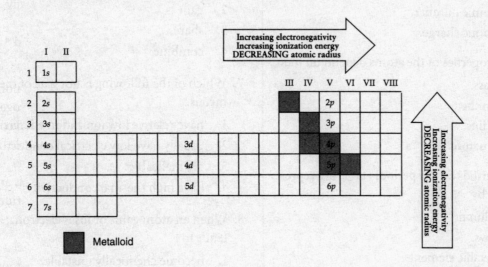

Questions

1. The modern periodic table is based on
   1. atomic radius.
   2. atomic mass.
   3. atomic number.
   4. atomic charge.

2. The properties of the atoms depend on their
   1. mass.
   2. number.
   3. radius.
   4. structure.

3. The periods on the periodic table are represented by
   1. columns.
   2. rows.
   3. metallic elements.
   4. inert gas members.

4. Columns on the periodic table are called
   1. gases.
   2. solids.
   3. periods.
   4. groups.

5. Metals tend to _____ electrons.
   1. lose
   2. gain
   3. share
   4. combine

6. Nonmetals tend to _____ electrons in combination with metals.
   1. lose
   2. gain
   3. share
   4. combine

7. Which of the following is not true of the metals?
   1. have relative low ionization energies
   2. usually have low electrical conductivity
   3. are malleable
   4. have high thermal conductivity

8. When an atom gains or loses electrons, it tends to
   1. become chemically unstable.
   2. become neutral.
   3. increase its oxidation number.
   4. change its size.

9. Nonmetals, in the solid phase, tend to
   1. have the same size.
   2. conduct electricity.
   3. lack metallic luster.
   4. All of the above are correct.

10. Nonmetals do not generally
    1. possess high ionization energy.
    2. gain electrons.
    3. have high electronegativities.
    4. tend to be malleable.

11. Metalloids tend to have characteristics of
    1. metals.
    2. nonmetals.
    3. both metals and nonmetals.
    4. inert gases.

12. Elements within a group have
    1. similar number of valence electrons.
    2. the same number of energy levels.
    3. the same atomic radii.
    4. similar masses.

13. In the "A" groups, as the atomic number increases,
    1. the electronegativity increases.
    2. the ionization energy decreases.
    3. the atomic radius decreases.
    4. the elements tend to have fewer metallic properties.

14. In each period, as the atomic number increases,
    1. the radius of the atom increases.
    2. there is a transition from negative to positive oxidation states.
    3. the electronegativity increases.
    4. the ionization energy decreases.

15. Sulfur is _____ oxygen.
    1. smaller than
    2. less reactive than
    3. equally as reactive as
    4. an ion of

16. Generally, nitrogen compounds are
    1. not found in living systems.
    2. relatively stable.
    3. essential for living systems.
    4. not found in nature.

17. A loss or gain of electrons by an atom causes a corresponding change in
    1. the number of protons.
    2. the number of neutrons.
    3. the atomic number.
    4. size.

18. Group VIIA elements are
    1. inert at room temperature.
    2. known as the halogens.
    3. the largest atoms on the periodic table.
    4. low in electronegativity.

19. As the atomic number increases in a group, the chemical properties
    1. change.
    2. stay roughly the same.
    3. decrease.
    4. stabilize.

20. Those elements in which electrons from the two outermost sublevels may be involved in a chemical reaction are known as
    1. Group VIIA.
    2. the metalloids.
    3. the nonmetals.
    4. the transition elements.

Answers

1. The correct answer is 3. The modern periodic table, after several false starts early in its history, is based on the atomic number. Such an arrangement reveals the periodic nature of the properties of the elements. While atomic charge may be used to refer to the number of protons and thus the atomic number, the link is confusing with the introduction of a signed number. Choice 3 is the most correct and most often used.

2. The correct answer is 4. The arrangement of the three particles in the atom—the structure—dictates the properties of that atom. It is not the mass of the atom since that is overly simplistic with no hope of establishing rules that make the mass the unit of structure. Number is too vague to be an answer and radius, while a descriptive term of one of the atom's characteristics, does little to suggest the atom's detailed structure.

3. The correct answer is 2. Period is a term used to designate rows on the table. This could go on infinitely, but our modern tables contain only 7 rows.

4. The correct answer is 4. Group is a term used to designate columns on the table. This system has been revised in recent years. Older periodic tables will indicate "A" and "B" columns, while newer tables simply number right across the top from "1" to "18."

5. The correct answer is 1. The tendency for metals is to lose electrons, becoming positive ions in the process. Nonmetals tend to gain electrons. Sharing electrons does not seem to be confined to one area, although the tendency is stronger on the right side of the table.

6. The correct answer is 2. When combining with metals, nonmetals tend to gain electrons and become negative ions in the process—just the opposite of metals. The combination of a metal and a nonmetal often makes what we call a "salt."

7. The correct answer is 2. Metals have all the properties listed except low electrical conductivity. They are good conductors of electricity. The reason we employ metals the way we do now is precisely because of properties like those listed in choices 1, 3, and 4, as well as the opposite of choice 2.

8. The correct answer is 4. A gain or loss of electrons makes the atoms more stable chemically, although they become electrically unstable by doing so. They do change size when they gain or lose electrons; however they also either increase the size of a principal energy level or decrease it by filling more orbitals or emptying them, respectively.

9. The correct answer is 3. In the solid phase, nonmetals lack the luster typical of metals. Having the same size is obviously not going to be an option, and there is no evidence they conduct electricity. Some substances show less resistance to the flow of electricity, but this doesn't seem to apply to nonmetals in the solid state.

10. The correct answer is 4. Metals are not known to be brittle substances; rather, the particles adhere quite well to each other, which accounts for their malleability and ductility. Nonmetals on the other hand do tend to be brittle. Choices 1 through 3 are correct in regard to nonmetals.

11. The correct answer is 3. The word *metalloid* is meant to convey the sense that they are part metal and part nonmetal in their properties. They can be slightly more metallic or slightly more nonmetallic but are always some mix of the two. They are certainly not inert gases.

12. The correct answer is 1. The groups are designated by the number of valence electrons in an element. Choices 2 through 4 cannot be true.

13. The correct answer is 2. All of the choices fail to characterize the "A" group elements as their atomic number increases except 2. Their ionization energy decreases since the atom is getting bigger. Therefore, choice 2 is the correct answer since electronegativity decreases, atomic radius increases, and the "A" group elements begin to take on more and more metallic properties.

14. The correct answer is 3. From left to right across the periods the atomic radii decrease, while electronegativity and ionization energy increase and the transition is from positive to negative oxidation numbers.

15. The correct answer is 2. Sulfur is none of the choices listed except less reactive than oxy-

gen. Its mass number is larger; therefore, the atom is larger. It is not an ion of oxygen; that would still be called oxygen.

16. The correct answer is 3. Nitrogen compounds, which are essential for protein formation, are far from nonessential to living systems. In addition, they tend to be unstable and are, obviously, found ubiquitously in nature.

17. The correct answer is 4. Gaining or losing electrons only causes a change in size compared to the other choices, since the orbitals define the size of an atom. Choices 1 and 2 are not possible from a mere change in electron number and since choice 1 is not possible, therefore choice 3 is not possible either. Choices 1, 2, and 3 all have to do with the nucleus.

18. The correct answer is 2. The Group VIIA elements are classically known as the halogens. They are very reactive at room temperature, are among the largest atoms by period, and are the highest in electronegativity.

19. The correct answer is 2. Elements in each group have fairly constant chemical properties (though not exactly the same) and this is why they are in the same groups. By the time you go from one element to the next below it, the properties come back to the same place—periodically!

20. The correct answer is 4. The properties of the metals are due to the fact that two outermost sublevels are involved in reactions as opposed to one outer sublevel in most other groups, including the choice listed.

Chapter 7

The Mathematics of Chemistry

I.   Mole Interpretation

Mole interpretation—A mole contains *Avogadro's number* (6.02×10^{23}) of particles and is also represented by the gram atomic/molecular mass of the substance,
and it occupies 22.4 L of ideal gas volume at STP. All of these are equivalent to
each other and are true for all substances (for ideal gases, all substances that are
actually gases at STP).

II.   Use of the Mole Concept

Use of the mole concept—It may be used in calculations involving the number of
particles (atoms, molecules, ions, electrons, etcetera). involved in chemical reactions, the mass of elements or compounds, or the volume relationships in gases.

A.   Gram atomic mass—represents the mass in grams of Avogadro's number of
atoms of the element. For example, from the periodic table the g.a.m. of Cu is
63.546 g.

B.   Gram molecular mass—the sum of the gram atomic masses of the atoms that
make up a particular molecule or its formula and is thus also called the gram
formula mass. For example, the g.m.m. or g.f.m. of H_2O is 18 g.

C.   Molar volume of an ideal gas—a mole of atoms/molecules of any gas occupies
a volume of 22.4 L at STP, if that gas behaves ideally. See Section IV in chapter 3, "Matter, Energy, and Measurement," for a description of an ideal gas.

III. Stoichiometry

Stoichiometry is the study of the quantitative relationships implied by chemical
formulas and chemical equations and makes full use of the concept of the mole,
including various calculations between representations of the mole, for example,
volume-mass, mass-mass, mole-mass, etcetera.

A. Problems involving formulas

1. Percent composition is calculated from the ratio of the mass of that element represented in the formula to the formula mass of the entire compound. For example, the total mass of a water molecule is 18 g and oxygen is 16 g of that, therefore oxygen is 89 percent by weight of water—16g/18g.

2. Empirical formula—represents the simplest ratio in which atoms combine to form a compound. For example, the empirical formula for H_2O_2 is HO.

B. Problems involving equations—The coefficients used in balancing a chemical equation represent moles. It is assumed the reaction is a single reaction, that it goes to completion, and that the reactants are completely consumed. If it is more than this, then each reaction is considered singly and, in the end, the sum of the reactions is represented as the total reaction.

1. Mass problems—A balanced equation shows the mole proportions of products and reactants. For example: $2H_2 + O_2 \rightarrow 2H_2O$. The ratio of hydrogen to oxygen to water in this reaction is 2:1:2.

2. Mass-volume problems—In a balanced equation, the mole unit serves to relate the quantities of products and reactants and make it possible to determine the quantitative results in desired units that may not necessarily be the same as the original units (i.e., we may start with a volume of a gas and wish to find its mass).

3. Volume problems—The volumes of gases involved in a reaction are proportional to the number of moles indicated by the numerical coefficients in a balanced equation. For example, the equation above for the synthesis of water requires 2 volumes of hydrogen. The word *volume* can be any correct designation for volume, such as L, dL, cL, mL, etcetera, as long as the same label is used throughout the calculation. It is similar to the use of the word *parts*.

IV. Solutions

A. Characteristics—a homogeneous mixture of two or more substances, the composition of which may vary within limits. The component which is usually a liquid and is present in excess is called the *solvent*, while the other component is called the *solute*.

B. Methods of indicating concentrations—simple definitions:

   1. Molarity—the number of moles of solute contained in a liter of solution.

      formula: $M = \dfrac{\text{number of moles of solute}}{\text{1 liter of solution}}$

   2. Molality—the number of moles of solute in a kilogram of solvent.

      formula: $m = \dfrac{\text{number of moles of solute}}{\text{1 kilogram of solution}}$

C. Formula from percent composition—The empirical formula of a compound can be found from the percent composition of each element in the compound and the atomic masses of the elements. For example, a compound was found to contain 80 percent carbon and 20 percent hydrogen. Assuming a 100 g sample, we have 80 g of carbon. One mole of carbon weighs 12 g, so we have 6.7 moles of carbon present in the 100 g sample. One mole of hydrogen weighs 1 gram, so we have 20 moles of hydrogen present in the 100 g sample. The ratio we have is 1 carbon for every 3 hydrogens, so the empirical formula is CH_3. Choosing to use a 100 g sample makes percentages directly convertible to grams and vice versa.

V. Gram Molecular Mass from Gas Density

Gram molecular mass from gas density can be determined by using the relationship between the molar volume (22.4 L) and the mass of 1 mole of gas. Since density is expressed in units of mass per unit of volume, knowing the density of the gas and measuring its volume at STP will yield the mass from a simple calculation, or knowing mass can yield volume in a similar way. Using the volume, for example, this is then compared with a mole of the gas which leads to the gram molecular mass.

VI. Effect of Solute on Solvent

A. Colligative properties—The presence of dissolved particles affects some of the properties of the solvent. Properties that depend on the relative number of particles rather than the nature of the particles are called colligative properties.

   1. Boiling point elevation—The presence of a nonvolatile solute raises the boiling point of the solvent by an amount that is proportional to the concentration of the dissolved solute particles. Double the concentration and the effect doubles, as in the case of electrolytes.

   2. Freezing point depression—The presence of a solute lowers the freezing point of the solvent by an amount that is proportional to the concentra-

tion of the dissolved solute particles. Changing the concentration has an effect that is proportional to the effect on the boiling point.

3. Abnormal behavior of electrolytes—An ionic solution changes the boiling and freezing points of a solvent more than a nonelectrolyte of equal molality, since it contributes more than one concentration of particles as it dissolves into, at the very least, one concentration of (+) particles and one concentration of (−) particles.

VII. Calorimetry

Calorimetry—The energy changes involved in chemical reactions are measured in calories with the use of a calorimeter.

A. Heat of vaporization—the energy required to vaporize one unit mass of a liquid at constant temperature. Of course we are talking about the boiling point if we are heating the substance or condensation if we are cooling it. The energy is seen as going into the substance if we are heating it and being released if we are cooling it. Farmers make use of cooling phenomena by constructing ponds at key locations on their land to keep the air warm during those marginal temperature conditions where crops might be damaged by excess cold.

B. Heat of fusion—is the energy required to melt one unit mass of a solid at constant temperature. We are, of course, talking about the melting point if we are heating the substance or the freezing point if we are cooling it. Once again, the energy is seen as going into the substance if we are heating it and being released if we are cooling it.

VIII. Combined Gas Laws.

Combined Gas Laws—Since changes in volume, pressure, and temperature often occur simultaneously, it is convenient to combine the gas laws into a single equation.

Example: $\dfrac{P_1 V_1}{T_1} = \dfrac{P_2 V_2}{T_2}$

IX. Graham's Law.

Graham's Law—under the same conditions of temperature and pressure, gases diffuse at a rate inversely proportional to the square roots of their molecular masses, meaning the smaller the particle, the faster (and farther) it will diffuse. Gases can also travel through small openings in materials, called effusion. Graham's law applies to effusion also.

Questions

1. Which of the following is not equivalent to a mole of a substance?

   1. 22.4L of an ideal gas at STP
   2. atomic number
   3. gram atomic mass
   4. 6.02×10^{23} atoms

2. _____ represents the mass in grams of Avogadro's number of atoms.

   1. gram atomic mass
   2. gram molecular mass
   3. 22.4 L at STP
   4. 6.02×10^{23} atoms

3. _____ is a molar volume of a gas.

   1. 22.4 L at STP
   2. 6.02×10^{23} molecules
   3. The gram formula mass
   4. None of the above is correct.

4. The gram molecular mass for H_2SO_4 is

   1. 64 grams.
   2. 196 grams.
   3. 7 grams.
   4. 98 grams.

5. If the gram atomic mass of sulfur is 32 g, then 80 g represents

   1. 1 mole.
   2. 2.5 moles.
   3. 25 moles.
   4. 2,560 moles.

6. In the following equation, how many total grams of water are formed?

$$2H_2 + O_2 \rightarrow 2H_2O$$

   1. 2 g
   2. 18 g
   3. 36 g
   4. 3.6 g

7. The coefficients used in balancing chemical equations represent

   1. grams of product.
   2. the molar volume of the reactants.
   3. moles.
   4. grams.

8. The percent composition by weight of oxygen in H_2SO_4 is

   1. 32 percent.
   2. 98 percent.
   3. 64 percent.
   4. 65.3 percent.

9. The empirical formula for H_2O_2 is

   1. H_2O.
   2. HO.
   3. a multiple of 4.
   4. H_2O_2.

10. The correct mole proportions for the following equation is

$$HCl + NaOH \rightarrow H_2O + NaCl$$

   1. 4:1.
   2. 2:2.
   3. 1:1:2:1.
   4. 1:1:1:1.

11. The balanced mole proportion in the following unbalanced equation is

$FeCl_3 + NaOH \rightarrow Fe(OH)_3 + NaCl$

1. 1:1:1:1.
2. 1:1.
3. 1:3:1:3.
4. 3:1.

12. If the NaCl produced in the equation in question 11 was dissolved in water to make a liter of solution, the molarity would be

1. .1 M.
2. 3 M.
3. 8 M.
4. .5 M.

13. What is the empirical formula of a compound found to contain 80 percent carbon and 20 percent hydrogen?

1. CH_3
2. CH_4
3. C_2H_8
4. CH_5

14. Colligative properties depend on the _____ of the dissolved particles.

1. nature
2. structure
3. number
4. size

15. Ionic solutions change the boiling and freezing points _____ nonelectrolytes.

1. more than
2. less than

3. the same as
4. inversely compared to

16. If the temperature is held constant and the pressure on a gas increases, the volume

1. increases.
2. decreases.
3. remains the same.
4. does not affect it.

17. If the pressure is held constant and the temperature of a gas increases, the volume

1. increases.
2. decreases.
3. remains the same.
4. does not affect it.

18. If the pressure on a gas increases, this will cause _____ in the temperature of the gas if the volume is held constant.

1. an increase
2. a decrease
3. no change
4. no effect

19. According to Graham's law, gases diffuse at a rate _____ proportional to the square roots of their molecular masses.

1. directly
2. inversely
3. equally
4. None of the above is correct.

20. 67.2 L of oxygen gas at STP (assume ideality) has a mass of

1. 32 g.
2. 48 g.
3. 96g.
4. cannot be determined.

Answers

1. The correct answer is 2. The atomic number is the number of protons and does not relate to a mole. Choices 1, 3, and 4 are the three ways that we define a mole: 22.4L is the volume of a mole at STP, the gram atomic mass is the mass of a mole of atoms, and 6.02×10^{23} is the number of particles in a mole of anything.

2. The correct answer is 1. The gram atomic mass is the way we represent Avogadro's number of atoms. Obviously, a gram molecular mass would have required choice 2. Choices 3 and 4 are the ways we describe a mole in terms other than mass.

3. The correct answer is 1. Choice 1, 22.4 L, is an expression of volume and is the amount equal to a mole of ideal gas at STP. Choices 2 and 3 are other ways we describe a mole, and 4 is not true.

4. The correct answer is 4. Adding up the individual gram atomic masses yields a total of 98 g. Hydrogen contributes 2 grams for 2 hydrogens, each having a mass of 1 gram. Sulfur has a mass of 32 grams and 4 oxygens, each having a mass of 16 grams, contribute a total of 64 grams. Adding this up, we arrive at a gram molecular mass of 98 g.

5. The correct answer is 2. If a mass of one mole of sulfur is 32 g, then 80 g represents 2.5 moles since 80 is 2.5 times larger than 32.

6. The correct answer is 3. If a gram atomic mass of one mole of water is 18 g, and the equation indicates 2 moles of water, then the total mass of water produced is 36 g. All of the other choices contain information about the other substances in the equation except choice 4; it is a decimal shift from the right answer.

7. The correct answer is 3. The number in front of the chemical formulas in an equation (coefficient) represents the moles of that substance. Grams of product would come from the periodic table, so choices 1 and 4 are wrong and it is certainly not a volume indication we want as choice 2 would indicate.

8. The correct answer is 4. Add up the total mass of all of the parts of the molecule indicated and compare that to just the oxygen mass in the molecule. When you divide the mass of oxygen in the compound by the mass of the total compound, you get 65.3 percent of oxygen by mass.

9. The correct answer is 2. The empirical formula is the simplest ratio of atoms in a compound. H_2O_2 then is reduced to HO. H_2O is water, of course. H_2O_2 is the same formula as given and a multiple of 4 means nothing here.

10. The correct answer is 4. The equation given is already balanced, implying a 1 in front of each formula. The correct mole proportion, therefore, is 1:1:1:1, meaning 1 mole of hydrogen chloride reacts with 1 mole of sodium hydroxide to produce 1 mole of water and 1 mole of sodium chloride.

11. The correct answer is 3. Balancing the equation gives the mole proportion of 1:3:1:3. We are given 3 moles of chloride, so we need 3 moles of sodium ions to balance that on the right-hand side. Only 1 mole of iron compounds is yielded.

12. The correct answer is 2. Dissolving 3 moles of sodium chloride to make a liter of solution yields a 3 M solution using the formula:

$$\text{Molarity} = \frac{\text{\# of moles}}{\text{L of solution}}$$

13. The correct answer is 1. See the calculation in part C of Section IV in this chapter for details.

14. The correct answer is 3. The colligative properties of substances depend only on the number of dissolved particles expressed as a concentration. The nature, structure, and size of the particles does not affect the freezing or boiling points, only the number of the particles—i.e., it's not the size or structure of the particles that gets in the way; it's how many there are.

15. The correct answer is 1. This is due to the fact that ions dissociate in solution into constituent parts and nonelectrolytes do not. It is possible, for example, that sodium chloride will contribute sodium ions and chloride ions, for a concentration of two particles per molecule. Sugar, on the other hand, does not dissociate, leaving sugar molecules intact in solution and thereby contributing a concentration of only one particle per molecule.

16. The correct answer is 2. Pressure and volume of a gas are inversely related, a statement of Boyle's Law. This is easy to remember since a gas can be the result of "boiling."

17. The correct answer is 1. Temperature and volume of a gas are directly related, a statement of Charles's Law.

18. The correct answer is 1. Pressure and temperature of a gas are directly related, a statement of Guy-Lussac's Law.

19. The correct answer is 2. This is just a simple statement of Graham's Law and says that the smaller the particle, the faster it will diffuse (or effuse as well).

20. The correct answer is 3. First, we must remember that oxygen exists in gaseous form as O_2, not O. It is possible to generate gaseous oxygen atoms but this would be a highly reactive, non-ideal behaving system that would not last long. Hence 22.4 L of O_2 contains $2 \times 16 = 32$g O (gram molecular mass), and 67.2 L = 3×22.4 L so 3×32g = 96g. Answer 4, "cannot be determined," would be true without giving more information if we could not assume ideal behavior (which means 22 L = 1.0 mole gas).

Chapter 8

Kinetics and Equilibrium

I. Kinetics

Kinetics—the branch of chemistry concerned with the rate of chemical reactions and the mechanism of stepwise chemical reactions by which the overall changes occur. The rate of a chemical reaction is governed by several things: concentration of reactants/products, temperature, surface area of materials involved, to name a few.

A. Role of energy in reactions—Energy is required to initiate a chemical reaction and may be released or absorbed during the course of the reaction. Depending on the materials, energy will be absorbed or released, which will dictate a number of things about the reaction.

> **Basic Concept**
>
> ΔH negative   = exothermic
>   = heat given off
>
> ΔH positive   = endothermic
>   = heat absorbed
>
> Bond–breaking is endothermic;
> bond formation is exothermic.

1. Activation—the minimum energy required to initiate a reaction and is very specific for each reaction. The amount of activation energy required can be changed by the presence of a catalyst.

2. Heat (enthalpy) of reaction—the heat released or absorbed in the formation of the products and represents the difference in energy content between the products and the reactants as illustrated by the equation:
   $\Delta H = H_{products} - H_{reactants}$

    a.   Endothermic reaction—one in which energy is absorbed, the products have a higher potential energy than the reactants, and the sign of ΔH is positive. The energy is shown on the left side of the equation as being added in to the products. An example would be the decomposition of water into hydrogen and oxygen gases.

    b.   Exothermic reaction—one in which energy is released, the products have a lower potential energy than the reactants, and the sign of ΔH is negative. The energy shows on the right side of the equation as being given off to the surroundings. An example would be any combustion reaction.

3.   Potential energy diagram—The activation energy and heat of reaction can be shown graphically when plotting potential energy against a reaction coordinate. From this diagram we can plot energy differences between reactants and products.

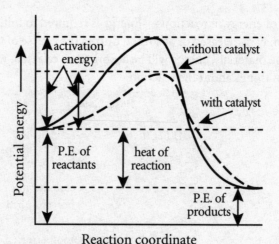

Reaction coordinate

B.   Factors affecting rate of reaction—These include collisions between the reacting particles, atoms, molecules or ions, principally the number of collisions and the fraction of the collisions that are effective. Since bonds may be broken or formed in a reaction—potentially releasing or absorbing energy—the nature of the bond is an important factor affecting reaction rates. An increase in the concentration of one or more reactants generally increases the rate of the reaction. An increase in temperature increases the rate of all chemical reactions. An increase in the surface area of reactants increases their rate of reaction. Catalysts change the rate of reaction by changing the activation energy required—they do not initiate the chemical reaction. It is important to clearly understand that catalysts not only increase the rate of the reaction, they can also decrease the rate of the reaction as in the case of enzymes in living systems.

II. Equilibrium

Equilibrium—the state of balance between two opposing (physical or chemical) reactions occurring at the same rate. Most reactions are reversible depending on the available energy.

A. Phase equilibrium—In general, phase changes are reversible, and in a closed environment, equilibrium can be achieved. This would be achieved simply with the addition or subtraction of heat. Increases in energy add more motion to the particles and vice versa.

B. Solution equilibrium

1. Gases in liquids—In a closed system (one in which no matter is exchanged with the surroundings), equilibrium may exist between a gas dissolved in a liquid and the undissolved gas above the liquid. This equilibrium is affected by both pressure and temperature.

2. Solids in liquids—Solution equilibrium exists when opposing processes of dissolving and crystallizing of a solute occur at equal rates. The solution exhibiting this state must be saturated. The material is just at the point of crystallizing.

3. Solubility—the maximum mass of solute dissolved in a given volume of solvent under specified conditions and may be defined as the concentration of solute in a saturated solution at a specified temperature.

C. Chemical equilibrium—occurs when the concentration of reactants and products remains constant.

1. Le Châtelier's principle—If stress (change) is applied to a system at equilibrium, the equilibrium is shifted in a way that tends to relieve the effects of the stress.

a. Concentration effect—Increasing the concentration of one substance in a reaction at equilibrium will cause the reaction to go in a direction that consumes the increase, thus creating a new equilibrium. This reasoning can be applied also to physical equilibria of ionic, slightly soluble solids dissolving in aqueous solution, but with an important catch: Adding more dissolved ions at equilibrium will cause solid to precipitate, but not vice versa—adding more solid will simply add to the undissolved solid amount. No further solvation will occur.

b. Effect of pressure—An increase in pressure will cause the equilibrium to shift in the direction that favors the formation of fewer moles of gases. If no change in the number of gas moles occurs, then a change in pressure has no effect on the equilibrium.

c. Effect of temperature—When the temperature of a system in equilibrium is raised, the equilibrium is displaced in such a way that energy is absorbed.

d. Effect of a catalyst—A catalyst increases the rate of both forward and reverse reactions equally and produces no net change in the equilibrium concentrations.

2. Law of chemical equilibrium—When a reversible reaction has attained equilibrium at a given temperature, the product of the molar concentration of the substances to the right of the equation, divided by the product of the molar concentrates of the substances to the left of the equation (each concentration raised to the power equal to the number of moles of that substance appearing in the equation) is a constant. Pure solids, or liquids acting as the solvent, do not appear in the expression for K_{eq}.

Example:

For the reaction $aM(g) + b N(g) \rightarrow c P(g) + d Q(g)$:

$\frac{[P]^c[Q]^d}{[M]^a[N]^b} = K_{eq} = $ a constant at a constant temperature.

This is known as the *equilibrium constant*. Usually the following designations are made for "K": K_a for acids and K_b for bases; K_{eq} for chemical reactions; K_{sp} for solubility of solids; and K_w for the ionization of water. A large value of "K" favors the formation of produ cts, and a small "K" indicates the reactants are favored.

C. Solubility constant (K_{sp})—A special class of equilibrium constants; a measure of the concentration of slightly soluble salts in water. An example would be in the reaction $AB(s) \rightarrow A^+(aq) + B^-(aq)$, $K_{sp} = [A^+] [B^-]$ where [ ] = the concentration of the ion in solution at a certain temperature. The addition of a common ion to the solution of a slightly soluble salt results in a decrease in the solubility of the salt and is known as the *common ion effect*.

D. Spontaneous reactions—depend on the balance between two tendencies found in nature: (a) toward a lower energy state, and (b) toward randomness.

1. Energy changes—A system tends to undergo a reaction that, in its final state, has lower energy than in its initial state.

2. Entropy changes—Entropy is a measure of the disorder of a system and is defined so that the more random a system is, the higher the entropy. High entropy is favored by high temperatures and at a constant temperature (T) a system tends to undergo a reaction that, in its final state, has higher entropy ($\Delta S > \Delta O$) than in its initial state. Entropy, therefore, is a state of loss of useful energy.

   a. Gibb's Free Energy change—The difference between energy change and entropy change is known as free energy change (ΔG) and is given by the relationship

   $$\Delta G = \Delta H - T \Delta S.$$

   b. Predicting spontaneous reactions—For this to occur in a system, its free energy change must be negative, from the above formula.

Basic Concept

$\Delta G°$ positive: small K,
reaction not favored

$\Delta G°$ negative: large K,
reaction favored

$\Delta G°$ is the "standard" free energy change of a reaction, when all species are in their standard states, defined as 1 atm for gases, 298K, 1M solutions, and pure solids or liquids.

Questions

1. The rate of a chemical reaction is
   1. determined from the balanced chemical equation.
   2. the change in concentration of products and reactants in a certain amount of time.
   3. not possible to determine experimentally.
   4. expressed in units of time.

2. The average rate of a chemical reaction can be expressed as the
   1. concentration of reactants minus the concentration of products.
   2. concentration of products and reactants multiplied by the time required for the reaction.
   3. change in concentration of products or reactants divided by the change in time.
   4. change in time divided by change in concentration of products or reactants.

3. For molecules to react they must collide, and an affected collision depends upon
   1. a molecule's colliding with the wall of a container.
   2. three or more molecules colliding.
   3. molecules having proper orientation only.
   4. molecules having proper orientation and enough energy.

4. The energy required to physically break bonds among reactant molecules comes from the reactant molecules' _____ energy.
   1. potential
   2. kinetic
   3. chemical
   4. electrical

5. Activation energy is the energy required to form the
   1. original bonds.
   2. activated complex.
   3. reaction complex.
   4. reactant molecules.

6. A catalyst increases the rate of a chemical reaction by
   1. causing more collisions between molecules.
   2. increasing the energy of the particles in a reaction.
   3. lowering the activation energy of the reaction.
   4. raising the activation energy.

7. A reaction that has a significant tendency to form products has a K_{eq}
   1. $= 1$.
   2. > 1.
   3. < 1.
   4. $= 0$.

8. A spontaneous reaction
   1. is always exothermic.
   2. is always endothermic.
   3. requires outside intervention.
   4. proceeds without outside intervention once started.

9. A change in concentration over time is the
   1. reaction rate.
   2. transition state.
   3. activated complex.
   4. intermediate rate.

10. $\Delta H°$ is
    1. the standard enthalpy change for a reaction.
    2. the heat transfer in a reaction.
    3. calculated at 25°C and one atmosphere.
    4. All of the above are correct.

11. A reaction is spontaneous when
    1. ΔS is positive and the reaction is exothermic.
    2. ΔS for the universe is positive.
    3. ΔG is negative.
    4. All the above are correct.

12. What is K_{eq} for a reaction when ΔG is much greater than 1?
    1. K_{eq} is greater than 1.
    2. K_{eq} is less than 1.
    3. K_{eq} equals 1.
    4. ΔG has no correlation with K_{eq}.

13. The rate of a chemical reaction can be increased by
    1. decreasing the concentration of the reactants.
    2. increasing the surface area of the reactants.
    3. removing the catalyst.
    4. decreasing the reaction temperature.

14. Which of the following is true?
    1. In a reversible reaction, products can react to form reactants.
    2. Reversible reactions are also always reversible on their own.
    3. A reversible reaction must be forced to undergo the forward reaction.
    4. A reversible reaction always goes to completion.

15. The equilibrium constant for a reaction
    1. is independent of temperature.
    2. is a measure of the extent to which the reaction proceeds to completion.
    3. is equal to the equilibrium.
    4. changes with different concentrations.

16. According to Le Châtelier's principle, an increase in the concentration of a reactant will cause a reaction to
    1. go to completion.
    2. consume the added reactant.
    3. never return to equilibrium.
    4. Both 1 and 3 are correct.

17. Increasing the pressure on an equilibrium system will

    1. affect only the gases.
    2. shift the equilibrium position for all reactions.
    3. cause the reaction to go toward the side that produces fewer molecules of gas.
    4. Answers 1 and 3 above are correct.

18. A reaction's equilibrium constant will change only if _____ is changed.

    1. temperature
    2. pressure
    3. concentration
    4. All of the above are correct.

19. The Haber process

    1. requires low pressure.
    2. decreases the amount of NH_3 produced in a reaction.
    3. is used in the production of explosives.
    4. All of the above are correct.

20. When the enthalpy of the products is greater than the enthalpy of the reactants, the reaction

    1. releases heat.
    2. absorbs heat.
    3. is spontaneous.
    4. can do work.

Answers

1. The correct answer is 2. Choice 4 is not true as the rate is determined by the concentration of materials over time, not just time by itself. Choice 3 is incorrect because the rate *can* be determined and choice 1 is only the start. Choice 2 is the definition of the rate of a chemical reaction—one must know concentration and time.

2. The correct answer is 3. This statement is an embellishment on the definition of the rate of a chemical reaction found in question 1 and is the word formula for calculating the rate of a chemical reaction. Choice 4 is the opposite and is wrong; choice 1 does not include time, an oddity when discussing rate; and choice 2 includes multiplication which, as described, would not translate into a rate.

3. The correct answer is 4. The collisions must be effective, and there must be enough of them. Choice 1 describes a collision with the wall of the container whereas we need to have particles collide with each other. The number of particles indicated in choice 2 is irrelevant, and choice 3 is only half right.

4. The correct answer is 2. The actual breaking of the bonds is nothing if not an active process whereby work can be done, and this requires kinetic energy. Chemical and electrical energies are too vague, and potential energy is not an active process that is needed here.

5. The correct answer is 2. This is our definition of the activated complex, the formation of which is critical for the reaction to occur.

Reactant molecules and the vagueness of that allows that we can only guess at their energies; we won't want original bonds formed, and reaction complex is too vague a term.

6. The correct answer is 3. The catalyst does not initiate the reaction; it lowers the activation energy required to allow the reaction to occur, causing the activation complex to have a greater effect. If the activation energy were increased, the reaction rate would decrease. Choice 2 does not specify which particles are being referred to, and choice 1 suggests catalysts have some source by which they can cause more collisions directly.

7. The correct answer is 2. A large (>1) value of K_{eq} has a tendency to form products. That is, with a positive reading, the energy of the products being greater than the energy of the reactants as an indication of reaction direction indicates a reaction that will form products.

8. The correct answer is 4. The simple definition of spontaneous means it will proceed on its own. It can be exothermic or endothermic depending on the value of ΔH. ΔG is given by the formula $\Delta G = \Delta H - T\Delta S$, where ΔH is enthalpy and ΔS is entropy and T is temperature, absolute. If ΔG is negative, the reaction is spontaneous.

9. The correct answer is 1. This is our definition of reaction rate, which is known as the change in concentration of reactants and products over a period of time.

10. The correct answer is 4. All of the choices (1–3) are correct when measuring ΔH making 4 the correct choice.

11. The correct answer is 4. All of the choices (1–3) are correct when calculating the likelihood of a spontaneous reaction.

12. The correct answer is 2. If $\Delta G > 1$, then the K_{eq} for that reaction must be <1. A free energy change >1 favors reactants. A $K_{eq} >1$ would, as has been indicated, favor products since the Gibb's free energy drops below 1. Choice 4 is very wrong.

13. The correct answer is 2. None of the choices works to increase a reaction rate except choice 2; all of the other choices are the reverse of how they would affect the reaction rate (e.g., raising the temperature increases the rate, not lowering it). The key things to be aware of are when the increases occur and when the decreases occur.

14. The correct answer is 1. In addition to being wrong, choices 2–4 are quite cut and dry and arbitrary. Choice 1, in addition to being true, covers all possibilities.

15. The correct answer is 2. Choice 4 is tricky because by Le Châtelier's principle, changes in concentration will shift the "position" of equilibrium, but the equilibrium constant K is still a constant as long as temperature stays constant (so choice 1 is wrong). Choice 3 is incorrect because K is a representation of the equilibrium taking place, but not the equilibrium itself (in the same way that a picture of you is not you).

16. The correct answer is 2. Le Châtelier's principle states that a system under stress (by the introduction of more reactant) will act in a way to consume the stressor, in this case the newly added reactant. In doing so, it will return to equilibrium and it may or may not go to completion.

17. The correct answer is 4. Pressure does not affect the equilibria of reactions in which there are no gases present, so choice 2 is incorrect. Choice 3 describes Le Châtelier's principle for gas phase reactions at equilibrium as they respond to an increase in pressure.

18. The correct answer is 3. The equilibrium constant is affected only by temperature. Pressure is too vague as it affects only gases. With a change in concentration, the equilibrium will shift, but not the equilibrium constant, for a given temperature.

19. The correct answer is 3. This is the process Fritz Haber was famous for perfecting in order to produce the ammonia needed to make explosives during WWI. It requires a higher pressure and is significant because it raises the amount of NH_3 produced in a reaction.

20. The correct answer is 2. This explains the difference in the enthalpy of the two components, wherein the products having greater enthalpy have absorbed heat.

Chapter 9

Acids and Bases

I.   Electrolytes

    A.   Electrolytes—will dissociate in water to form a solution that will conduct an electric current due to the presence of ions that are free to move.

    B.   Weak electrolytes in aqueous solution attain an equilibrium between ions and the undissociated compound. The equilibrium constant for such a system is known as the dissociation constant.

II. Acids and Bases—Acids and bases may be defined in terms of operational properties that have been extended as the understanding of acid-base reactions has grown and as principles of these reactions have been applied to reactions not in aqueous solutions.

    A.   Acids—aqueous solutions that conduct electricity and have a sour taste. Acids will react with certain metals to liberate hydrogen gas; will cause color changes in certain acid-base indicators and will react with hydroxides to form water and a salt. The two principal theories listed here each add an understanding as to the function of acids and bases.

        1.   Arrhenius's theory—An acid yields hydrogen ions as the only positive ion in solution, the excess of which accounts for the characteristic properties of an acid in aqueous solution.

        2.   Brønsted-Lowry theory—An acid is a species (molecule or ion) that can donate a proton (hydrogen ion) to another species.

    B.   Bases—aqueous solutions that conduct electricity. Bases cause color changes in certain acid-base indicators; react with acids to form water and a salt; and feel slippery.

1. Arrhenius's theory—A base yields hydroxide ions as the only negative ion in aqueous solution, the excess of which leads to the characteristic properties of a base in aqueous solution.

2. Brønsted-Lowry theory—A base is any species (molecule or ion) that can combine with a proton (hydrogen ion).

C. Amphoteric (amphiprotic) substance—one that can act as either an acid or a base depending on its chemical environment. An amino acid is a base at the amine end and an acid at the carboxyl end.

III. Acid-Base Reactions

A. Neutralization—occurs when an equivalent amount of a strong acid and strong base are mixed, is usually determined by titration and leads to the formation of a salt if carried to completion. The resulting pH of the solution will be 7.0.

1. Titration—The molarity of an acid (or base) may be determined by slowly combining it with a base (or acid) of known concentration until the equivalence point is reached (when equal moles of base and acid are present). The end point (very close to, but not the same as, the equivalence point) may be determined by the use of an appropriate indicator, by a temperature change, or by an electrode potential change. The figure below illustrates the change in pH that occurs when a strong acid (low pH) is titrated with a strong base, NaOH.

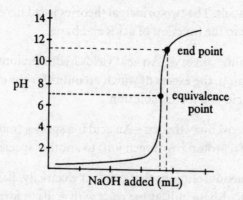

2. Salts—ionic compounds containing positive ions other than hydrogen and negative ions other than hydroxide. Some, in aqueous solution, react

with the water to form solutions that are acidic or basic in a process called *hydrolysis*.

B. Conjugate acid-base pair—According to the Brønsted-Lowry theory, acid-base reactions involve a transfer of protons from the acid to the base. The acid transfers a proton to become a conjugate base, the two forming a conjugate acid-base pair, while the base receives a proton to become a conjugate acid, the two forming a second acid-base pair. The strongest acids have the weakest conjugate bases and the strongest bases have the weakest conjugate acids.

Example: $Base_1 + Acid_1 = Acid_2 + Base_2$
$H_2O + HCl = H_3O^+ + Cl^-$
$NH_3 + H_2O = NH_4+ + OH^-$

IV. Ionization Constant

A. K_a— a measure of the strength of an acid. A $K_a <1$ indicates only partial dissociation.

Example: for the reaction $HB(aq) \rightarrow H^+(aq) + B^-(aq)$,

$K_a = \frac{[H^+][B^-]}{[HB]}$ where [ ] = concentration of this substance.

B. K_w—in water and aqueous solutions, the product of the hydrogen ion concentration and the hydroxide concentration is a constant at a constant temperature and is useful in problems involving the concentration of these two ions.

Example: $K_w = [H^+][OH^-]$

C. pH—a measure of the concentration of hydrogen ions in a solution and is the negative log of the $[H^+]$. A pH of 7 is neutral at 25°C, <7 is acidic and >7 is basic, and pH is given by the formula:

$$pH = \log \frac{1}{[H^+]} = -\log[H^+].$$

The pH scale goes from 0 to 14 but has validity only between 1 and 13. For pure water at 25°C, $[H^+] = [OH^-] = 10^{-7}M$, and for any pH value at 25°C, $[H^+][DH^-] = 1.0 \times 10^{-14} M^2$.

Questions

1. H_3O^+ represents a(n)
   1. conjugate base.
   2. hydronium ion.
   3. salt.
   4. amphoteric.

2. The chloride ion (Cl^-) is the _____ of hydrochloric acid (HCl).
   1. conjugate acid
   2. conjugate base
   3. hydronium ion
   4. salt

3. Which of the following is not a characteristic of a base?
   1. feels smooth and slippery
   2. turns litmus from red to blue
   3. has a bitter taste
   4. typically reacts vigorously with metals

4. Which of the following is characteristic of an acid only?
   1. is an electrolyte
   2. has a bitter taste
   3. typically reacts vigorously with metals
   4. typically does not react with metals

5. The best way to determine if a substance is an acid or a base is to
   1. taste it.
   2. touch it.
   3. dilute it with water.
   4. test it with litmus paper.

6. In neutralization,
   1. the base is neutralized.
   2. the acid is neutralized.
   3. a salt is formed.
   4. All of the above are correct.

7. Which of the following is not true?
   1. Water is a good conductor of electricity.
   2. A solution that contains electrolytes conducts electricity.
   3. A water solution of an acid conducts electricity.
   4. A water solution of a base conducts electricity.

8. An Arrhenius acid is one that
   1. produces OH^- ions
   2. produces H^+ ions
   3. accepts OH^- ions
   4. accepts H^+ ions

9. Brønsted-Lowry theory says that
   1. a base accepts H^+ ions.
   2. a base is a proton donor.
   3. an acid is a proton acceptor.
   4. Both 1 and 2 are correct.

10. A strong acid
    1. is a weak electrolyte.
    2. transfers H^+ to water to form H_3O^+.
    3. never reaches equilibrium in a reaction.
    4. has a K_a near 0.

11. A weak acid
    1. reacts with water to completely form H_3O^+ ions.
    2. has a weak conjugate base also.
    3. has a $K_a > 1$.
    4. has a $K_a < 1$.

12. The salt solution formed from a strong acid and a weak base is
    1. acidic.
    2. basic.
    3. neutral.
    4. always soluble in water.

13. The self-ionization of water
    1. creates H_2O_2.
    2. creates H_3O^+ and OH^- ions.
    3. involves the transfer of OH^- ions.
    4. produces H_3O^+ and OH^- in large concentrations.

14. If the pH of a solution is 3,
    1. the solution is acidic.
    2. the solution is basic.
    3. the solution is neutral.
    4. the H_3O^+ ion concentration is 3×10^1.

15. A buffer solution
    1. can release H^+ ions.
    2. can absorb H^+ ions.
    3. is often a mixture of an acid and a base.
    4. All of the above are correct.

16. The concentration of a weak acid in a solution is determined by

    1. measuring the concentration of H_3O^+ ions in solution.
    2. measuring the concentration of OH^- ions in solution.
    3. titration.
    4. All of the above are correct.

17. A standard solution
    1. has an unknown concentration.
    2. contains an acid and a base.
    3. contains an acid or a base.
    4. None of the above is correct.

18. Which if the following statements is false?
    1. A titration curve represents pH data on a graph.
    2. An acid-base titration involves a known and an unknown concentration.
    3. The standard solution for an unknown base should be a strong base.
    4. Phenolphthalein is an indicator used in strong acid-base titrations.

19. The end point for a titration
    1. should be close to the equivalence point.
    2. occurs at pH = 7.
    3. occurs only in acidic solution.
    4. None of the above is correct.

20. Which of the following is not true of acids?
    1. They react with metals to produce O_2 gas.
    2. They react with hydroxides to form a salt and water.
    3. They have a sour taste.
    4. Aqueous solutions conduct electricity.

Answers

1. The correct answer is 2. The ion represented would more likely be called a conjugate acid, which is not a choice. It is also known by the term "hydronium ion," which is a choice. It is not a salt, as it still has a charge, and it is not amphoteric, a reference to substances that can act as acids and bases.

2. The correct answer is 2. According to the Brønsted-Lowry theory, the H^+ from HCl combines with water to form the conjugate acid H_3O^+, leaving Cl^- as the conjugate base in this reaction. It is not a hydronium ion (see answer 1). It is also not a salt, although it forms the nonmetallic part of many salts.

3. The correct answer is 4. Bases are characterized by all the properties listed except combining vigorously with metals. Metals have a network of free electrons which an acid, not a base, will react with quite vigorously under certain circumstances.

4. The correct answer is 3. Acids, strictly speaking (i.e., in a nonaqueous setting), are not electrolytes, although in aqueous solution they do help conduct electricity. They are not bitter (a property of bases); instead they are sour to the taste, e.g., vinegar, lemon, etcetera. They do react with metals readily, thus making choice 4 incorrect and choice 3 correct.

5. The correct answer is 4. The first two choices are never an option in a chemistry lab, and choice 3 serves no purpose other than to dilute the unknown substance, leaving it still as an unknown. Litmus paper identifies acids and bases.

6. The correct answer is 4. All three choices offered are true of neutralization. The base neutralizes the acid or vice versa, leading to the formation of a salt, the nonmetal part of the acid combined with the metal part of the base.

7. The correct answer is 1. Water, here taken to be pure water, contains very few ions and, therefore, is not a good conductor of electricity. All the other choices refer to an excess of ions that will conduct electricity.

8. The correct answer is 2. By definition choice 2 is the answer. Arrhenius bases produce OH^- ions in water, so 1 is incorrect for this question; an Arrhenius acid accepts neither OH^- nor H^+ ions.

9. The correct answer is 1. By definition, choice 1 is the correct answer; therefore choices 2, 3, and 4 are incorrect. For example, a base is a proton acceptor, not a donor as choice 2 indicates, and an acid is a proton donor, according to theory, not an acceptor as choice 3 indicates.

10. The correct answer is 2. The K_a of a strong acid would be >1. Choice 1 is the opposite; a strong acid is also a strong electrolyte, part of the reason we call it "strong." Choice 3 is opposite of the truth, because strong acids

and bases always reach equilibrium and go to completion (products strongly favored). In fact, all chemical reactions, once started, will reach equilibrium eventually.

11. The correct answer is 4. A weak acid will have a very low hydrogen ion concentration and, as such, does not completely form H_3O^+ ions. By definition, it also has a strong conjugate base.

12. The correct answer is 1. It is almost self-evident that this would be true unlike the conjugate acid-base inversion.

13. The correct answer is 2. The only logical outcome would be to have the H^+ attach to the H_2O molecule and leave OH^- as the conjugate base. It doesn't involve the "transfer" of OH^- ions—a vague term at best—and it does not produce ions in large concentrations, unless the supply of "parts" is large and the question does not state that this is the case.

14. The correct answer is 1. A pH, by definition, of <7 is acidic, >7 is basic and 7 is neutral.

15. The correct answer is 4. Buffers are mixtures of an acid and a base that can stabilize the concentration of H^+. The most common buffers are combinations of weak acids and their conjugate bases. Buffers do all three things indicated by choices 1–3, making choice 4 the right answer.

16. The correct answer is 3. By titration, one is measuring the $[H_3O^+]$ and $[OH^-]$ ions, but one cannot measure the $[H_3O^+]$ or $[OH^-]$ alone without a process like titration. Choice 3 comes before choices 1 and 2.

17. The correct answer is 4. A standard solution must have a known concentration and can be any substance about which the characteristics are known (e.g., is it an acid or a base, and is its concentration known?).

18. The correct answer is 3. There is no need for a standard to be a weak or a strong anything, but merely that its characteristics, e.g., concentration, be known. Choice 1 is certainly true, choice 2 is why we titrate, and choice 4 is true for the indicator we often use.

19. The correct answer is 1. The pH of the end point of a titration is going to be very close to the pH at the equivalence point. The end point is not necessarily 7—see question 12 as an example.

20. The correct answer is 1. Acids react with metals to release hydrogen gas, not oxygen gas. The other three choices are accurate descriptions of what we know of acids.

Chapter 10

Redox and Electrochemistry

I. Redox (Oxidation-Reduction)

    A. Oxidation—represents a loss, or apparent loss, of electrons and refers to any chemical change in which there is an increase in oxidation number of a particle, at which time it is said to have been oxidized. The particle being oxidized acts as a reducing agent.

    B. Reduction—represents a gain, or apparent gain, of electrons and refers to any chemical change in which there is a decrease in oxidation number of a particle, at which time it is said to have been reduced. The particle being reduced acts as an oxidizing agent.

    C. Oxidation number—is the charge an atom has, or appears to have, when electrons are counted by certain arbitrary rules. The sharing between two unlike atoms counts the electrons as belonging to the more electronegative atom while sharing between two like atoms divides the electrons equally between the sharing atoms.

        1. Free elements—Each atom has an oxidation number of zero.

        2. Simple ion—has an oxidation number equal to the charge on the atom.

        3. Group IA—All metals in this group have an oxidation number of $^{+}1$ in all compounds.

        4. Group IIA—All metals in this group have an oxidation number of $^{+}2$ in all compounds.

        5. Oxygen—has an oxidation number of $^{-}2$ in all its compounds except peroxides (such as H_2O_2) when it is $^{-}1$ and may be $^{+}1$ or $^{+}2$ in compounds with fluorine.

        6. Hydrogen—has an oxidation number of $^{+}1$ in all its compounds except in the metal hydrides (such as LiH) when it is $^{-}1$.

7. Conservation of charge—All oxidation numbers must be consistent with the conservation of charge. For all neutral molecules, the oxidation numbers must add up to zero.

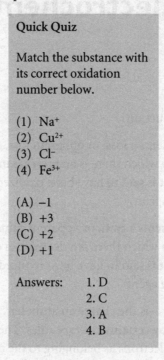

Quick Quiz

Match the substance with its correct oxidation number below.

(1) Na^+
(2) Cu^{2+}
(3) Cl^-
(4) Fe^{3+}

(A) −1
(B) +3
(C) +2
(D) +1

Answers: 1. D
            2. C
            3. A
            4. B

D. Redox reactions—occur simultaneously (reduction cannot occur without oxidation).

II. Electrochemistry

A. Half-reactions—Each reaction in redox is known as a half-reaction, with oxidation being one half and reduction being the other half.

B. Half-cells—It is possible to set up reactions so that each half of a redox reaction takes place in a separate vessel, provided the vessels are connected by an external conductor and a salt bridge or porous partition is placed between them which permits the migration of ions while not allowing the solutions to mix.

1. Half-cell potential—When the driving force of a half-reaction is compared with the hydrogen standard, a scale of voltage can be established, allowing the standard electrode potential to be obtained.

   Example: The half-reaction for hydrogen has been adopted as the standard: $2H^+ + 2e^- \rightarrow H_2$.

2. Electrode potentials—useful in determining whether a redox reaction will take place. Any pair of half-reactions can be combined to give the complete reaction for a cell whose potential difference can be calculated by adding the appropriate half-cell potentials.

C. Galvanic (Voltaic) cells—redox reactions that occur spontaneously and provide a source of electricity when connected by an external conductor, causing a flow of electrons (electric current) to occur.

D. Electrolytic cells—Redox reactions that do not occur spontaneously can be forced to take place by supplying energy with an externally applied electric current. The reaction produced is called *electrolysis*.

   1. Electrodes

      a. Cathode—the electrode at which reduction occurs. In a chemical cell, it is the positive electrode, and in an electrolytic cell, it is the negative cell.

      b. Anode—the electrode at which oxidation occurs. In a chemical cell, it is the negative electrode, and in an electrolytic cell, it is the positive cell.

III. Balancing Simple Redox Equations

Balancing Simple Redox Equations—In any reaction, the loss of electrons by the species oxidized must equal the gain of electrons by the species reduced. Both charge and mass must be conserved.

A common example of a galvanic cell is the Daniell cell, shown below:

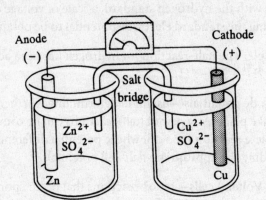

In the Daniell cell, a zinc bar is placed in an aqueous $ZnSO_4$ solution, and a copper bar is placed in an aqueous $CuSO_4$ solution. The anode of this cell is the zinc bar where Zn (s) is oxidized to $Zn^{2+}(aq)$. The cathode is the copper bar, and it is the site of the reduction of $Cu^{2+}(aq)$ to Cu (s). The half-cell reactions are written as follows:

$Zn\ (s) \rightarrow Zn^{2+}\ (aq) + 2e^-$ (anode)

$Cu^{2+}\ (aq) + 2e^- \rightarrow Cu\ (s)$ (cathode)

The salt bridge is meant to allow current to complete the circuit (electons through the wire and ions through the solutions), but also to keep the anode solution away from the cathode solution, which would result in the reaction "shorting out," producing no electric current in the wire.

Questions

1. The oxidation number of atoms in an uncombined element is
   1. positive if a nonmetal.
   2. zero.
   3. negative if a metal.
   4. none of the above.

2. A redox reaction is a process
   1. of losing electrons.
   2. where electrons are transferred between reactants.
   3. of gaining electrons.
   4. where steps repeat themselves.

3. The oxidation number of a monatomic ion is always
   1. equal to its ionic charge.
   2. neutral.
   3. positive if in Group VIIA.
   4. negative.

4. Elements in Group IA all have oxidation numbers of
   1. zero.
   2. −7.
   3. +1.
   4. none of the above.

5. When combined with nonmetals, hydrogen's oxidation number is
   1. +1.
   2. −1.
   3. zero.
   4. none of the above.

6. An oxidizing agent is
   1. one that remains neutral.
   2. always becomes positive.
   3. mostly found in Groups IA or IIA.
   4. one that accepts electrons from another substance.

7. In most compounds, aluminum has an oxidation number of
   1. −3.
   2. +3.
   3. −5.
   4. +5.

8. Oxidation involves reactions in which
   1. oxygen has been removed from the reactants.
   2. oxygen is gained by the reactants.
   3. a substance loses one or more electrons.
   4. a substance gains one or more electrons.

9. Reduction involves reactions in which
   1. oxygen has been removed from the reactants.
   2. oxygen is gained by the reactants.
   3. a substance loses one or more electrons.
   4. a substance gains one or more electrons.

10. A reducing agent
    1. contains the atom that shows a decrease in oxidation number.
    2. is the substance that is reduced.
    3. is the substance that is oxidized.
    4. causes oxidation.

11. Which of the following metals is most reactive according to the activity series of metals?
    1. zinc
    2. magnesium
    3. copper
    4. silver

12. Bleaches act on stains by
    1. removing electrons during the oxidation process.
    2. reducing the colored compound by adding electrons.
    3. exciting electrons to move between energy levels.
    4. adding hydrogen ions to the stain.

13. A salt bridge
    1. acts as an anode.
    2. connects two half-cells.
    3. contains an electrolytic solution.
    4. Both 2 and 3 are correct.

14. A voltaic cell
    1. uses spontaneous redox reactions.
    2. uses nonspontaneous redox reactions.
    3. uses the reverse of a spontaneous redox reaction.
    4. None of these is correct.

15. An anode
    1. is where reduction takes place.
    2. is where oxidation takes place.
    3. is the positive end of a battery.
    4. Both 1 and 3 are correct.

16. In a cell, standard-state conditions include all of the following EXCEPT
    1. concentration of 1 M.
    2. partial pressure of 1 atm.
    3. 25°C.
    4. 0°C.

17. A molecule with a positive standard reduction potential is
    1. harder to reduce than H^+.
    2. easier to reduce than H^+.
    3. harder to oxidize than H^+.
    4. easier to oxidize than H^+.

18. A common dry cell
    1. contains KOH.
    2. oxidizes MnO_2.
    3. has a paste electrolyte.
    4. is rechargeable.

19. A lead storage battery
    1. contains NH_4.
    2. contains H_2SO_4.
    3. Both 1 and 2 are correct.
    4. Neither 1 nor 2 is correct.

20. The electrolysis of aqueous sodium chloride
    1. is used in electroplating.
    2. produces hydrogen for commercial purposes.
    3. is a voltaic cell reaction.
    4. oxidizes chlorine.

Answers

1. The correct answer is 2. Elements of the periodic table and yet uncombined (i.e., unreacted), have not had any electrons transferred. Therefore, there is no charge. The practice is to use the oxidation number for an element as if it happened before the reaction. This is good only for predicting reactions, but the reality is that any element in its elemental state has not yet been assigned an oxidation number.

2. The correct answer is 2. The definition of a reduction-oxidation reaction is one where electrons are transferred between reactions. Choices 1 and 3 are half right and choice 4 is incorrect.

3. The correct answer is 1. This is one of the unique situations where the oxidation number is equal to its ionic charge. Since there is only one atom, as it takes on a charge, it will be a monatomic ion with the same charge as its oxidation number. This is just one of several ways of saying the same thing.

4. The correct answer is 3. Although the metals have the potential of gaining seven electrons in a chemical reaction, they classically are treated as losing the one electron in their outermost energy level—something they always seem to do under normal circumstances—to achieve an oxidation number of $+1$.

5. The correct answer is 1. In combination with nonmetals, hydrogen donates an electron, thus achieving an oxidation number of $+1$. The nonmetals will have negative oxidation numbers, so the hydrogen will take on the positive oxidation number, whether it donates the electron or shares it.

6. The correct answer is 4. An oxidizing agent is defined as the substance that accepts electrons from another substance. By doing so, the agent is reduced. Since it accepts electrons, it will always become less positive, sometimes negative. It would not be found in Groups IA or IIA (1 or 2) since it is an electron acceptor.

7. The correct answer is 2. Being in Group IIIA, aluminum normally loses three electrons to achieve an oxidation number of $+3$ in most compounds.

8. The correct answer is 3. The oxidation reaction is named after and follows the behavior of oxygen. During a chemical reaction, the substance being oxidized loses electrons to oxygen or a substance like it that will gain electrons. Anything that loses electrons in a chemical reaction is said to have been oxidized, and the process is no longer limited to oxygen as the oxidizing agent.

9. The correct answer is 4. Substances that gain electrons—thereby becoming more negative, like oxygen—are said to be reduced. Any oxidizing agent is itself reduced and vice versa. See question 8.

10. The correct answer is 3. Any substances that can take the lost electrons of a substance that is being oxidized are themselves reduced. All substances that are oxidized and have lost electrons are agents of reduction and vice versa.

11. The correct answer is 2. According to the metal activity series, magnesium will replace the other three metals listed in a chemical reaction.

12. The correct answer is 1. Most bleaches are better oxidizers than oxygen; they act the same as oxygen except better.

13. The correct answer is 4. A salt bridge has both two half-cells and an electrolytic solution to connect them, thus the name "bridge."

14. The correct answer is 1. A voltaic cell produces energy on its own by making use of spontaneous redox reactions once the cells are connected. The reading of choice 2 reveals that it is saying the same thing as choice 3.

15. The correct answer is 2. The anode is the electrode that provides the excess electrons needed for oxidation to occur. In the classic treatment of electrolytics, the cathode is where they collect.

16. The correct answer is 4. Standard-state conditions in a cell are defined as indicated in choices 1, 2, and 3. Only one temperature defines the conditions, which makes choice 4 incorrect.

17. The correct answer is 2. A positive standard reduction potential for any molecule places it above H^+ in its ability to be reduced, and is therefore easier to reduce than H^+.

18. The correct answer is 3. Since it does not contain a liquid, the paste cell is often referred to as a dry cell. The paste allows for the migration of ions in a similar way to aqueous solutions, only at a slower rate.

19. The correct answer is 2. A lead storage battery contains sulfuric acid as the electrolyte, making choice 2 the only right choice. It would hardly contain ammonia.

20. The correct answer is 2. In solution, the electrolysis of sodium chloride will produce sodium, just as the electrolysis of molten sodium chloride would, except that in the aqueous setup, Na reacts with water to liberate H_2.

Chapter 11

Organic Chemistry

I. Definition

   Definition—The chemistry of carbon compounds formerly referred to mainly as organic chemistry, is now more specifically referred to as *carbon chemistry*. The principles behind the formation of carbon compounds more acurately reflect what used to be known vaguely as organics.

II. Characteristics of organic compounds

   Characteristics of organic compounds—Organic compounds are insoluble in water and soluble in nonpolar solvents. Generally, organic compounds are non-electrolytes, with relatively low melting points and unstable under high heat.

   A. Bonding—Carbon atoms usually form compounds by means of covalent bonds, have four valence electrons, and can form four covalent bonds with other elements or with other carbon atoms. The covalent bonding results in compounds that are molecular in nature.

   B. Structural formula—A formula showing the sharing of a pair of electrons as a short line is known as a structural formula, for example a single bond is pictured as C–C and a double bond as C=C.

   C. Isomers—Compounds that have the same molecular formula but different structural formula are known as isomers.

   D. Saturated-Unsaturated compounds—When a single pair of electrons is shared, the bond is said to be saturated. When more than a single pair of electrons are shared, the bond is said to be unsaturated.

III. Homologous Series

   Homologous series—Organic compounds can be classified into groups called homologous series.

A. Hydrocarbons—Compounds containing only carbon and hydrogen are known as hydrocarbons.

   1. Alkanes—saturated (i.e., only single bonds throughout) hydrocarbons with the general formula C_nH_{2n+2}; for example, C_2H_6 (ethane).

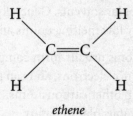

ethane

   2. Alkenes—unsaturated hydrocarbons containing one double bond and having the general formula C_nH_{2n}. In the I.U.P.A.C. system of nomenclature, the alkenes are named from the corresponding alkane by replacing the "-ane" ending with "-ene." Alkenes are also called olefins.

$$H \diagdown \diagup H$$
$$C = C$$
$$H \diagup \diagdown H$$

ethene

   3. Alkynes—unsaturated hydrocarbons containing one triple bond and having the general formula C_nH_{2n-2}. In the I.U.P.A.C. system of nomenclature, the alkynes are named from the corresponding alkane by replacing the "-ane" ending with "-yne."

   4. Benzene series—aromatic ring hydrocarbons having the general formula C_nH_{2n-6}. All of the carbon-carbon bonds are the same, intermediate between single and double bonds. It is common practice, however, to

draw the compound with alternating single and double bonds between the 6 carbon atoms.

Benzene with its two equivalent structures

IV. Other Organic Compounds

Other organic compounds—these homologous structures occur when one or more hydrogens have been replaced by other elements in a hydrocarbon and are named from their corresponding hydrocarbons. A functional group is a particular arrangement of a few atoms which gives characteristic properties to an organic molecule. Organic compounds can be thought of as being composed of one or more functional groups attached to a hydrocarbon group.

Structure of glucose showing both alcohol and aldehyde functional groups

A. Alcohols—One or more hydrogens of a hydrocarbon have been replaced by an –OH group.

1. Primary alcohols—The –OH is attached to the end carbon and contains the functional group –CH$_2$OH. In the I.U.P.A.C. system of nomencla-

ture, the alcohols are named from the corresponding hydrocarbon by replacing the "-e" ending with "-ol."

B. Organic Acids—Organic acids contain the functional group $-\overset{\overset{\displaystyle O}{\|}}{C}-O-H$, abbreviated as –COOH. In the I.U.P.A.C. system of nomenclature, the organic acids are named from the corresponding hydrocarbon by replacing the "-e" ending with "-oic" and adding the name "acid."

C. Aldehydes—contain the functional group –COH. In the I.U.P.A.C. system of nomenclature, the aldehydes are named from the corresponding hydrocarbon by replacing the "-e" ending with "-al."

D. Ketones—contain the functional group $R_1-\overset{\overset{\displaystyle O}{\|}}{C}-R_2$.

E. Ethers—contain the functional group R_1-O-R_2.

F. Polymers—composed of repeating units called monomers.

G. Esters—contain the functional group $R_1-\overset{\overset{\displaystyle }{C}}{\underset{\underset{\displaystyle O}{\|}}{}}-O-R_2$, or $R_1-COO-R_2$ abbreviated.

Questions

1. A carbon atom needs _____ additional electrons to satisfy the octet rules.
   1. 2
   2. 4
   3. 6
   4. none of the above

2. Which of the following is not an organic compound?
   1. CH_4
   2. $C_6H_{12}O_6$
   3. CH_3OH
   4. $CaCO_3$

3. Which of the following is an organic compound?
   1. C_2H_6
   2. NH_3
   3. CO_2
   4. $CaCO_3$

4. An alkane with 22 carbon atoms has the molecular formula
   1. $C_{22}H_{44}$.
   2. $C_{22}H_{32}$.
   3. $C_{22}H_{46}$.
   4. $C_{22}H_{12}$.

5. Which of the following is not an allotrope of carbon?
   1. coke
   2. methane
   3. diamond
   4. graphite

6. The carbon atom
   1. exists diatomically.
   2. has 4 valence electrons.
   3. needs only 2 electrons to satisfy the octet rule.
   4. forms 4 ionic bonds.

7. An organic compound
   1. contains carbon.
   2. can be produced synthetically.
   3. Both 1 and 2 are correct.
   4. Neither 1 nor 2 is correct.

8. A fossil fuel
   1. is formed from the decomposition of remains of ancient plants and animals.
   2. is recycled naturally in the carbon cycle.
   3. contains mainly methane.
   4. is not an organic compound.

9. An alkene with 16 carbons has a molecular formula of
   1. $C_{16}H_{16}$.
   2. $C_{16}H_{34}$.
   3. $C_{16}H_8$.
   4. $C_{16}H_{32}$.

10. A cyclic arrangement of 6 carbon and 6 hydrogen atoms is
    1. benzene.
    2. alkane.
    3. butane.
    4. alkene.

11. Natural polymers
    1. include Teflon.
    2. are not assembled from monomers.
    3. include polonium
    4. are biodegradable.

12. Glucose is metabolized by
    1. plants only.
    2. plants and animals.
    3. animals only.
    4. monerans only.

13. The process by which plants convert radiant energy into chemical energy is called
    1. hydrolysis.
    4. depolymerization.
    3. cellular respiration.
    4. photosynthesis.

14. A functional group
    1. consists only of hydrogen and carbon.
    2. is given in the general formula as "X."
    3. determines the properties of a hydro-carbon derivative.
    4. None of the above is correct.

15. A secondary alcohol has a hydroxyl group
    1. on the end of the the hydrocarbon chain.
    2. attached to a carbon that is attached to one other carbon atom.
    3. attached to a carbon that is attached to three other carbon atoms.
    4. on the interior of the hydrocarbon chain.

16. An aldehyde
    1. has a carbonyl group at the end of the hydrocarbon chain.
    2. can contain only an alkyl group.
    3. is given by the general formula R–CHO.
    4. All of the above are correct.

17. Which of the following is a ketone?
    1. acetone
    2. formaldehyde
    3. formic acid
    4. propanol

18. Which of the following is not an ester?
    1. propanoate
    2. hexanoic acid
    3. butanoate
    4. methyl acetate

19. An amino group
    1. forms hydrocarbons.
    2. is nonpolar.
    3. acts as a base.
    4. acts as a strong acid.

20. Compounds that have the same molecular formula, but a different structural formula are known as
    1. isomers.
    2. polymers.
    3. monomers.
    4. dinomers.

Answers

1. The correct answer is 2. Carbon resides in Group IVA, a group with four electrons in their outer energy level needing four more electrons to satisfy the octet rule. In addition to taking four electrons, carbon can also give four electrons. In reality, carbon most often shares electrons to satisfy the octet rule, forming the basis for organic or carbon chemistry.

2. The correct answer is 4. Calcium carbonate, choice 4, is not an organic compound, despite the fact that it contains carbon. Carbon, in this compound, is acting as part of a polyatomic ion, not in its usual way in an organic compound.

3. The correct answer is 1. Choice 1 is the organic compound, specifically a hydrocarbon. Choice 2 is the ammonium complex and can be found in organic molecules but it does not define organic molecules. Choice 3 is the result of the combustion of an organic molecule but is not usually considered organic itself. Choice 4 was discussed in answer 2.

4. The correct answer is 3. The rule for alkanes is to assign carbon a number, usually called n. The number of hydrogens bonded to those carbons is then calculated from the formula $2n + 2$ where n is the number of carbons, as previously indicated. In this question, the only compound that satisfies that formula is choice 3. Choice 1 uses the formula $2n$ to find the hydrogens, choice 2 uses $n + 10$ and choice 4 appears to use $n - 10$.

5. The correct answer is 2. All of the items listed are forms, or allotropes, of carbon except methane, which is a compound of carbon that has the formula CH_4. An allotrope must be identical in composition.

6. The correct answer is 2. Our understanding of the properties of carbon atoms is that they contain four electrons in their outer energy level, putting them in Group IVA (meaning they have four available electrons for bonding). Group IVA is now more often referred to as Group 14.

7. The correct answer is 3. Both choices 1 and 2 are correct for organic compounds; they contain carbon and can be synthesized. Produced synthetically usually means in a lab, not in nature.

8. The correct answer is 1. The only valid choice for this question is the statement as to the origin of fossil fuels. They do not "recycle" naturally since it takes incorporation into living matter after they are decomposed in cycles beyond the carbon cycle, such as cellular respiration, and combustion to name only two.

9. The correct answer is 4. The general formula used for alkenes is to first assign n as the number of carbons in the molecule. The number of hydrogens in this group of hydrocarbons is then found by the formula $2n$. Choice 4 is the only formula arrived at using this designation. Choice 1 appears to use n for carbon as well as hydrogen, choice 2 uses

the formula for alkanes, and choice 3 uses $n/2$. None of these is correct for alkenes.

10. The correct answer is 1. Benzene is the only substance on the list with a cyclic arrangement of carbon atoms with six equivalent bonds between each C atom. Alkanes and alkenes are linear and butane is an alkane with four carbons.

11. The correct answer is 4. Polymers found in nature are, as one might expect, degradable in the very environment from which they came. Teflon is a synthetic polymer; polymers are assembled from smaller monomers; and polonium is a radioactive element not likely to be found in any monomer or polymer in nature.

12. The correct answer is 2. Both plants and animals metabolize the glucose that plants produce during photosynthesis. Monerans also metabolize glucose released from the decomposition of carbohydrates, but choice 4 says "only," which is not true.

13. The correct answer is 4. This is the classic definition of the fourth item listed, photosynthesis. Hydrolysis occurs within the light reactions of photosynthesis, but it is only one phase of the energy conversion. Rather than depolymerization, photosynthesis involves polymerization of 3-carbon units into glucose. Cellular respiration is, of course, the opposite of photosynthesis.

14. The correct answer is 3. The definition of a functional group is that when attached onto the basic structure of a molecule within a group of organic compounds, it accounts for the differences among the members of that group. It can consist of far more than just carbon and hydrogen as in the case of the disulfide bonds in insulin.

15. The correct answer is 4. The placement of the hydroxyl (−OH) group on the interior of a hydrocarbon chain is what makes the hydrocarbon a secondary alcohol, as opposed to a primary alcohol, which has the −OH on the end. Choice 2 is too vague, and Choice 3 represents a tertiary alcohol.

16. The correct answer is 4. All three choices are correct in describing the properties and characteristics of an aldehyde, where "R" stands for the variable group.

17. The correct answer is 1. Acetone is the only ketone on the list, the rest being an aldehyde, an organic acid, and an alcohol, respectively (choices 2 through 4).

18. The correct answer is 2. Hexanoic acid is an organic acid and not an ester. Esters have an R-group in place of the hydrogen on the carboxyl group found in carboxylic acids.

19. The correct answer is 3. NH_3 is a weak base and promotes the ionization of water, forming NH_4OH. While amino acids are amphoteric (able to act as an acid and a base), the NH_3 side acts as a stronger base than the acid side does as an acid.

20. The correct answer is 1. Of course, this is the definition of an isomer. A polymer, as has been noted, is many monomers bonded together, thus giving us the idea of what a monomer is, and dinomer is a contrived term.

Chapter 12

Nuclear Chemistry

I. Artificial Radioactivity

Elements can be made radioactive by bombarding their nuclei with high-energy particles such as protons, neutrons, and alpha particles.

A. Artificial transmutation—Bombardment of nuclei by accelerated particles may result in the formation of new elements.

B. Accelerators—Electric and magnetic fields are used to accelerate charged particles.

II. Nuclear Energy

In nuclear reactions, mass is converted to energy.

A. Fission—can be brought about by *neutron capture* by an atom, which results in splitting the atom (fission fragments), liberation of energy, and release of two or more neutrons. The liberation of energy is the result of conversion of mass into energy. Nuclei such as uranium-235 fission spontaneously—a natural form of radioactivity.

1. Fuels—Uranium-233, uranium-235, and plutonium-239 are fissionable.

2. Moderators—For efficient nuclear fission, it is necessary to slow the speed of the neutrons using "moderators," which are materials that have the ability to slow down the neutrons without absorbing them.

3. Control rods—made of material with good ability to absorb neutrons, these work with moderators to control the reaction by adjusting the number of neutrons available.

4. Coolants—are used to keep the temperatures generated at reasonable levels within the reactor and to carry heat to the exchangers and turbines.

5. Shielding—Internally, it protects the walls of the reactor from radiation damage, and externally, it protects the employees from exposure to radiation.

B. Fusion reaction—the process of combining two nuclei to form a heavier one. The energy released in some fusion reactions is much greater than in a fission reaction.

   1. Fuels—The isotopes of hydrogen, deuterium [^{2}H], and tritium [^{3}H], are used as fuels in fusion reactions designed to produce commercial energy in the future, and used in nuclear weapons.

   2. High-energy requirement—Since each nucleus carries a positive charge, they repel each other the closer they get. In order for them to interact, they must travel at enormous speeds (have enough kinetic energy) to overcome the repulsion.

C. Radioactive waste—Fission products are very radioactive and must be isolated from the general population and stored for a long time or disposed of in special ways.

D. Radioisotopes

   1. Based on chemical activity—Since they are chemically similar to their more stable relatives (the same element) they can be used as tracers in chemical reactions.

   2. Based on radioactivity—Radioisotopes are used in medical diagnoses, therapy, and food preservation and as a means of measuring physical dimensions of many industrial products.

   3. Based on half-life—They give a fairly consistent method of dating some geologic events.

   4. When the atomic mass for an element on the Periodic Table is given as an integer, this indicates both the longest lived isotope of that element and the fact that there are no stable isotopes of that element (examples are Po, Tc, and all elements heavier than Np).

Questions

1. Which of the following cannot be used to bombard atoms?

   1. protons
   2. neutrons
   3. electrons
   4. all of the above can be used to bombard atoms

2. An isotope is

   1. a different form of the same element.
   2. a charged atom.
   3. always radioactive.
   4. an atom that is not charged.

3. Splitting of atoms is also called

   1. merging.
   2. moderating.
   3. fusion.
   4. fission.

4. If U–238 is the form of uranium listed on the periodic table, then U–233

   1. does not exist.
   2. weighs more than U–238.
   3. has five fewer neutrons then U–238.
   4. has five more neutrons than U–238.

5. The speed of a chain reaction is regulated in a nuclear reactor

   1. by using coolants.
   2. with internal shielding.
   3. with external shielding.
   4. by using moderators.

6. Which of the following is not true of a fission reaction?

   1. an atom is split
   2. neutrons are released
   3. it results in fission fragments
   4. lightweight nuclei interact

7. Radioactive decay

   1. occurs in unstable isotopes.
   2. is spontaneous.
   3. Both 1 and 2 are correct.
   4. Neither 1 nor 2 is correct.

8. The half-life of a radioactive isotope

   1. is the time it takes for one half of the sample to decay.
   2. is the time it takes for all of the sample to decay.
   3. is always more than 10,000 years for any given isotope.
   4. cannot be mathematically calculated.

9. Carbon-14

   1. is oxidized to produce a fixed ratio of $^{14}CO^2$ to $^{12}CO_2$.
   2. decays into Nitrogen-14.
   3. incorporation continues after the death of the animal plant.
   4. None of the above is correct.

10. Nuclear bombardment reactions are useful because

    1. they are inexpensive to produce.
    2. they require no kinetic energy to initiate.
    3. they create many artificial radioactive isotopes.
    4. None of the above is correct.

11. Radiation
    1. can be useful in food preparation.
    2. causes disruption of cells in living tissue.
    3. can be useful in the treatment of cancer.
    4. All of the above are correct.

12. Which of the following is true?
    1. Fission of U-235, pound for pound, produces more energy than fusion of hydrogen isotopes.
    2. Fission provides less energy than fusion.
    3. Fission and fusion provide exactly the same amount of energy.
    4. None of the above are true.

13. Which of the following is true of a fusion reaction?
    1. An atom is split.
    2. Neutrons are released.
    3. It results in fragments.
    4. Lightweight nuclei interact.

14. Cancer is suitable for radioactive therapy
    1. because cancer cells are more susceptible than normal cells to radiation.
    2. only for lymph tissue.
    3. only as a last resort.
    4. Cancer is not suitable for radiotherapy.

15. Which of the following is false?
    1. Nuclear fission involves the splitting of one nucleus into two smaller nuclei.
    2. The mass lost in a fission reaction is converted to energy.
    3. Fission reactions provide nuclear power.
    4. A "runaway" nuclear chain reaction is not possible.

16. Which of the following is true about cold fusion?
    1. Cold fusion theory states that nuclear fusion reactions can be performed under ordinary laboratory conditions.
    2. Cold fusion involves the electrolysis of ordinary water.
    3. Cold fusion research strongly supports the original cold fusion theory.
    4. All of the above are true.

17. Nuclear power plants transfer the heat given off by nuclear materials by using
    1. moderators.
    2. water.
    3. uranium.
    4. lead shielding.

18. Which of the following is used as a coolant in nuclear power plants?
    1. asbestos
    2. water
    3. uranium
    4. lead shielding

19. Which of the following is true of moderators in a nuclear reactor?
    1. They are optional.
    2. They are necessary.
    3. They are not necessary.
    4. None of the above is correct.

20. Which of the following is false?
    1. Matter can be converted to energy.
    2. Energy can be converted to matter.
    3. When matter is converted to energy, some is destroyed.
    4. Matter can be neither destroyed nor created.

Answers

1. The correct answer is 4. Atoms can be bombarded with any particle; the ones small enough to hit the atom would have the most significant effect. Since all three of these particles help make up the atom, the likelihood is that, given enough of them over a long enough period of time, they would hit the atom.

2. The correct answer is 1. Our definition uses the prefix "iso-" for "same" and the root "-tope" for conveying the fact that two substances are the same element in a different form.

3. The correct answer is 4. Fusion relates to fusing of things and fission relates to fissures or cracks that occur when things split. Therefore, *fission* is our word for splitting atoms.

4. The correct answer is 3. The 238 and the 233 indicated here refer to mass numbers of the two isotopes of uranium noted in the question. Since they both refer to uranium, the number of protons is the same, but the difference in mass must be five fewer neutrons in U-233.

5. The correct answer is 4. Nuclear reactions are controlled by rods called moderators or control rods made of a material designed to absorb neutrons.

6. The correct answer is 4. A fission reaction is one in which large nuclei are split into smaller nuclei, so it is not true that a fission reaction involves the interaction of light-weight nuclei.

7. The correct answer is 3. The nature and definition of radioactivity is that it involves the spontaneous loss (or emission) of radiation (in the form of rays or particles) from an unstable isotope.

8. The correct answer is 1. Half-life was originally designed to be able to predict, from the constant rate of loss of particles and/or energy in radioactive substances, how much of the substance in question would remain after a known period of time. This became known as the half-life.

9. The correct answer is 2. Carbon-14 does not oxidize to produce a C-14/C-12 ratio of CO_2 or of any compound of C-12; it decays radioactively. Therefore choice 2 is the answer and not choice 1.

10. The correct answer is 3. One rich area of study in nuclear chemistry is the artificial isotopes that spring from nuclear bombardment of atoms.

11. The correct answer is 4. All of the answers (1, 2, and 3) offered are true about radiation.

12. The correct answer is 4. Choice 1 is the exact opposite of the correct answer as it is the fusion of H-2 and H-3 together that yields the greatest amount of energy per reaction and therefore per gram of material. Almost any two nuclei can be fused to pro-

duce a third nucleus—the energy release, however, in almost all of these fusion reactions is not significant if at all. Choice 3 cannot be correct since the processes are very different. Choice 2 is tricky because it is true only if you compare the two processes for the same amount of starting material and only if you compare those reactions actually used in the nuclear energy/weapons industry. As it stands, however, the statement is too general to be correct.

13. The correct answer is 4. In the more familiar process of fusion, the nuclei of lightweight atoms are fused to produce energy (see answer 6).

14. The correct answer is 1. Cancer-cell growth is accelerated usually because the nucleus is somehow made more active. This very act makes it absorb more radioactive energy as well, spelling doom for the cancer cells that are bombarded with (and therefore take up most of the) radiation than the surrounding normal tissue.

15. The correct answer is 4. A runaway nuclear reaction is entirely possible and is what occurs in nuclear bombs. Unfortunately, it also occurs in a state yielding far less energy than a nuclear bomb does in a short period of time but is nonetheless damaging such as the accident at Chernobyl. Nuclear power plants do not contain enough critical mass to become bombs, but their total energy output can be damaging when they become "runaway."

16. The correct answer is 1. This is the fundamental and yet to be substantiated theory behind cold fusion. Present-day investigations into cold-fusion research do not support the original cold-fusion theory; the group is, in fact, seeking a way to formulate the theory, and the process is certainly not the simple electrolysis of water.

17. The correct answer is 2. This water heats other water not in contact with the reactor by use of a heat exchanger. The secondary heated water is then used to run a steam turbine that turns a generator. The other materials are not employed in running turbines.

18. The correct answer is 2. The coolant used in nuclear reactors is large pools of water. The other materials simply will not do it. Asbestos is probably outlawed, and lead acts as a shield, not a coolant.

19. The correct answer is 2. Moderators are not optional: They are necessary in nuclear reactors to capture stray neutrons and thereby slow or shut down the reaction. Failure to do so results in massive amounts of heat and possible fires. There is not enough uranium in a nuclear power plant to explode.

20. The correct answer is 3. When converting matter to energy or vice versa, it is important to point out that nothing is lost. All matter and converted energy are accounted for.

Chapter 13

Laboratory Activities

I. Measurement

A. Measuring devices—You should be proficient in using, as well as be able to accurately describe the use of, balances, graduated cylinders, beakers, flasks, thermometers, burettes, and other laboratory devices. All of these devices have scales divided into equal parts. You should be able to accurately interpolate to 1/10th of the smallest division on the scale.

B. Significant figures—The use of significant figures helps us know the precision of the instrument used to generate the figures. The accepted technique is to allow an estimation of a measurement to one place beyond the markings on a scale: e.g., if a scale is marked to tenths of units, we are allowed a guess to hundredths of units. When we manipulate measurements mathematically, the answer we report can have no more significant figures than the measurement recorded with the least number of significant figures. And when adding or subtracting significant figures, the answer we report should not have more decimal places than the least number of decimal places among the figures given. This ensures that our result is not indicating more accuracy than our least accurate device. All nonzero digits are significant, as are all nonplaceholding zeros. Therefore, any zero in between nonzero digits is significant. Whole numbers that are multiples of 10 (whole numbers larger than zero and ending in zero) should be written in scientific notation. This will ensure that the correct number of significant figures will be used. For example, in the following operation, the number 1.7 has only two significant figures. The answer would then be 1,100, since the accurate answer would be rounded off so that we present only two significant figures.

$$634 \times 1.7 = 1,077.8$$

C. Percent error—Our work in the lab often involves the measurement of a value—the observed value—for which a standard or accepted value exists, whether by direct observation, such as the volume of a mole of gas, or one that was calculated from direct measurements, such as density. We want to be able to communicate how accurate our observations have been compared to the standard. We do this by indicating the difference between the observed and the accepted value. The equation would present the percent of error as [(observed value) − (accepted value)] / (accepted value) × 100. The accepted value is always subtracted from the observed value, as this will give us a positive percent if our observed value is above the accepted value and a negative percent if we are below the accepted value. Students should use this on every measurement for which there is a standard or accepted value. In the following example, the percent error is −5.2%.

Observed value = $118.9 g/cm^3$

Accepted value = $125.4 g/cm^3$

$$\frac{118.9 - 125.4}{125.4} \times 100 = -5.183\%$$

II. Laboratory Skills

A. Bunsen burner—In using the Bunsen burner, students should make proper connections between the hose, the burner, and the gas outlet. The hose should not be corroded or defective in any way. Proper adjustment of any part that regulates the oxygen flow (usually on the underside of the burner) must be made with the amount of oxygen initially set higher than might be needed in order to ensure the flame will light. After this, adjustments based on need may be made. One should always strike the match first—or have the striker ready—before turning on the gas. Once ready and with the gas turned on, the lighted match or striker should be introduced from the side until the flame is lighted. Adjustment of the oxygen, noted by the color of the flame and the amount of gas regulated at the outlet, can now be made based on the needs of the activity. Extinguishing the flame should always be done by turning off the gas at the outlet. If the flame should go out accidentally, the gas jet should be turned off and time should be allowed for any unburned gas to dissipate before lighting the burner again. At the end of every activity, care should be taken to turn off properly all gas jets in the lab.

B. Glass tubing—As with every piece of equipment, glass should be handled with care. In the lab, in addition to simply using glass tubing, you may want to (1) cut, (2) bend, or (3) fire-polish it.

1. Cutting—There are two devices for cutting glass, a triangular file and a tubing cutter. The former is a file in the shape of a triangle, i.e., it has three filing surfaces. The first step in cutting the tubing is to place the inner corner of any two sides of the file on the tubing at the desired cutting point. While properly supporting both the file and the tubing, scratch the tubing with the file at the cutting point. Next, place both hands on either side of the scratch and pull the ends of the tubing towards you while pushing the section with the scratch away from you. This should produce a clean break at the point of the scratch. The other device, the tubing cutter, has a wheel much like those in a glass cutter found in a hardware store. The cutter has a place to sit the tubing in while making a complete 360° cut with the blade. The tubing is then snapped as with the technique using the triangular file.

2. Bending—A metal piece called a flame spreader, pictured below, is placed on top of a Bunsen burner. When the burner is lighted, it provides a wide flame in which to turn the tubing. Once the tubing feels soft enough to bend, it is removed from the flame and quickly and deliberately bent into the desired shape and held that way for approximately one minute to make sure it will retain that shape until it can be placed in a safe, secure place.

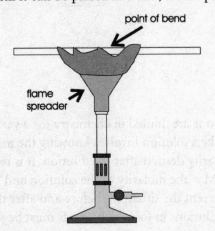

point of bend

flame spreader

3. Fire polishing—After a piece of glass tubing is cut (see "Cutting" above) the edges will be dangerously sharp. Placing the cut end of a piece of tubing

into the Bunsen burner flame until it takes on a rounded appearance will ensure that the end is rounded and smooth. In effect, we are melting the end of the tubing just long enough for it to be rounded. At this point it is removed from the flame, allowed to cool, and placed in a dry, secure place.

C. Funnel and filter paper—Funnels are mostly used in the filtering process along with a piece of filter paper. In a tight space, the funnel might be used simply for pouring. Filter paper comes in various circle sizes and tightness of weave in the paper. The finer the paper, the smaller the particle it filters. The filter paper is folded in half to form equal halves, and then folded in the same way again into quarters. Finding a place where one quarter of the folded filter paper is on one side and the other three quarters are on the other side, you can now open the folded filter paper into the shape of a funnel itself and this is placed in the real funnel. The mixtures to be separated using this setup are then poured down the middle of this "paper funnel."

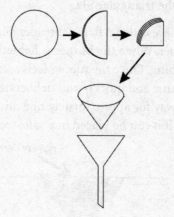

D. Dilution—Solutions are diluted in chemistry for a variety of reasons. One equation often used to make a dilution involves knowing the molarity of the current solution and the molarity desired after the dilution. It is represented by $M_1 \times V_1 = M_2 \times V_2$, where M = the molarity of the solution and V is the volume. The numbers 1 and 2 represent the situations before and after the dilution. Acids and bases are special case dilutions in form only. Acids must be slowly poured (see "Pouring liquids" below) into water, not the reverse, and water is poured into bases.

E. Solid chemicals—Solid chemicals are always handled in the lab by removing them from containers with spatulas, scoops, or tongs depending on whether the solid is in powder form or in large pieces. Placing the chemical on a piece of filter paper or in a glass container of some kind is the preferred method for transporting. Chemicals should not come in contact with skin, eyes, or membranes.

F. Pouring liquids—One of the safest and surest ways to pour liquids is to place a glass stirring rod in the container into which the liquid will be poured. Slowly tilting the container holding the liquid against the stirring rod until the liquid slowly flows down the stirring rod will deliver the liquid into the container where it belongs.

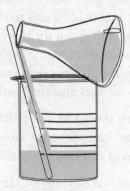

G. Heating materials—One must heat all materials with caution as they may all be potentially dangerous in some way. Substances in a test tube, for example, are always heated with the mouth of the test tube pointed away from anyone in the lab. At times a water bath is employed as a means of heating to ensure that the temperature will not rise above 100°C. Heated solids are kept from being placed directly on the lab table tops; instead, they should be placed in a ceramic container or Pyrex glass. Glass tubing that has been heated should be kept away from drops or puddles of water as it may otherwise crack. Boiling chips are often employed to regulate the boiling process of some solutions. Some substances should be heated only in a hood with a good working fan and ventilating system.

H. Evaporation of a liquid—Most liquids should be evaporated in an evaporating dish under a chemical hood for as long as the evaporation needs to take place. If the fan is used at all in this process, it should be on its minimum setting.

I. Drying a solid—A solid is placed in a container called a desiccator that has a desiccant (a substance that promotes drying) in an area where the solid will not touch it. (NOTE: The solid should be in an open container in the desiccator so that the liquid can easily leave the solid.) Usually the solid will be dried of all liquid in a day or so.

III. Laboratory Activities

A. Phase change—Students of chemistry should be able to set up a phase change experiment, e.g., one that goes from the melting of ice to the boiling of the water from that melting. They should be able to record the temperatures and times in a table, graph the results, and, given the mass of ice used, be able to calculate the heats of fusion and vaporization in the experiment. The student should also be able to recognize what the plateaus represent on a phase change graph; namely, points of equilibrium for heat absorbed and heat released.

B. Calorimetry—Students should be able to set up a calorimeter containing a measured quantity of water, heat the setup with a candle to a desired temperature, and then calculate the heat of combustion of the candle.

C. Endothermic/Exothermic reactions—Students should be able to measure the temperature changes associated with certain chemical events and recognize the change as exothermic (gives off heat) or endothermic (absorbs heat). The dissolution of $NaOH$ is exothermic and NH_4Cl is the endothermic.

D. Solubility—Students should be able to record the amount of a substance that dissolves in a solvent at various temperatures on a chart, graph the data, and then interpolate or predict from the graph a solubility point at a temperature or mass not investigated. Finally, they should be able to measure that solubility in the lab.

E. Organic/Inorganic substances—Students should be able to recognize the difference between organic—carbon based—and inorganic substances using such properties as melting point, stability, and electrical conductivity. Organic compounds are principally molecular carbon compounds, most often covalently bonded.

F. Flame test—Students should be able to identify a variety of metallic ions by use of a flame test; namely, copper, strontium, lithium, sodium, potassium, and calcium.

G. Percent mass of water—Students should be able to calculate the percent mass of water that is part of a compound, e.g., $BaSO_4 \bullet 2H_2O$. Calculate the difference between the mass of the water in the compound (by itself) and the mass of the compound including the water. This difference is divided by the mass of the compound and water together and multiplied by 100. This gives the percent water in the compound by mass.

H. Molar volume—Students should at least recognize the volume of a mole of any ideal gas at STP(273K, 1 atm) as 22.4 L. In the lab, the student should be able to set up an apparatus for collecting a gas, whether a mole or a portion of a mole. If the gas is not soluble in water, an inverted bottle of water set in a water bath tub, with a tube running from the container that will generate the gas to the inverted bottle, will provide for collection of the gas.

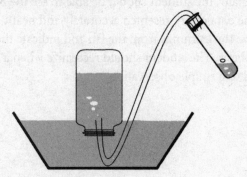

I. Titration—students should be able to set up two burets on a buret stand, place in one the solution to be titrated and in the other a standard solution, and successfully perform a titration of the unknown solution to completion. For example, in an acid-base titration, with the use of phenolphthalein as the indicator, the student should recognize that a change to pink after one drop of base indicates that the titration is close to the endpoint. Using the equation in IID—"Dilution," the student should be able to calculate the molarity of the unknown.

IV. Laboratory Reports

A. Organization—Lab notebooks and lab reports should be neat, organized, and presentable. It is a journal of activities and in the corporate world becomes a legal document of discovery. There ought to be a place for everything (and everything in its place) in the report as well as the notebook. It should start from a title or hypothesis, through materials, to the procedure, results, and conclusion.

B. Graphs/Tables—Space should be made for the recording of data in a lab notebook, including charts, tables, graphs, etcetera. Before the experiment is carried out, a plan for just what is to be recorded and how it is going to be recorded should be decided. The student should be able to interpret and interpolate the data from the charts, tables, and graphs as well.

C. Observations—Following the statement of a plan, the student should provide for ample space in which to record observations. These should be recorded accurately and neatly and properly labelled. Any calculation should be done in this area with an indication of how it was done. In addition, the student should be able to recognize when a statement is an observation and when it is not.

D. Conclusions—Finally, the student should be able to see the big picture and the overall meaning of the data once presented accurately and neatly. The student should be able to summarize the learnings from the lab and indicate their relationships to the title or the hypothesis. The student should recognize when a conclusion is being made as opposed to a simple observation.

Questions

1. What is the correct volume in the graduated cylinder pictured here?

   1. 2.5 mL
   2. 2.75 mL
   3. 3.0 mL
   4. 2.5 L

2. The precision of an instrument can be indicated on paper by the use of
   1. estimation
   2. significant figures
   3. careful measurement
   4. all of these

3. Report the answer for the indicated operation to the correct number of significant figures:

$$72.149 + 291.23 + 2392.5$$

   1. 2800
   2. 2755.879
   3. 2755.8
   4. 2755.9

4. Report the answer for the following operation to the correct number of significant figures:

$$2.74 \times 6.3$$

   1. 17.3
   2. 17.26
   3. 17.2
   4. 17

5. A student calculates the density of copper to be 8.3 g/cm^3. Following this, she finds a chart with the accepted value for the density of copper as 8.92 g/cm^3. What is her percent error?
   1. 8.3%
   2. 6.9%
   3. −6.9%
   4. 93%

6. In order to properly cut a piece of glass tubing, a scratch must be made with a triangular file at the place where the break is desired and the tubing is then
   1. snapped away from you with the scratch facing toward you
   2. snapped away from you with the scratch facing away from you
   3. cut the rest of the way through at the scratch with a tubing saw
   4. placed in a flame and allowed to break at the point of the scratch

7. When diluting acids in the lab
   1. add water to the acid
   2. add acid to the water
   3. carefully add equal volumes of acid and water to each other at the same time
   4. acids are purchased in dilute form and not diluted in the lab

8. Heating materials safely in a test tube means
   1. securing a stopper in the test tube before heating
   2. looking in the test tube often to check for boiling
   3. using a stopper only when you are certain the contents will not boil
   4. holding the opening away from people, including yourself, throughout the heating

9. The formation of one mole of CO^2 from the following reaction:

$$C + O_2 \rightarrow CO_2$$

   1. is endothermic
   2. produces 94.1 kcal/mole of energy
   3. absorbs 94.1 kcal/mole of energy
   4. favors enthalpy

10. Flame tests are performed to identify
    1. halogens
    2. inert gases
    3. metallic ions
    4. nonmetallic ions

11. From Table D, the solubility of HCl in 100g of water at 45°C is approximately
    1. 83g
    2. 60g
    3. 43g
    4. 90g

12. The percent mass of water in the compound $CuSO_4 \cdot 5H_2O$ is
    1. 56%
    2. 36%
    3. 18%
    4. 16%

13. The following graph indicates how many phase changes?

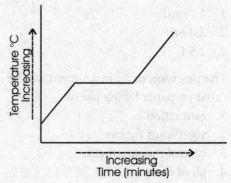

    1. 1
    2. 2
    3. 3
    4. none of these

14. How many moles of NaOH are required to neutralize 0.20 mol of HNO_3?
    1. 2.0 moles
    2. 0.10 moles
    3. 0.20 moles
    4. 0.40 moles

15. Which of the following is an observation?
    1. Density is calculated to be 2.75 g/cm3.
    2. The percent error was +4.3%.
    3. The green flame indicated that the salt was copper.
    4. The mass was 21.73g.

16. What is the volume of gas produced when 0.05g Mg reacts with excess dilute HCl at STP²?
    1. 4.7 L
    2. 0.47 L
    3. 0.047 L
    4. 0.0047 L

17. The order of events in determining the melting point of water from the following list of events is:
    a. record the temperature of the mixture
    b. fill the beaker almost to the top of the ice with water
    c. place ice in a beaker
    d. read the temperature when about half of the ice has melted
    1. a, b, c, d
    2. c, b, a, d
    3. c, a, b, d
    4. c, b, d, a

18. Which of the following is NOT true of titration of an acid with a base?
    1. Neutralization is achieved at the end point.
    2. Pink indicates the base is neutralized.
    3. A solution of known molarity is called a standard solution.
    4. It is the addition of a known amount of solution to determine the concentration of another solution.

19. Upon heating a sample of a white crystal in the lab, a student finds the result to produce a dark powder which gives off a colorless gas. The student can conclude:
    1. the crystal was an element.
    2. the crystal contained 2 elements.
    3. the crystal was not a compound.
    4. the crystal was not an element.

20. If 1 atm = 760 mmHg (or 1 torr), then according to Table O, water boils at
    1. 100°C
    2. 100°F
    3. 100°K
    4. 100°A

Answers

1. The correct answer is 2. The correct volume of most liquids—mercury is an exception—is read from the bottom of the curved line formed by the surface tension of the liquid and adhesion to the sides of the container. The spacing of the marks on the graduated cylinder and the label "mL" indicates that the smallest division is in fourths of milliliters. The bottom of the curve lines up with the third line after 2 mL, indicating a measurement of 2.75 mL.

2. The correct answer is 2. Significant figures are used to convey the accuracy of measurement of an instrument by allowing for the measurement to be as accurate as the smallest measurement on the instrument plus one place. So if a scientist reports a figure of 52.78g to the correct number of significant figures, then his scale is accurate to tenths of grams and he has estimated the mass to the next decimal or hundredths.

3. The correct answer is 4. In dealing with significant figures in addition, it is agreed that we will report no answer to have more decimal places than the least number of decimal places among the figures given. Choice 4 is the correct one because the answer of 2,755.879 has been correctly rounded to 2,755.9.

4. The correct answer is 4. Once again, not reporting an answer more accurate than the number with the least significant fig-

ures in the answer gives us choice 4 as the correct answer. It has been properly rounded off to 17 from 17.262. Note the absence of a zero at the end. A number of 17.0 would be incorrect as the decimal makes the zero significant. If it were a simple placeholder to the left of the decimal, it would not be significant.

5. The correct answer is 3. Percent error is calculated by comparing the accepted value with the observed value and then dividing by the accepted (correct) value. This answer is then multiplied by 100 to become a percent. The equation is always [(observed) − (accepted)] / (accepted) × 100. In this manner, if the observed value is larger than the accepted value, the result will be a positive number indicating the experimenter had a value higher than the accepted. Likewise, if the observed value is less than the accepted value, the result will be a negative number indicating that the experimenter had a value less than the accepted value.

6. The correct answer is 2. The scratch made by the triangular file is intended to introduce a place of weakness in the glass. Applying stress to this area in the proper way snaps the tubing with a clean break. We introduce stress by using the method in choice 2. When you use this method, snapping the tubing away from you, it places stress on the scratch. Choice 1

would place stress on the tubing on the side opposite from the scratch, achieving nothing but a shattered piece of glass.

7. The correct answer is 2. The preferred method for diluting acid is to pour the acid into water. Either way, the water ionizes the acid, but pouring acid into water introduces only a few ionized particles at a time. Pouring water into the acid creates a rush of ionized particles—potentially the entire container at once—an undesirable effect. In addition, it is best to pour the acid or any liquid when mixing liquids, down a glass stirring rod, to avoid drips over the edge of the container.

8. The correct answer is 4. Choices 1 through 3 are all dangerous under any circumstance. Test tubes are never heated with stoppers in them, whether or not we suspect boiling will occur; we always assume it will. We also assume solids can send material out the test tube explosively. We never look in the test tube either. Check for activity from the side of the test tube—that is why they are made from glass. And always point it away from anyone, including yourself.

9. The correct answer is 2. Using Table G, we see that in forming, CO_2 gives off—indicated by the negative number—94.1 kcal/mole of energy. This reaction is exothermic. If it absorbed 94.1 kcal/mole, it would be endothermic.

10. The correct answer is 3. Flame tests, where we place a dilute sample of the salt in a hot Bunsen burner flame—the color of which should be blue, not yellowish—give a characteristic color by which we are able to identify metallic ions. Upon absorbing energy from the flame, electrons are stimulated to jump to a higher energy level. When they do so, they immediately fall back to the original level and give the energy they absorbed back as light. Various metals have characteristic colors they impart to the flame, acting like a fingerprint for that ion.

11. The correct answer is 2. Following the line for HCl from the low temperature of 0° C on the left side of the graph (where it starts at a solubility of approximately 83 g/100g of water), we trace the line to 45° C where it crosses the 60g line on the graph indicating that, at 45° C, HCl dissolves 60g for every 100g of water.

12. The correct answer is 2. The percent of water in a compound is calculated by adding up the atomic mass of each atom present in the hydrated form of the compound and then adding up just the atomic mass of the atoms in the water. Next, divide the mass of the water by the mass of the compound and water and multiply this by 100 to arrive at the percent of water in the compound. For $CuSO_4 \cdot 5H_2O$ the percent water is 36%.

13. The correct answer is 1. The graph illustrates one phase change. The flat line or plateau indicates an equilibrium between heat entering the system and heat leaving. Since the line is flat, it indicates that no heat is being used to raise the temperature—i.e., add to the average motion of the particles. Therefore, energy is being absorbed internally to cause the particles to separate further from each other—an increase in total energy, but no increase in the average heat in the system.

14. The correct answer is 3. Balancing this reaction gives us $NaOH + HNO_3 \rightarrow NaNO_3 + H_2O$. In other words, one mole of NaOH neutralizes 1 mole of HNO_3 or, put another way, they neutralize on a 1:1 ratio. (NOTE: If 2 moles of NaOH neutralized 2 moles of HNO_3, they would still react on a 1:1 ratio.) This means that for every mole of HNO_3 we have, a mole of NaOH will neutralize it. Therefore 0.20 moles of NaOH will neutralize 0.20 moles of HNO_3.

15. The correct answer is 4. An observation is a simple statement of fact, an event has occurred and it is written down as it is seen. Choice 4 is the statement of fact in this question. An object was weighed and the scale read 21.73g and this information was recorded as read. Density is a calculated number from two observed numbers. Likewise, percent error is calculated from the known value and the observed value. Saying copper caused the green flame is an interpretation. The fact that one saw a green flame alone would be an observation.

16. The correct answer is 3. When we balance the equation for this reaction, we get: $2HCl + Mg \rightarrow MgCl_2 + H_2$ noting that 1 mole of Mg reacts with excess HCl to form 1 mole of H_2. We need to find out how many moles of Mg there are in 0.05g. Dividing by 24.3, the number of grams in 1 mole of Mg, we get 0.0021 moles. That means 0.0021 moles of hydrogen gas will be formed or 0.0042 g. There are 2g of hydrogen gas in one mole of hydrogen, which occupies 22.4 L of volume at STP. The 0.0042g of hydrogen gas will occupy 0.047 L of space.

17. The correct answer is 4. The order of events will be to place the ice in the beaker, fill with water, read the thermometer when about half the ice is melted and record the temperature. The last step of recording the temperature is deceptive, but it has to be read first to be recorded.

18. The correct answer is 2. All of the choices given are true all the time except choice 2. The indicator may not be one that turns pink, and when neutralizing a base with an acid, the pink color will actually disappear on neutralization. Choice 4 is the definition of titration, choice 1 one tells us at what point neutralization occurs, and choice 3 is a requirement for titration.

19. The correct answer is 4. Since the student started out with what appears to be one substance and, through the simple act of heating it in the lab, ended up with what appears to be two entirely different substances, we can assume the original substance was composed of at least two components combined chemically. The act of heating provided enough energy to break the bonds. The original substance appears to have been a compound and not an element. An element is one substance that cannot be broken down by ordinary (laboratory) means.

20. The correct answer is 1. According to Table O, if the pressure is 760 mm Hg, then water will boil at 100° C. The other choices, 2, 3, and 4, respectively, are in the Fahrenheit scale (for which 100 is too low), Kelvin, and Absolute (also in error, both being too low).

Part IV

Practice Exams and Answers

Note: The first page of each Regents exam shows the original date the exam was administered in New York State. The Board of Regents has consistently maintained the structure and content of the Regents exams over the years, so tests that were administered more recently are in no way more "accurate" or "up-to date" than the older tests. The Regents exam to be given this year is as similar to the exams given last year as the exams given ten years ago.

Reference Tables for Chemistry

PHYSICAL CONSTANTS AND CONVERSION FACTORS

Name	Symbol	Value(s)	Units
Angstrom unit	Å	1×10^{-10} m	meter
Avogadro number	N_A	6.02×10^{23} per mol	
Charge of electron	e	1.60×10^{-19} C	coulomb
Electron volt	eV	1.60×10^{-19} J	joule
Speed of light	c	3.00×10^8 m/s	meters/second
Planck's constant	h	6.63×10^{-34} J·s	joule-second
		1.58×10^{-37} kcal·s	kilocalorie-second
Universal gas constant	R	0.0821 L·atm/mol·K	liter-atmosphere/mole-kelvin
		1.98 cal/mol·K	calories/mole-kelvin
		8.31 J/mol·K	joules/mole-kelvin
Atomic mass unit	μ(amu)	1.66×10^{-24} g	gram
Volume standard, liter	L	1×10^3 cm^3 = 1 dm^3	cubic centimeters, cubic decimeter
Standard pressure, atmosphere	atm	101.3 kPa	kilopascals
		760 mmHg	millimeters of mercury
		760 torr	torr
Heat equivalent, kilocalorie	kcal	4.18×10^3 J	joules

Physical Constants for H_2O

Molal freezing point depression	1.86°C
Molal boiling point elevation	0.52°C
Heat of fusion	79.72 cal/g
Heat of vaporization	539.4 cal/g

STANDARD UNITS

Symbol	Name	Quantity
m	meter	length
kg	kilogram	mass
Pa	pascal	pressure
K	kelvin	thermodynamic temperature
mol	mole	amount of substance
J	joule	energy, work, quantity of heat
s	second	time
C	coulomb	quantity of electricity
V	volt	electric potential, potential difference
L	liter	volume

Selected Prefixes		
Factor	Prefix	Symbol
10^6	mega	M
10^3	kilo	k
10^{-1}	deci	d
10^{-2}	centi	c
10^{-3}	milli	m
10^{-6}	micro	μ
10^{-9}	nano	n

C

DENSITY AND BOILING POINTS OF SOME COMMON GASES			
Name		*Density grams/liter at STP**	*Boiling Point (at 1 atm) K*
Air	—	1.29	—
Ammonia	NH_3	0.771	240
Carbon dioxide	CO_2	1.98	195
Carbon monoxide	CO	1.25	82
Chlorine	Cl_2	3.21	238
Hydrogen	H_2	0.0899	20
Hydrogen chloride	HCl	1.64	188
Hydrogen sulfide	H_2S	1.54	212
Methane	CH_4	0.716	109
Nitrogen	N_2	1.25	77
Nitrogen (II) oxide	NO	1.34	121
Oxygen	O_2	1.43	90
Sulfur dioxide	SO_2	2.92	263

*STP is defined as 273 K and 1 atm

D

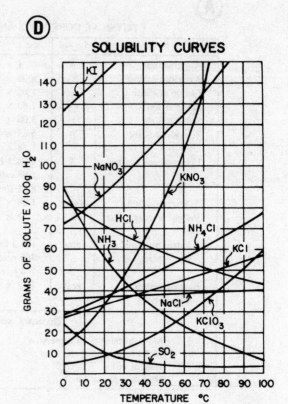

SOLUBILITY CURVES

E

TABLE OF SOLUBILITIES IN WATER											
i — nearly insoluble ss — slightly soluble s — soluble d — decomposes n — not isolated	acetate	bromide	carbonate	chloride	chromate	hydroxide	iodide	nitrate	phosphate	sulfate	sulfide
Aluminum	ss	s	n	s	n	i	s	s	i	s	d
Ammonium	s	s	s	s	s	s	s	s	s	s	s
Barium	s	s	i	s	i	s	s	s	i	i	d
Calcium	s	s	i	s	s	ss	s	s	i	ss	d
Copper II	s	s	i	s	i	i	n	s	i	s	i
Iron II	s	s	i	s	n	i	s	s	i	s	i
Iron III	s	s	n	s	i	i	n	s	i	ss	d
Lead	s	ss	i	ss	i	i	ss	s	i	i	i
Magnesium	s	s	i	s	s	i	s	s	i	s	d
Mercury I	ss	i	i	i	ss	n	i	s	i	ss	i
Mercury II	s	ss	i	ss	i	i	s	s	d	i	i
Potassium	s	s	s	s	s	s	s	s	s	s	s
Silver	ss	i	i	i	ss	n	i	s	i	ss	i
Sodium	s	s	s	s	s	s	s	s	s	s	s
Zinc	s	s	i	s	s	i	s	s	i	s	i

F

SELECTED POLYATOMIC IONS			
Hg_2^{2+}	dimercury (I)	CrO_4^{2-}	chromate
NH_4^+	ammonium	$Cr_2O_7^{2-}$	dichromate
$C_2H_3O_2^-$	acetate	MnO_4^-	permanganate
CH_3COO^-		MnO_4^{2-}	manganate
CN^-	cyanide	NO_2^-	nitrite
CO_3^{2-}	carbonate	NO_3^-	nitrate
HCO_3^-	hydrogen carbonate	OH^-	hydroxide
		PO_4^{3-}	phosphate
$C_2O_4^{2-}$	oxalate	SCN^-	thiocyanate
ClO^-	hypochlorite	SO_3^{2-}	sulfite
ClO_2^-	chlorite	SO_4^{2-}	sulfate
ClO_3^-	chlorate	HSO_4^-	hydrogen sulfate
ClO_4^-	perchlorate	$S_2O_3^{2-}$	thiosulfate

SELECTED RADIOISOTOPES

Nuclide	Half-Life	Decay Mode
^{198}Au	2.69 d	β^-
^{14}C	5730 y	β^-
^{60}Co	5.26 y	β^-
^{137}Cs	30.23 y	β^-
^{220}Fr	27.5 s	α
^{3}H	12.26 y	β^-
^{131}I	8.07 d	β^-
^{37}K	1.23 s	β^+
^{42}K	12.4 h	β^-
^{85}Kr	10.76 y	β^-
^{85m}Kr*	4.39 h	γ
^{16}N	7.2 s	β^-
^{32}P	14.3 d	β^-
^{239}Pu	2.44×10^4 y	α
^{226}Ra	1600 y	α
^{222}Rn	3.82 d	α
^{90}Sr	28.1 y	β^-
^{99}Tc	2.13×10^5 y	β^-
^{99m}Tc*	6.01 h	γ
^{232}Th	1.4×10^{10} y	α
^{233}U	1.62×10^5 y	α
^{235}U	7.1×10^8 y	α
^{238}U	4.51×10^9 y	α

y=years; d=days; h=hours; s=seconds
*m = meta stable or excited state of the same nucleus. Gamma decay from such a state is called an isomeric transition (IT).
Nuclear isomers are different energy states of the same nucleus, each having a different measurable lifetime.

STANDARD ENERGIES OF FORMATION OF COMPOUNDS AT 1 atm AND 298 K

Compound	Heat (Enthalpy) of Formation* kcal/mol ($\triangle H_f^o$)	Free Energy of Formation kcal/mol ($\triangle G_f^o$)
Aluminum oxide Al_2O_3(s)	−400.5	−378.2
Ammonia NH_3(g)	−11.0	−3.9
Barium sulfate $BaSO_4$(s)	−352.1	−325.6
Calcium hydroxide $Ca(OH)_2$(s)	−235.7	−214.8
Carbon dioxide CO_2(g)	−94.1	−94.3
Carbon monoxide CO(g)	−26.4	−32.8
Copper (II) sulfate $CuSO_4$(s)	−184.4	−158.2
Ethane C_2H_6(g)	−20.2	−7.9
Ethene (ethylene) C_2H_4(g)	12.5	16.3
Ethyne (acetylene) C_2H_2(g)	54.2	50.0
Hydrogen fluoride HF(g)	−64.8	−65.3
Hydrogen iodide HI(g)	6.3	0.4
Iodine chloride ICl(g)	4.3	−1.3
Lead (II) oxide PbO(s)	−51.5	−45.0
Magnesium oxide MgO(s)	−143.8	−136.1
Nitrogen (II) oxide NO(g)	21.6	20.7
Nitrogen (IV) oxide NO_2(g)	7.9	12.3
Potassium chloride KCl(s)	−104.4	−97.8
Sodium chloride $NaCl$(s)	−98.3	−91.8
Sulfur dioxide SO_2(g)	−70.9	−71.7
Water H_2O(g)	−57.8	−54.6
Water H_2O(ℓ)	−68.3	−56.7

* Minus sign indicates an exothermic reaction.

Sample equations:

$$2Al(s) + \frac{3}{2} O_2(g) \rightarrow Al_2O_3(s) + 400.5 \text{ kcal}$$

$$2Al(s) + \frac{3}{2} O_2(g) \rightarrow Al_2O_3(s) \quad \triangle H = -400.5 \text{ kcal/mol}$$

HEATS OF REACTION AT 1 atm and 298 K	
Reaction	$\triangle H$ (kcal)
$CH_4(g) + 2O_2(g) \rightarrow CO_2(g) + 2H_2O(\ell)$	-212.8
$C_3H_8(g) + 5O_2(g) \rightarrow 3CO_2(g) + 4H_2O(\ell)$	-530.6
$CH_3OH(\ell) + \frac{3}{2}O_2(g) \rightarrow CO_2(g) + 2H_2O(\ell)$	-173.6
$C_6H_{12}O_6(s) + 6O_2(g) \rightarrow 6CO_2(g) + 6H_2O(\ell)$	-669.9
$CO(g) + \frac{1}{2}O_2(g) \rightarrow CO_2(g)$	-67.7
$C_8H_{18}(\ell) + \frac{25}{2}O_2(g) \rightarrow 8CO_2(g) + 9H_2O(\ell)$	-1302.7
$KNO_3(s) \xrightarrow{H_2O} K^+(aq) + NO_3^-(aq)$	$+8.3$
$NaOH(s) \xrightarrow{H_2O} Na^+(aq) + OH^-(aq)$	-10.6
$NH_4Cl(s) \xrightarrow{H_2O} NH_4^+(aq) + Cl^-(aq)$	$+3.5$
$NH_4NO_3(s) \xrightarrow{H_2O} NH_4^+(aq) + NO_3^-(aq)$	$+6.1$
$NaCl(s) \xrightarrow{H_2O} Na^+(aq) + Cl^-(aq)$	$+0.9$
$KClO_3(s) \xrightarrow{H_2O} K^+(aq) + ClO_3^-(aq)$	$+9.9$
$LiBr(s) \xrightarrow{H_2O} Li^+(aq) + Br^-(aq)$	-11.7
$H^+(aq) + OH^-(aq) \rightarrow H_2O(\ell)$	-13.8

SYMBOLS USED IN NUCLEAR CHEMISTRY		
alpha particle	^4_2He	α
beta particle (electron)	$^0_{-1}e$	β^-
gamma radiation		γ
neutron	^1_0n	n
proton	^1_1H	p
deuteron	^2_1H	
triton	^3_1H	
positron	$^0_{+1}e$	β^+

IONIZATION ENERGIES AND ELECTRONEGATIVITIES

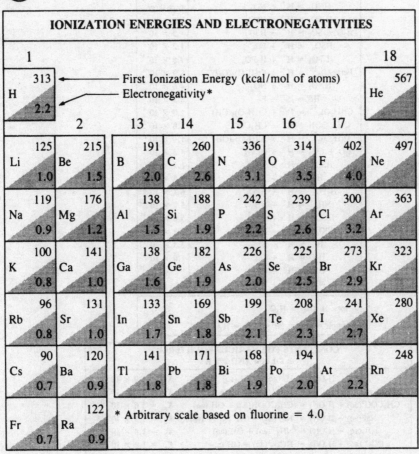

1							18
H 313 / 2.2		First Ionization Energy (kcal/mol of atoms) — Electronegativity*					**He** 567

	2	13	14	15	16	17	
Li 125 / 1.0	**Be** 215 / 1.5	**B** 191 / 2.0	**C** 260 / 2.6	**N** 336 / 3.1	**O** 314 / 3.5	**F** 402 / 4.0	**Ne** 497
Na 119 / 0.9	**Mg** 176 / 1.2	**Al** 138 / 1.5	**Si** 188 / 1.9	**P** 242 / 2.2	**S** 239 / 2.6	**Cl** 300 / 3.2	**Ar** 363
K 100 / 0.8	**Ca** 141 / 1.0	**Ga** 138 / 1.6	**Ge** 182 / 1.9	**As** 226 / 2.0	**Se** 225 / 2.5	**Br** 273 / 2.9	**Kr** 323
Rb 96 / 0.8	**Sr** 131 / 1.0	**In** 133 / 1.7	**Sn** 169 / 1.8	**Sb** 199 / 2.1	**Te** 208 / 2.3	**I** 241 / 2.7	**Xe** 280
Cs 90 / 0.7	**Ba** 120 / 0.9	**Tl** 141 / 1.8	**Pb** 171 / 1.8	**Bi** 168 / 1.9	**Po** 194 / 2.0	**At** / 2.2	**Rn** 248
Fr / 0.7	**Ra** 122 / 0.9	* Arbitrary scale based on fluorine = 4.0					

RELATIVE STRENGTHS OF ACIDS IN AQUEOUS SOLUTION AT 1 atm AND 298 K	
Conjugate Pairs *ACID BASE*	K_a
$HI = H^+ + I^-$	very large
$HBr = H^+ + Br^-$	very large
$HCl = H^+ + Cl^-$	very large
$HNO_3 = H^+ + NO_3^-$	very large
$H_2SO_4 = H^+ + HSO_4^-$	large
$H_2O + SO_2 = H^+ + HSO_3^-$	1.5×10^{-2}
$HSO_4^- = H^+ + SO_4^{2-}$	1.2×10^{-2}
$H_3PO_4 = H^+ + H_2PO_4^-$	7.5×10^{-3}
$Fe(H_2O)_6^{3+} = H^+ + Fe(H_2O)_5(OH)^{2+}$	8.9×10^{-4}
$HNO_2 = H^+ + NO_2^-$	4.6×10^{-4}
$HF = H^+ + F^-$	3.5×10^{-4}
$Cr(H_2O)_6^{3+} = H^+ + Cr(H_2O)_5(OH)^{2+}$	1.0×10^{-4}
$CH_3COOH = H^+ + CH_3COO^-$	1.8×10^{-5}
$Al(H_2O)_6^{3+} = H^+ + Al(H_2O)_5(OH)^{2+}$	1.1×10^{-5}
$H_2O + CO_2 = H^+ + HCO_3^-$	4.3×10^{-7}
$HSO_3^- = H^+ + SO_3^{2-}$	1.1×10^{-7}
$H_2S = H^+ + HS^-$	9.5×10^{-8}
$H_2PO_4^- = H^+ + HPO_4^{2-}$	6.2×10^{-8}
$NH_4^+ = H^+ + NH_3$	5.7×10^{-10}
$HCO_3^- = H^+ + CO_3^{2-}$	5.6×10^{-11}
$HPO_4^{2-} = H^+ + PO_4^{3-}$	2.2×10^{-13}
$HS^- = H^+ + S^{2-}$	1.3×10^{-14}
$H_2O = H^+ + OH^-$	1.0×10^{-14}
$OH^- = H^+ + O^{2-}$	$< 10^{-36}$
$NH_3 = H^+ + NH_2^-$	very small

Note: $H^+(aq) = H_3O^+$

Sample equation: $HI + H_2O = H_3O^+ + I^-$

CONSTANTS FOR VARIOUS EQUILIBRIA AT 1 atm AND 298 K	
$H_2O(\ell) = H^+(aq) + OH^-(aq)$	$K_w = 1.0 \times 10^{-14}$
$H_2O(\ell) + H_2O(\ell) = H_3O^+(aq) + OH^-(aq)$	$K_w = 1.0 \times 10^{-14}$
$CH_3COO^-(aq) + H_2O(\ell) = CH_3COOH(aq) + OH^-(aq)$	$K_b = 5.6 \times 10^{-10}$
$NaF(aq) + H_2O(\ell) = Na^+(aq) + OH^-(aq) + HF(aq)$	$K_b = 1.5 \times 10^{-11}$
$NH_3(aq) + H_2O(\ell) = NH_4^+(aq) + OH^-(aq)$	$K_b = 1.8 \times 10^{-5}$
$CO_3^{2-}(aq) + H_2O(\ell) = HCO_3^-(aq) + OH^-(aq)$	$K_b = 1.8 \times 10^{-4}$
$Ag(NH_3)_2^+(aq) = Ag^+(aq) + 2NH_3(aq)$	$K_{eq} = 8.9 \times 10^{-8}$
$N_2(g) + 3H_2(g) = 2NH_3(g)$	$K_{eq} = 6.7 \times 10^5$
$H_2(g) + I_2(g) = 2HI(g)$	$K_{eq} = 3.5 \times 10^{-1}$

Compound	K_{sp}	Compound	K_{sp}
$AgBr$	5.0×10^{-13}	Li_2CO_3	2.5×10^{-2}
$AgCl$	1.8×10^{-10}	$PbCl_2$	1.6×10^{-5}
Ag_2CrO_4	1.1×10^{-12}	$PbCO_3$	7.4×10^{-14}
AgI	8.3×10^{-17}	$PbCrO_4$	2.8×10^{-13}
$BaSO_4$	1.1×10^{-10}	PbI_2	7.1×10^{-9}
$CaSO_4$	9.1×10^{-6}	$ZnCO_3$	1.4×10^{-11}

STANDARD ELECTRODE POTENTIALS	
Ionic Concentrations 1 M Water At 298 K, 1 atm	
Half-Reaction	E^0 (volts)
$F_2(g) + 2e^- \rightarrow 2F^-$	+2.87
$8H^+ + MnO_4^- + 5e^- \rightarrow Mn^{2+} + 4H_2O$	+1.51
$Au^{3+} + 3e^- \rightarrow Au(s)$	+1.50
$Cl_2(g) + 2e^- \rightarrow 2Cl^-$	+1.36
$14H^+ + Cr_2O_7^{2-} + 6e^- \rightarrow 2Cr^{3+} + 7H_2O$	+1.23
$4H^+ + O_2(g) + 4e^- \rightarrow 2H_2O$	+1.23
$4H^+ + MnO_2(s) + 2e^- \rightarrow Mn^{2+} + 2H_2O$	+1.22
$Br_2(\ell) + 2e^- \rightarrow 2Br^-$	+1.09
$Hg^{2+} + 2e^- \rightarrow Hg(\ell)$	+0.85
$Ag^+ + e^- \rightarrow Ag(s)$	+0.80
$Hg_2^{2+} + 2e^- \rightarrow 2Hg(\ell)$	+0.80
$Fe^{3+} + e^- \rightarrow Fe^{2+}$	+0.77
$I_2(s) + 2e^- \rightarrow 2I^-$	+0.54
$Cu^+ + e^- \rightarrow Cu(s)$	+0.52
$Cu^{2+} + 2e^- \rightarrow Cu(s)$	+0.34
$4H^+ + SO_4^{2-} + 2e^- \rightarrow SO_2(aq) + 2H_2O$	+0.17
$Sn^{4+} + 2e^- \rightarrow Sn^{2+}$	+0.15
$2H^+ + 2e^- \rightarrow H_2(g)$	0.00
$Pb^{2+} + 2e^- \rightarrow Pb(s)$	−0.13
$Sn^{2+} + 2e^- \rightarrow Sn(s)$	−0.14
$Ni^{2+} + 2e^- \rightarrow Ni(s)$	−0.26
$Co^{2+} + 2e^- \rightarrow Co(s)$	−0.28
$Fe^{2+} + 2e^- \rightarrow Fe(s)$	−0.45
$Cr^{3+} + 3e^- \rightarrow Cr(s)$	−0.74
$Zn^{2+} + 2e^- \rightarrow Zn(s)$	−0.76
$2H_2O + 2e^- \rightarrow 2OH^- + H_2(g)$	−0.83
$Mn^{2+} + 2e^- \rightarrow Mn(s)$	−1.19
$Al^{3+} + 3e^- \rightarrow Al(s)$	−1.66
$Mg^{2+} + 2e^- \rightarrow Mg(s)$	−2.37
$Na^+ + e^- \rightarrow Na(s)$	−2.71
$Ca^{2+} + 2e^- \rightarrow Ca(s)$	−2.87
$Sr^{2+} + 2e^- \rightarrow Sr(s)$	−2.89
$Ba^{2+} + 2e^- \rightarrow Ba(s)$	−2.91
$Cs^+ + e^- \rightarrow Cs(s)$	−2.92
$K^+ + e^- \rightarrow K(s)$	−2.93
$Rb^+ + e^- \rightarrow Rb(s)$	−2.98
$Li^+ + e^- \rightarrow Li(s)$	−3.04

VAPOR PRESSURE OF WATER			
°C	torr (mmHg)	°C	torr (mmHg)
0	4.6	26	25.2
5	6.5	27	26.7
10	9.2	28	28.3
15	12.8	29	30.0
16	13.6	30	31.8
17	14.5	40	55.3
18	15.5	50	92.5
19	16.5	60	149.4
20	17.5	70	233.7
21	18.7	80	355.1
22	19.8	90	525.8
23	21.1	100	760.0
24	22.4	105	906.1
25	23.8	110	1074.6

RADII OF ATOMS

KEY

Symbol →	F
Covalent Radius, Å →	0.64
Atomic Radius in Metals, Å →	(—)
Van der Waals Radius, Å →	1.35

A dash (—) indicates data are not available.

Each cell below lists the element symbol followed by: Covalent Radius, Å / Atomic Radius in Metals, Å / Van der Waals Radius, Å.

Element	Covalent	Atomic (Metals)	Van der Waals
H	0.37	(—)	1.2
He	(—)	(—)	1.22
Li	1.23	1.52	(—)
Be	0.89	1.13	(—)
B	0.88	(—)	2.08
C	0.77	(—)	1.85
N	0.70	(—)	1.54
O	0.66	(—)	1.40
F	0.64	(—)	1.35
Ne	(—)	(—)	1.60
Na	1.57	1.54	(—)
Mg	1.36	1.60	(—)
Al	1.25	1.43	2.0
Si	1.17	(—)	2.0
P	1.10	(—)	1.90
S	1.04	(—)	1.85
Cl	0.99	(—)	1.81
Ar	(—)	(—)	1.91
K	2.03	2.27	2.31
Ca	1.74	1.97	(—)
Sc	1.44	1.61	(—)
Ti	1.32	1.45	(—)
V	1.22	1.32	(—)
Cr	1.17	1.25	(—)
Mn	1.17	1.24	(—)
Fe	1.17	1.24	(—)
Co	1.16	1.25	(—)
Ni	1.15	1.25	(—)
Cu	1.17	1.28	(—)
Zn	1.25	1.33	(—)
Ga	1.25	1.22	(—)
Ge	1.22	1.23	(—)
As	1.21	(—)	2.0
Se	1.17	(—)	1.85
Br	1.14	(—)	1.95
Kr	(—)	(—)	1.98
Rb	2.16	2.48	(—)
Sr	1.92	2.15	(—)
Y	1.62	1.81	(—)
Zr	1.45	1.60	(—)
Nb	1.34	1.43	(—)
Mo	1.29	1.36	(—)
Tc	(—)	1.36	(—)
Ru	1.24	1.33	(—)
Rh	1.25	1.35	(—)
Pd	1.28	1.38	(—)
Ag	1.34	1.44	(—)
Cd	1.41	1.49	(—)
In	1.50	1.63	(—)
Sn	1.40	1.41	(—)
Sb	1.41	(—)	2.2
Te	1.37	(—)	2.20
I	1.33	(—)	2.15
Xe	(—)	(—)	1.98
Cs	2.35	2.65	2.62
Ba	1.98	2.17	(—)
Hf	1.44	1.56	(—)
Ta	1.34	1.43	(—)
W	1.30	1.37	(—)
Re	1.28	1.37	(—)
Os	1.26	1.34	(—)
Ir	1.26	1.36	(—)
Pt	1.29	1.38	(—)
Au	1.34	1.44	(—)
Hg	1.44	1.60	(—)
Tl	1.55	1.70	(—)
Pb	1.54	1.75	(—)
Bi	1.52	(—)	2.2
Po	1.53	1.67	2.20
At	(—)	(—)	2.15
Rn	(—)	(—)	2.14
Fr	2.7	(—)	(—)
Ra	(—)	2.20	(—)

La – Lu

Element	Covalent	Atomic (Metals)	Van der Waals
La	1.69	1.88	(—)
Ce	1.65	1.83	(—)
Pr	1.65	1.83	(—)
Nd	1.64	1.82	(—)
Pm	(—)	1.81	(—)
Sm	1.66	1.80	(—)
Eu	1.85	2.04	(—)
Gd	1.61	1.80	(—)
Tb	1.59	1.78	(—)
Dy	1.59	1.77	(—)
Ho	1.58	1.77	(—)
Er	1.57	1.76	(—)
Tm	1.56	1.75	(—)
Yb	1.70	1.94	(—)
Lu	1.56	1.73	(—)

Ac – Lr

Element	Covalent	Atomic (Metals)	Van der Waals
Ac	(—)	1.88	(—)
Th	(—)	1.80	(—)
Pa	(—)	1.61	(—)
U	(—)	1.39	(—)
Np	(—)	1.31	(—)
Pu	(—)	1.51	(—)
Am	(—)	1.84	(—)
Cm	(—)	(—)	(—)
Bk	(—)	(—)	(—)
Cf	(—)	(—)	(—)
Es	(—)	(—)	(—)
Fm	(—)	(—)	(—)
Md	(—)	(—)	(—)
No	(—)	(—)	(—)
Lr	(—)	(—)	(—)

Periodic Table of the Elements

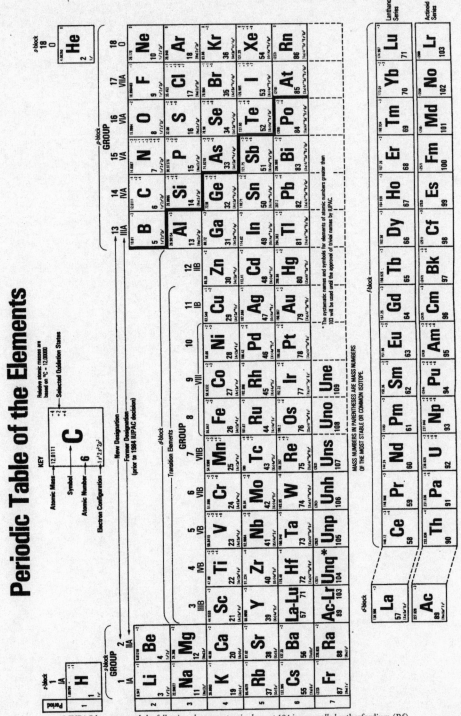

* IUPAC has approved the following changes: atomic element 104 is now called rutherfordium (Rf),
and atomic element 105 is now known as dubnium (Db).

Sample Regents Exam 2—June 1996

Part I

Answer all 56 questions in this part. [65]

Directions (1–56): For *each* statement or question, select the word or expression that, of those given, best completes the statement or answers the question. Record your answer on the separate answer sheet in accordance with the directions on the front page of this booklet.

1 What is the vapor pressure of a liquid at its normal boiling temperature?

(1) 1 atm   (3) 273 atm
(2) 2 atm   (4) 760 atm

2 A sealed container has 1 mole of helium and 2 moles of nitrogen at 30°C. When the total pressure of the mixture is 600 torr, what is the partial pressure of the nitrogen?

(1) 100 torr   (3) 400 torr
(2) 200 torr   (4) 600 torr

3 Solid X is placed in contact with solid Y. Heat will flow spontaneously from X to Y when

(1) X is 20°C and Y is 20°C
(2) X is 10°C and Y is 5°C
(3) X is –25°C and Y is –10°C
(4) X is 25°C and Y is 30°C

4 Which graph represents the relationship between volume and Kelvin temperature for an ideal gas at constant pressure?

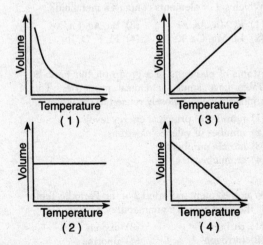

(1)   (3)

(2)   (4)

5 An example of a binary compound is

(1) potassium chloride
(2) ammonium chloride
(3) potassium chlorate
(4) ammonium chlorate

6 Which kind of radiation will travel through an electric field on a pathway that remains unaffected by the field?

(1) a proton   (3) an electron
(2) a gamma ray   (4) an alpha particle

7 The major portion of an atom's mass consists of

(1) electrons and protons
(2) electrons and neutrons
(3) neutrons and positrons
(4) neutrons and protons

8 Which atom contains exactly 15 protons?

(1) phosphorus-32   (3) oxygen-15
(2) sulfur-32   (4) nitrogen-15

9 Element X has two isotopes. If 72.0% of the element has an isotopic mass of 84.9 atomic mass units, and 28.0% of the element has an isotopic mass of 87.0 atomic mass units, the average atomic mass of element X is numerically equal to

(1) $(72.0 + 84.9) \times (28.0 + 87.0)$
(2) $(72.0 - 84.9) \times (28.0 + 87.0)$
(3) $\dfrac{(72.0 \times 84.9)}{100} + \dfrac{(28.0 \times 87.0)}{100}$
(4) $(72.0 \times 84.9) + (28.0 \times 87.0)$

10 Given the equation: $^{14}_{6}C \rightarrow \, ^{14}_{7}N + X$

Which particle is represented by the letter X?

(1) an alpha particle   (3) a neutron
(2) a beta particle   (4) a proton

11 The atom of which element in the ground state has 2 unpaired electrons in the $2p$ sublevel?

(1) fluorine   (3) beryllium
(2) nitrogen   (4) carbon

12 Which atoms contain the same number of neutrons?

(1) ^1_1H and ^3_2He (3) ^3_1H and ^3_2He
(2) ^2_1H and ^4_2He (4) ^3_1H and ^4_2He

13 Which hydrocarbon formula is also an empirical formula?

(1) CH_4 (3) C_3H_6
(2) C_2H_4 (4) C_4H_8

14 The potential energy possessed by a molecule is dependent upon

(1) its composition, only
(2) its structure, only
(3) both its composition and its structure
(4) neither its composition nor its structure

15 Which is a correctly balanced equation for a reaction between hydrogen gas and oxygen gas?

(1) $H_2(g) + O_2(g) \rightarrow H_2O(\ell) + heat$
(2) $H_2(g) + O_2(g) \rightarrow 2H_2O(\ell) + heat$
(3) $2H_2(g) + 2O_2(g) \rightarrow H_2O(\ell) + heat$
(4) $2H_2(g) + O_2(g) \rightarrow 2H_2O(\ell) + heat$

16 The atom of which element has an ionic radius smaller than its atomic radius?

(1) N   (3) Br
(2) S   (4) Rb

17 Which molecule contains a polar covalent bond?

(1) $\overset{\times\times}{\underset{\times\times}{\times}} I \overset{..}{\underset{..}{\times}} I \overset{..}{\underset{..}{:}}$ (3) $H \overset{..}{\times} N \overset{..}{\times} H$
                             $\overset{..}{H}$

(2) $H \overset{}{\times} H$ (4) $: N \overset{\times\times}{\underset{\times\times}{}} N \overset{\times}{\underset{\times}{}}$

18 Which is the correct formula for nitrogen (I) oxide?

(1) NO   (3) NO_2
(2) N_2O (4) N_2O_3

19 Which element in Group 15 has the strongest metallic character?

(1) Bi   (3) P
(2) As   (4) N

20 Which halogens are gases at STP?

(1) chlorine and fluorine
(2) chlorine and bromine
(3) iodine and fluorine
(4) iodine and bromine

21 What is the total number of atoms represented in the formula $CuSO_4 \cdot 5H_2O$?

(1) 8   (3) 21
(2) 13   (4) 27

22 When combining with nonmetallic atoms, metallic atoms generally will

(1) lose electrons and form negative ions
(2) lose electrons and form positive ions
(3) gain electrons and form negative ions
(4) gain electrons and form positive ions

23 Which set of elements contains a metalloid?

(1) K, Mn, As, Ar   (3) Ba, Ag, Sn, Xe
(2) Li, Mg, Ca, Kr   (4) Fr, F, O, Rn

24 Atoms of elements in a group on the Periodic Table have similar chemical properties. This similarity is most closely related to the atoms'

(1) number of principal energy levels
(2) number of valence electrons
(3) atomic numbers
(4) atomic masses

25 Which element in Period 2 of the Periodic Table is the most reactive nonmetal?

(1) carbon   (3) oxygen
(2) nitrogen   (4) fluorine

26 What is the gram formula mass of $(NH_4)_3PO_4$?

(1) 113 g (3) 149 g
(2) 121 g (4) 404 g

27 Given the reaction:

$$CH_4 + 2O_2 \rightarrow CO_2 + 2H_2O$$

What amount of oxygen is needed to completely react with 1 mole of CH_4?

(1) 2 moles (3) 2 grams
(2) 2 atoms (4) 2 molecules

28 Based on Reference Table E, which of the following saturated solutions would be the *least* concentrated?

(1) sodium sulfate
(2) potassium sulfate
(3) copper (II) sulfate
(4) barium sulfate

29 What is the total number of moles of H_2SO_4 needed to prepare 5.0 liters of a 2.0 M solution of H_2SO_4?

(1) 2.5 (3) 10.
(2) 5.0 (4) 20.

30 Given the reaction:

$$Ca(s) + 2H_2O(\ell) \rightarrow Ca(OH)_2(aq) + H_2(g)$$

When 40.1 grams of Ca(s) reacts completely with the water, what is the total volume, at STP, of $H_2(g)$ produced?

(1) 1.00 L (3) 22.4 L
(2) 2.00 L (4) 44.8 L

31 Which is the correct equilibrium expression for the reaction below?

$$4NH_3(g) + 7O_2(g) \rightleftarrows 4NO_2(g) + 6H_2O(g)$$

(1) $K = \dfrac{[NO_2][H_2O]}{[NH_3][O_2]}$

(3) $K = \dfrac{[NH_3][O_2]}{[NO_2][H_2O]}$

(2) $K = \dfrac{[NO_2]^4[H_2O]^6}{[NH_3]^4[O_2]^7}$

(4) $K = \dfrac{[NH_3]^4[O_2]^7}{[NO_2]^4[H_2O]^6}$

32 The potential energy diagram below shows the reaction $X + Y \rightleftarrows Z$.

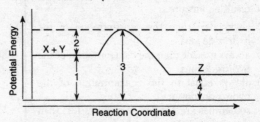

When a catalyst is added to the reaction, it will change the value of

(1) 1 and 2 (3) 2 and 3
(2) 1 and 3 (4) 3 and 4

33 Which conditions will increase the rate of a chemical reaction?

(1) decreased temperature and decreased concentration of reactants
(2) decreased temperature and increased concentration of reactants
(3) increased temperature and decreased concentration of reactants
(4) increased temperature and increased concentration of reactants

34 A solution exhibiting equilibrium between the dissolved and undissolved solute must be

(1) saturated (3) dilute
(2) unsaturated (4) concentrated

35 Which 0.1 M solution has a pH greater than 7?

(1) $C_6H_{12}O_6$ (3) KCl
(2) CH_3COOH (4) KOH

36 What color is phenolphthalein in a basic solution?

(1) blue (3) yellow
(2) pink (4) colorless

37 According to Reference Table L, which of the following is the strongest Brönsted-Lowry acid?

(1) HS^- (3) HNO_2
(2) H_2S (4) HNO_3

38 When HCl(aq) is exactly neutralized by NaOH(aq), the hydrogen ion concentration in the resulting mixture is

(1) always less than the concentration of the hydroxide ions
(2) always greater than the concentration of the hydroxide ions
(3) always equal to the concentration of the hydroxide ions
(4) sometimes greater and sometimes less than the concentration of the hydroxide ions

39 If 20. milliliters of 4.0 M NaOH is exactly neutralized by 20. milliliters of HCl, the molarity of the HCl is

(1) 1.0 M   (3) 5.0 M
(2) 2.0 M   (4) 4.0 M

40 The value of the ionization constant of water, K_w, will change when there is a change in

(1) temperature
(2) pressure
(3) hydrogen ion concentration
(4) hydroxide ion concentration

41 Based on Reference Table L, which species is amphoteric?

(1) NH_2^- (3) I^-
(2) NH_3 (4) HI

42 A redox reaction is a reaction in which

(1) only reduction occurs
(2) only oxidation occurs
(3) reduction and oxidation occur at the same time
(4) reduction occurs first and then oxidation occurs

43 Given the reaction:

___Mg + ___Cr^{3+} → ___Mg^{2+} + ___Cr

When the equation is correctly balanced using smallest whole numbers, the sum of the coefficients will be

(1) 10   (3) 5
(2) 7   (4) 4

44 Oxygen has an oxidation number of –2 in

(1) O_2 (3) Na_2O_2
(2) NO_2 (4) OF_2

45 Given the statements:

A   The salt bridge prevents electrical contact between solutions of half-cells.
B   The salt bridge prevents direct mixing of one half-cell solution with the other.
C   The salt bridge allows electrons to migrate from one half-cell to the other.
D   The salt bridge allows ions to migrate from one half-cell to the other.

Which two statements explain the purpose of a salt bridge used as part of a chemical cell?

(1) A and C   (3) C and D
(2) A and D   (4) B and D

46 When a substance is oxidized, it

(1) loses protons
(2) gains protons
(3) acts as an oxidizing agent
(4) acts as a reducing agent

47 In the reaction Cu + 2Ag^+ → Cu^{2+} + 2Ag, the oxidizing agent is

(1) Cu   (3) Ag^+
(2) Cu^{2+} (4) Ag

48 A compound that is classified as organic must contain the element

(1) carbon   (3) oxygen
(2) nitrogen   (4) hydrogen

49 Which substance is a product of a fermentation reaction?

(1) glucose   (3) ethanol
(2) zymase   (4) water

50 Which of the following hydrocarbons has the *lowest* normal boiling point?

(1) ethane   (3) butane
(2) propane   (4) pentane

51 What type of reaction is

$$CH_3CH_3 + Cl_2 \rightarrow CH_3CH_2Cl + HCl?$$

(1) an addition reaction
(2) a substitution reaction
(3) a saponification reaction
(4) an esterification reaction

52 Which compound is a saturated hydrocarbon?

(1) ethane   (3) ethyne
(2) ethene   (4) ethanol

Note that questions 53 through 56 have only three choices.

53 As atoms of elements in Group 16 are considered in order from top to bottom, the electronegativity of each successive element

(1) decreases
(2) increases
(3) remains the same

54 As the pressure of a gas at 760 torr is changed to 380 torr at constant temperature, the volume of the gas

(1) decreases
(2) increases
(3) remains the same

55 Given the change of phase: $CO_2(g) \rightarrow CO_2(s)$

As $CO_2(g)$ changes to $CO_2(s)$, the entropy of the system

(1) decreases
(2) increases
(3) remains the same

56 In heterogeneous reactions, as the surface area of the reactants increases, the rate of the reaction

(1) decreases
(2) increases
(3) remains the same

Part II

This part consists of twelve groups, each containing five questions. Each group tests a major area of the course. Choose seven of these twelve groups. Be sure that you answer all five questions in each group chosen. Record the answers to these questions on the separate answer sheet in accordance with the directions on the front page of this booklet.   [35]

Group 1 — Matter and Energy

If you choose this group, be sure to answer questions 57–61.

57 What is the total number of calories of heat energy absorbed by 15 grams of water when it is heated from 30.°C to 40.°C?

(1) 10.   (3) 25
(2) 15   (4) 150

58 The graph below represents the uniform cooling of a sample of a substance, starting with the substance as a gas above its boiling point.

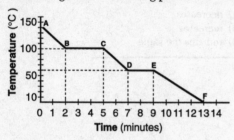

Which segment of the curve represents a time when both the liquid and the solid phases are present?

(1) EF   (3) CD
(2) BC   (4) DE

59 Which change of phase is exothermic?

(1) $NaCl(s) \rightarrow NaCl(\ell)$
(2) $CO_2(s) \rightarrow CO_2(g)$
(3) $H_2O(\ell) \rightarrow H_2O(s)$
(4) $H_2O(\ell) \rightarrow H_2O(g)$

60 According to the kinetic theory of gases, which assumption is correct?

(1) Gas particles strongly attract each other.
(2) Gas particles travel in curved paths.
(3) The volume of gas particles prevents random motion.
(4) Energy may be transferred between colliding particles.

61 A compound differs from a mixture in that a compound always has a

(1) homogeneous composition
(2) maximum of two components
(3) minimum of three components
(4) heterogeneous composition

Group 2 — Atomic Structure

If you choose this group, be sure to answer questions 62–66.

62 An ion with 5 protons, 6 neutrons, and a charge of 3+ has an atomic number of
(1) 5   (3) 8
(2) 6   (4) 11

63 Electron X can change to a higher energy level or a lower energy level. Which statement is true of electron X?
(1) Electron X emits energy when it changes to a higher energy level.
(2) Electron X absorbs energy when it changes to a higher energy level.
(3) Electron X absorbs energy when it changes to a lower energy level.
(4) Electron X neither emits nor absorbs energy when it changes energy level.

64 What is the highest principal quantum number assigned to an electron in an atom of zinc in the ground state?
(1) 1   (3) 5
(2) 2   (4) 4

65 The first ionization energy of an element is 176 kilocalories per mole of atoms. An atom of this element in the ground state has a total of how many valence electrons?
(1) 1   (3) 3
(2) 2   (4) 4

66 What is the total number of occupied s orbitals in an atom of nickel in the ground state?
(1) 1   (3) 3
(2) 2   (4) 4

Group 3 — Bonding

If you choose this group, be sure to answer questions 67–71.

67 What is the chemical formula for nickel (II) hypochlorite?
(1) $NiCl_2$ (3) $NiClO_2$
(2) $Ni(ClO)_2$ (4) $Ni(ClO)_3$

68 Based on Reference Table G, which of the following compounds is most stable?
(1) $CO(g)$ (3) $NO(g)$
(2) $CO_2(g)$ (4) $NO_2(g)$

69 The attractions that allow molecules of krypton to exist in the solid phase are due to
(1) ionic bonds
(2) covalent bonds
(3) molecule-ion forces
(4) van der Waals forces

70 Oxygen, nitrogen, and fluorine bond with hydrogen to form molecules. These molecules are attracted to each other by
(1) ionic bonds
(2) hydrogen bonds
(3) electrovalent bonds
(4) coordinate covalent bonds

71 An atom of which of the following elements has the greatest ability to attract electrons?
(1) silicon   (3) nitrogen
(2) sulfur   (4) bromine

Group 4 — Periodic Table

If you choose this group, be sure to answer questions 72–76.

72 Which electron configuration represents the atom with the largest covalent radius?

(1) $1s^1$
(2) $1s^2 2s^1$
(3) $1s^2 2s^2$
(4) $1s^2 2s^2 2p^1$

73 A solution of $Cu(NO_3)_2$ is colored because of the presence of the ion

(1) Cu^{2+}
(2) N^{5+}
(3) O^{2-}
(4) NO_3^{1-}

74 Which element is more reactive than strontium?

(1) potassium
(2) calcium
(3) iron
(4) copper

75 At STP, which substance is the best conductor of electricity?

(1) nitrogen
(2) neon
(3) sulfur
(4) silver

76 The oxide of metal X has the formula XO. Which group in the Periodic Table contains metal X?

(1) Group 1
(2) Group 2
(3) Group 13
(4) Group 17

Group 5 — Mathematics of Chemistry

If you choose this group, be sure to answer questions 77–81.

77 Given the same conditions of temperature and pressure, which noble gas will diffuse most rapidly?

(1) He
(2) Ne
(3) Ar
(4) Kr

78 What is the total number of molecules of hydrogen in 0.25 mole of hydrogen?

(1) 6.0×10^{23}
(2) 4.5×10^{23}
(3) 3.0×10^{23}
(4) 1.5×10^{23}

79 The volume of a 1.00-mole sample of an ideal gas will decrease when the

(1) pressure decreases and the temperature decreases
(2) pressure decreases and the temperature increases
(3) pressure increases and the temperature decreases
(4) pressure increases and the temperature increases

80 A 0.100-molal aqueous solution of which compound has the *lowest* freezing point?

(1) $C_6H_{12}O_6$
(2) CH_3OH
(3) $C_{12}H_{22}O_{11}$
(4) NaOH

81 What is the empirical formula of a compound that contains 85% Ag and 15% F by mass?

(1) AgF
(2) Ag_2F
(3) AgF_2
(4) Ag_2F_2

Group 6 — Kinetics and Equilibrium

If you choose this group, be sure to answer questions 82–86.

82 Based on Reference Table M, which compound is less soluble in water than $PbCO_3$ at 298 K and 1 atmosphere?

(1) AgI   (3) $CaSO_4$

(2) AgCl   (4) $BaSO_4$

83 Given the equilibrium reaction at constant pressure:

$$2HBr(g) + 17.4\,kcal \rightleftarrows H_2(g) + Br_2(g)$$

When the temperature is increased, the equilibrium will shift to the

(1) right, and the concentration of HBr(g) will decrease
(2) right, and the concentration of HBr(g) will increase
(3) left, and the concentration of HBr(g) will decrease
(4) left, and the concentration of HBr(g) will increase

84 A system is said to be in a state of dynamic equilibrium when the

(1) concentration of products is greater than the concentration of reactants
(2) concentration of products is the same as the concentration of reactants
(3) rate at which products are formed is greater than the rate at which reactants are formed
(4) rate at which products are formed is the same as the rate at which reactants are formed

85 Which reaction will occur spontaneously? [Refer to Reference Table G.]

(1) $\frac{1}{2}N_2(g) + \frac{1}{2}O_2(g) \rightarrow NO(g)$

(2) $\frac{1}{2}N_2(g) + O_2(g) \rightarrow NO_2(g)$

(3) $2C(s) + 3H_2(g) \rightarrow C_2H_6(g)$

(4) $2C(s) + 2H_2(g) \rightarrow C_2H_4(g)$

86 Which potential energy diagram represents the reaction $A + B \rightarrow C + $ energy?

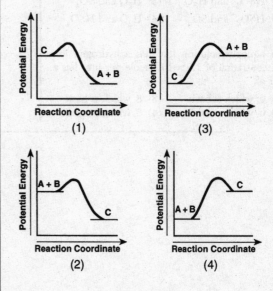

Group 7 — Acids and Bases

If you choose this group, be sure to answer questions 87–91.

87 Potassium chloride, KCl, is a salt derived from the neutralization of a

(1) weak acid and a weak base
(2) weak acid and a strong base
(3) strong acid and a weak base
(4) strong acid and a strong base

88 Given the reaction:

$$HSO_4^- + H_2O \rightleftarrows H_3O^+ + SO_4^{2-}$$

Which is a Brönsted-Lowry conjugate acid-base pair?

(1) HSO_4^- and H_3O^+ (3) H_2O and SO_4^{2-}
(2) HSO_4^- and SO_4^{2-} (4) H_2O and HSO_4^-

89 An aqueous solution that has a hydrogen ion concentration of 1.0×10^{-8} mole per liter has a pH of

(1) 6, which is basic (3) 8, which is basic
(2) 6, which is acidic (4) 8, which is acidic

90 The $[OH^-]$ of a solution is 1×10^{-6}. At 298 K and 1 atmosphere, the product $[H_3O^+][OH^-]$ is

(1) 1×10^{-2} (3) 1×10^{-8}
(2) 1×10^{-6} (4) 1×10^{-14}

91 Given the reaction:

$$KOH + HNO_3 \rightarrow KNO_3 + H_2O$$

Which process is taking place?

(1) neutralization (3) substitution
(2) esterification (4) addition

Group 8 — Redox and Electrochemistry

If you choose this group, be sure to answer questions 92–96.

92 Given the unbalanced equation:

__MnO$_2$ + __HCl → __MnCl$_2$ + __H$_2$O + __Cl$_2$

When the equation is correctly balanced using smallest whole-number coefficients, the coefficient of HCl is

(1) 1   (3) 3
(2) 2   (4) 4

93 Based on Reference Table N, which half-cell has a lower electrode potential than the standard hydrogen half-cell?

(1) Au^{3+} + 3e$^-$ → Au(s)
(2) Hg^{2+} + 2e$^-$ → Hg(ℓ)
(3) Cu$^+$ + e$^-$ → Cu(s)
(4) Pb^{2+} + 2e$^-$ → Pb(s)

94 According to Reference Table N, which reaction will take place spontaneously?

(1) Ni^{2+} + Pb(s) → Ni(s) + Pb^{2+}
(2) Au^{3+} + Al(s) → Au(s) + Al^{3+}
(3) Sr^{2+} + Sn(s) → Sr(s) + Sn^{2+}
(4) Fe^{2+} + Cu(s) → Fe(s) + Cu^{2+}

95 Given the reaction:

Mg(s) + Zn^{2+}(aq) → Mg^{2+}(aq) + Zn(s)

What is the cell voltage (E^0) for the overall reaction?

(1) +1.61 V   (3) +3.13 V
(2) –1.61 V   (4) –3.13 V

96 The diagram below represents a chemical cell at 298 K.

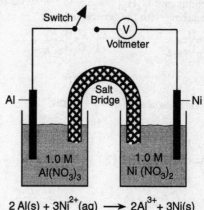

2 Al(s) + 3Ni^{2+}(aq) ⟶ 2Al^{3+} + 3Ni(s)

When the switch is closed, electrons flow from

(1) Al(s) to Ni(s)
(2) Ni(s) to Al(s)
(3) Al^{3+}(aq) to Ni^{2+}(aq)
(4) Ni^{2+}(aq) to Al^{3+}(aq)

Group 9 — Organic Chemistry

If you choose this group, be sure to answer questions 97–101.

97 The compound C_4H_{10} belongs to the series of hydrocarbons with the general formula

(1) C_nH_{2n} (3) C_nH_{2n-2}
(2) C_nH_{2n+2} (4) C_nH_{2n-6}

98 Which is an isomer of

$$H-\overset{\overset{\displaystyle H}{|}}{C}-\overset{\overset{\displaystyle H}{|}}{\underset{\underset{\displaystyle H}{|}}{C}}-OH\,?$$

(1)
$$H-\overset{\overset{\displaystyle H}{|}}{\underset{\underset{\displaystyle H}{|}}{C}}-O-\overset{\overset{\displaystyle H}{|}}{\underset{\underset{\displaystyle H}{|}}{C}}-H$$

(3)
$$H-\overset{\overset{\displaystyle H}{|}}{\underset{\underset{\displaystyle H}{|}}{C}}-\overset{\overset{\displaystyle O}{\parallel}}{C}-H$$

(2)
$$HO-\overset{\overset{\displaystyle H}{|}}{\underset{\underset{\displaystyle H}{|}}{C}}-\overset{\overset{\displaystyle H}{|}}{\underset{\underset{\displaystyle H}{|}}{C}}-H$$

(4)
$$H-\overset{\overset{\displaystyle H}{|}}{\underset{\underset{\displaystyle H}{|}}{C}}-\overset{\overset{\displaystyle H}{|}}{\underset{\underset{\displaystyle H}{|}}{C}}-O-\overset{\overset{\displaystyle H}{|}}{\underset{\underset{\displaystyle H}{|}}{C}}-H$$

99 To be classified as a tertiary alcohol, the functional —OH group is bonded to a carbon atom that must be bonded to a total of how many additional carbon atoms?

(1) 1   (3) 3
(2) 2   (4) 4

100 Which substance is made up of monomers joined together in long chains?

(1) ketone   (3) ester
(2) protein   (4) acid

101 What is the total number of carbon atoms in a molecule of glycerol?

(1) 1   (3) 3
(2) 2   (4) 4

Group 10 — Applications of Chemical Principles

If you choose this group, be sure to answer questions 102–106.

102 Which type of reaction is occurring when a metal undergoes corrosion?

(1) oxidation-reduction
(2) neutralization
(3) polymerization
(4) saponification

103 Which process is used to separate the components of a petroleum mixture?

(1) addition polymerization
(2) condensation polymerization
(3) fractional distillation
(4) fractional crystallization

104 Which substance functions as the electrolyte in an automobile battery?

(1) PbO_2 (3) H_2SO_4
(2) $PbSO_4$ (4) H_2O

105 A battery consists of which type of cells?

(1) electrolytic   (3) electroplating
(2) electrochemical   (4) electromagnetic

106 Which element can be found in nature in the free (uncombined) state?

(1) Ca   (3) Au
(2) Ba   (4) Al

Group 11 — Nuclear Chemistry
If you choose this group, be sure to answer questions 107–111.

107 Which radioactive isotope is used in geological dating?

(1) uranium–238   (3) cobalt–60
(2) iodine–131   (4) technetium–99

108 Which equation represents a fusion reaction?

(1) $^3_1H + ^1_1H \rightarrow ^4_2He$

(2) $^{40}_{18}Ar + ^1_1H \rightarrow ^{40}_{19}K + ^1_0n$

(3) $^{234}_{91}Pa \rightarrow ^{234}_{92}U + ^0_1e$

(4) $^{226}_{88}Ra \rightarrow ^{226}_{86}Rn + ^4_2He$

109 Which substance is used as a coolant in a nuclear reactor?

(1) neutrons   (3) hydrogen
(2) plutonium   (4) heavy water

110 Which substance has chemical properties similar to those of radioactive ^{235}U?

(1) ^{235}Pa (3) ^{233}U
(2) ^{233}Pa (4) ^{206}Pb

111 Control rods in nuclear reactors are commonly made of boron and cadmium because these two elements have the ability to

(1) absorb neutrons
(2) emit neutrons
(3) decrease the speed of neutrons
(4) increase the speed of neutrons

Group 12 — Laboratory Activities
If you choose this group, be sure to answer questions 112–116.

Base your answers to questions 112 and 113 on the table below, which represents the production of 50 milliliters of CO_2 in the reaction of HCl with $NaHCO_3$. Five trials were performed under different conditions as shown. (The same mass of $NaHCO_3$ was used in each trial.)

Trial	Particle Size of $NaHCO_3$	Concentration of HCl	Temperature (°C) of HCl
A	small	1 M	20
B	large	1 M	20
C	large	1 M	40
D	small	2 M	40
E	large	2 M	40

112 Which two trials could be used to measure the effect of surface area?

(1) trials A and B (3) trials A and D
(2) trials A and C (4) trials B and D

113 Which trial would produce the fastest reaction?

(1) trial A (3) trial C
(2) trial B (4) trial D

114 A student determined the heat of fusion of water to be 88 calories per gram. If the accepted value is 80. calories per gram, what is the student's percent error?

(1) 8.0%   (3) 11%
(2) 10.%   (4) 90.%

115 Given: (52.6 cm) (1.214 cm)

What is the product expressed to the correct number of significant figures?

(1) 64 cm^2 (3) 63.86 cm^2
(2) 63.9 cm^2 (4) 63.8564 cm^2

116 The diagram below represents a metal bar and two centimeter rulers, A and B. Portions of the rulers have been enlarged to show detail.

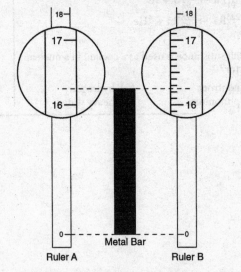

What is the greatest degree of precision to which the metal bar can be measured by ruler A and by ruler B?

(1) to the nearest tenth by both rulers
(2) to the nearest hundredth by both rulers
(3) to the nearest tenth by ruler A and to the nearest hundredth by ruler B
(4) to the nearest hundredth by ruler A and to the nearest tenth by ruler B

Sample Regents Exam 2

Answers

1. The correct answer is 1. When any liquid boils, this means it has enough energy to raise its vapor pressure to that of the atmosphere. The vapor pressure of any liquid at the normal boiling point is defined as 1 atmosphere.

2. The correct answer is 3. According to Dalton's partial pressure law, each gas contributes to the total pressure in an amount equal to its makeup of the volume. Since nitrogen makes up two thirds of the total amount of the gas, the pressure it exerts is two thirds, or 400 torr, of the total amount.

3. The correct answer is 2. Heat always flows from the area of greatest activity to the area of least activity. Choice 2 fits these criteria with solid X being 10°C and solid Y being 5°C. One must be careful of answers like choice 3, where the temperature of solid X is actually less than that of solid Y, although the numerals are larger since we are dealing with negative numbers.

4. The correct answer is 3. The relationship between volume and Kelvin temperature is a direct one. That is, when the temperature increases, the volume increases by the same factor, and this would be satisfied in the graph in choice 3 as long as pressure is held constant.

5. The correct answer is 1. A binary compound is known as a compound with only two elements in its makeup, and choice one contains only two elements. Choices 2 and 4 contain two words but three elements: Recall that ammonia contains nitrogen and hydrogen and is a polyatomic cation. Choice 2 has the anion as the polyatomic, containing chlorine and oxygen. Add to that the potassium and we have more than a binary.

6. The correct answer is 2. Gamma rays pass through an electric field unaffected since they have no charge. Choice 1 is a positive particle, choice 3 is a negative particle, and choice 4 is a positive particle, namely the nucleus of a helium atom, which contains two protons and two neutrons.

7. The correct answer is 4. The nucleus is where the majority of the mass of an atom is found. This contains neutrons and protons, so our correct answer is choice 4.

8. The correct answer is 1. Choices 3 and 4 are meant to mislead by giving mass numbers as 15, not proton numbers. Looking at the periodic chart shows phosphorus to have an atomic number of 15, meaning it has fifteen protons. P–32 is just one of the isotopes of phosphorus. Sulfur is atomic number 16.

9. The correct answer is 3. We find the average atomic mass by multiplying the percent abundance of each isotope by its atomic mass, and then adding all the isotope results, which is choice 3. Choice 4 is close to the way it should be done but leaves out the percentage factor.

10. The correct answer is 2. Particle X has no mass—the mass number of the two elements C and N is given as 14 and stays the same—yet it affects the atomic number of the elements involved by an increase of 1. If we lose only an electron from the nucleus, that "converts" a neutron into a proton which, when "added" in this way to carbon (number 6), makes it nitrogen (number 7), and preserves the mass number (14). Choice 2 is the answer.

11. The correct answer is 4. "In the ground state" means all electrons are as close to the nucleus as possible. If this element has two unpaired electrons in the 2p sublevel, this means that the only other electrons that this element would have would be in a filled 2s with two electrons and a filled 1s with two electrons. This gives us a total of six electrons which, in the ground state, would be matched by six protons making this element number 6, carbon.

12. The correct answer is 4. The top number shown in each example is the mass—the number of neutrons and protons—of the atom, and the bottom number is the atomic number—the number of protons. Subtracting the bottom from the top gives us the

number of neutrons. The only choice in which the pair of atoms contains the same number of neutrons is choice 4. For the isotope of hydrogen given—tritium—there are two neutrons and for the isotope of helium given, there are also two neutrons.

13. The correct answer is 1. An empirical formula is the formula of a substance reduced to its lowest terms. Choice 1 cannot be reduced beyond the one carbon, making the formula for methane both an empirical and a molecular formula. H_2O is another example.

14. The correct answer is 3. Both structure and composition affect the potential energy of a molecule. The ways in which a molecule's energy could be released depend both on the materials involved and the way they are arranged in the molecule.

15. The correct answer is 4. Only choice 4 balances by having the numbers of all of the atoms in the reactant molecules exactly equal to the numbers of all of the atoms in the product molecules.

16. The correct answer is 4. Rubidium gives up a lone electron in the number 5 principal energy level, leaving it with one less principal energy level. This makes the ionic form smaller in diameter than the atomic form. All the other choices offered add electrons.

17. The correct answer is 3. A polar covalent bond cannot exist between two identical atoms.

18. The correct answer is 2. Nitrogen (I) oxide indicates to us that the oxidation number for the nitrogen is (+1). Oxygen most typically has an oxidation number of (−2). In order to form a compound, we need two nitrogens to balance out the one oxygen or choice 2. Choice 1 would be nitrogen (II), choice 3 would be nitrogen (IV), and choice 4 would be nitrogen (III).

19. The correct answer is 1. As you travel down the groups in the periodic table, the elements take on more and more metallic, or fewer and fewer nonmetallic, properties. The farthest down of the choices given is bismuth, choice 1.

20. The correct answer is 1. The two smallest, and lowest atomic-numbered halogens, fluorine and chlorine, are gases at STP. Bromine is a liquid, and iodine is a solid.

21. The correct answer is 3. By adding up the number of atoms in the copper salt and the attached water molecules, we get 1—Cu, 1—S, 9—O, and 10—H, making a total of 21.

22. The correct answer is 2. Part of the definition of a metallic atom is that it readily loses electrons and thus becomes a positive ion (choice 2).

23. The correct answer is 1. The choice with the element As in the list contains the metalloid. It is sufficiently far down in Group 15 to have fewer nonmetal properties than nitrogen and phosphorus, yet not far enough down to have more fully metallic properties like bismuth.

24. The correct answer is 2. The similarities in atoms found in the groups are due to the atoms in the same group having the same number of electrons in their outer principal energy level, also known as valence electrons. For example, elements in Group I all have one valence electron.

25. The correct answer is 4. Moving through the choices from 1 to 4, we find the atoms becoming more reactive. We are also moving more to the nonmetallic end of the period. The reason we are encountering greater reactivity is because principal energy level 2, the outermost energy level in this period, is filling up. By the time we get to fluorine, we need only one electron to complete principal energy level 2.

26. The correct answer is 3. The gram formula mass is arrived at by adding up all of the atomic masses—taken from the periodic table—for all of the atoms in a compound. Choice 3 is the correct total for ammonium phosphate.

27. The correct answer is 1. The molar ratio is given in the balanced equation and for methane to oxygen, respectively, it is 1:2. Therefore, we will need 2 moles of oxygen to completely react with 1 mole of methane, choice 1. All of the other choices use the number 2 but with the wrong labels.

28. The correct answer is 4. According to the chart, barium sulfate is "nearly insoluble." We can then conclude that very few ions would be in solution, making its concentration (dissociation in aqueous solution) the lowest. All the others are indicated to be at least soluble.

29. The correct answer is 3. Using the equation for molarity of

$$M = \frac{\text{number of moles of solute}}{\text{liters of solution}}$$

and rearranging for # moles solute, we find that for 5 L of a 2.0 M solution of H_2SO_4, we need 10 moles of H_2SO_4 or choice 3.

30. The correct answer is 3. It is known that 40.1 grams of calcium is one mole of calcium. The balanced equation indicates that 1 mole of calcium produces 1 mole of $H_2(g)$. At STP, 1 mole of hydrogen occupies 22.4 L of volume, choice 3.

31. The correct answer is 2. The equilibrium expression is found using the formula in choice 2. That is, the concentration of each product, raised to the power of its coefficient in the balanced equation, is multiplied times each other. A similar operation is done for the reactants. The result of this operation for the products of the reaction is divided by the result of this operation for the reactants of the reaction, which gives us K_{eq}.

32. The correct answer is 3. The area indicated by the 2 represents what is called activation energy. This amount of energy is changed (not necessarily reduced, but changed as it could be increased) by the addition of a catalyst. This would affect the values of both 2 and 3, since these two areas both have the same high point.

33. The correct answer is 4. There are some reactions where adding more reactant will slow down the rate, but normally choice 4 will speed things up.

34. The correct answer is 1. When a solution attains equilibrium between the dissolved and undissolved components, it is said to be saturated, a very specific condition. Dilute is very vague and means "a little," unsaturated means anything less than saturated, and concentrated, like "dilute," is vague and simply means "a lot" (concentrated does not necessarily mean saturated, and vice versa).

35. The correct answer is 4. Potassium hydroxide has OH^- ions available in the molecule in addition to any it will cause by being ionized in water. Each of the other compounds either (a) does not ionize, as in the case of $C_6H_{12}O_6$, or (b) does not have additional OH^- ions available when ionized, as in the cases of both KCl and CH_3COOH.

36. The correct answer is 2. This is the color of phenolphthalein in a basic solution. This color is helpful during titration as the

change from pink to clear denotes the equivalence point.

37. The correct answer is 4. According to definition, a Brönsted-Lowry acid is one that donates hydrogen ions. A strong Brönsted-Lowry acid, then, is one that is a strong donor (meaning, the most) of hydrogen ions. From Reference Table L, we can see that, among the choices listed, HNO_3 is the strongest acid in aqueous solution (its K_a listed as "very large"). All the other choices have a K_a of < 1.

38. The correct answer is 3. The key to this question is the use of the words *exactly neutralized*. This means only answer 3 will do.

39. The correct answer is 4. Given the concept that an equal molarity of a base is neutralized by an equal molarity of an acid, the only correct choice is 4; the molarity of the acid must be 4.0 M.

40. The correct answer is 1. Pressure will not measurably affect the K_w of liquid water and the addition of ions would not affect the value of K_w at that temperature. It is the temperature that affects the ionization constant of a substance.

41. The correct answer is 2. An amphoteric substance is one that can act like an acid or a base, able to donate hydrogen ions and receive them. A good example is water. Among the choices given, and according to their K_a on Reference Table L, it appears that NH_3 is the amphoteric

substance. The last row on the chart indicates it can disassociate into NH_2 in small amounts as it donates an H^+, and further up the chart, it can receive an H^+ in small amounts in the formation of NH_4. The K_a for HI is very large, making it primarily an H^+ donor. Taking I^- alone is misleading, as is NH_2^-.

42. The correct answer is 3. Reduction, the gain of electrons, must take place at the same time as the loss of electrons, or oxidation, is taking place. Atoms will not tolerate an imbalance in their particles for long; on the atomic scale, the reaction probably takes place in a very short period of time.

43. The correct answer is 1. When the equation is balanced, we get a 3 in front of each form of magnesium and a 2 in front of each form of chromium. This adds up to a sum of 5 in the coefficients on each side of the equation or 10 total.

44. The correct answer is 2. Assuming the other elements are in their normal oxidation state, choice 1, of course, is 0; choice 3 makes oxygen take the $^-1$; and choice 4 has oxygen as a cation.

45. The correct answer is 4. The purpose of a salt bridge is twofold and is summarized in choice 4: to provide a connection between the two solutions without allowing them to mix while allowing the ions to migrate from one half-cell to the other, which will also allow electrons to migrate through the circuit.

46. The correct answer is 4. If a substance is oxidized, it loses electrons to a substance that will gain them, meaning that this second substance will be reduced. Therefore, our original substance will be the reducing agent.

47. The correct answer is 3. The copper is losing electrons when it goes from the 0 state on the left to the $^+2$ state on the right and is therefore being oxidized. The silver is gaining those electrons and is therefore being reduced.

48. The correct answer is 1. The fundamental definition of an organic compound is one that contains carbon, thus making it one of the compounds involved in the reactions that take place uniquely in living systems.

49. The correct answer is 3. Fermentation is the incomplete metabolism of an organic substance, often a carbohydrate, the result of which is usually carbon dioxide and an alcohol. Choice 3, an alcohol, is the answer.

50. The correct answer is 1. Ethane, the smallest hydrocarbon listed, has the lowest boiling point. The molecules are nonpolar and, ethane being the smallest, requires the least amount of energy to be vaporized.

51. The correct answer is 2. The reaction we are given is a substitution reaction wherein one of the chlorines from the Cl_2 replaces one of the hydrogens from ethane to make hydrochloric acid and ethyl chloride.

52. The correct answer is 1. Saturated hydrocarbons are so named because all of their bonds are in the ground state or saturated. They do this by having all single covalent bonds, the condition we would find ethane in (choice 1). Choices 2 and 3 have double and triple bonds, respectively, and choice 4 is not a hydrocarbon.

53. The correct answer is 1. The electronegativity of an atom is defined as its ability to attract electrons in a molecule. As we consider the elements in Group 16 from top to bottom, we notice they all need two electrons in their valence shell. However, the lowest members of Group 16 are fairly large, meaning the nucleus (a positive entity) is further and further from this valence shell; therefore, reducing the attractiveness to available electrons. Their electronegativity is less than the atoms at the top of the group.

54. The correct answer is 2. Pressure is inversely related to volume, which means if the pressure is reduced as the question states, the volume will increase if the temperature is maintained throughout.

55. The correct answer is 1. Entropy increases as substances change from solids to liquids to gases—in that order. The distance between the particles increases as we go from solid to gas, thus increasing their tendency toward randomness. Therefore, going from a gas to a solid decreases entropy and increases order and enthalpy.

56. The correct answer is 3. In heterogeneous reactions, the surface area of the solids has no effect on the reactions involving the gases as long as the density of the solids remains the same. In considering the reaction rate of a heterogeneous reaction, only the concentration of the gases is considered as affecting the reaction rate. The surface area of the gases will not change.

57. The correct answer is 4. Simply heating liquid water adds energy and raises the temperature as a result. The per calorie value of water is 1°C per gram, so raising 15 grams a total of 10°C would require 15 × 10 or 150 calories of energy. If we were to involve a phase change, an additional amount of energy per gram would have to be figured in.

58. The correct answer is 4. If the substance involved starts as a gas, then its temperature in the gaseous form declines until it reaches point B. At this point, the gas is condensing to a liquid and both are present from B to C where no energy is being given off (evidenced by a constant temperature), since it is being absorbed in the rearrangement of particles from gaseous to liquid form. Likewise, from points D to E, the next plateau, we have the liquid and solid phases present at the same time (choice 4). From C to D, the liquid is cooling to eventually become the solid phase.

59. The correct answer is 3. If a substance cools down, it is giving off heat. Doing so is our definition of an exothermic reaction or choice 3. All the other choices absorb heat.

60. The correct answer is 4. Choices 1 through 3 are almost directly opposite to the exact wording of the kinetic molecular theory as it applies to gases (including the definition of an ideal gas). Choice 4 is the only correct statement; energy is transferred between particles that collide, also known as elastic collisions if the total energy of the system does not change during the collision.

61. The correct answer is 1. Part of the definition of a compound includes the concept of definite proportions, i.e., the components of any compound are in the same ratios to each other no matter where that compound is and no matter what its source. If we take sodium and chlorine off the shelf and let them react, we get a salt with a ratio of one sodium for every one chlorine. If we react HCl and NaOH, we get a salt with a ratio of one sodium for every one of chlorine. They are both called sodium chloride, and both have a formula of NaCl.

62. The correct answer is 1. The only information one needs to be able to determine the atomic number is the number of protons. The number of neutrons and the charge on the atom both are unnecessary pieces of information here. If they had given us the charge on the nucleus, that would have been the number of protons and the atomic number.

63. The correct answer is 2. Any electron, when it moves to a higher principal energy level, must absorb energy in order to do

so. Once it falls back to its original position, it emits that energy in packets of light, a phenomenon we can use to identify the element in the substance.

64. The correct answer is 4. Since zinc is in the fourth period, the highest principal energy level it has is the fourth level. The highest quantum number we can assign, then, to an electron in zinc in the ground state—when all electrons are as close as they can get to the nucleus—is 4.

65. The correct answer is 2. It is known from Table K that 176 k-cal/mol (738 J/mol) is the first ionization energy for magnesium, which in the ground state has two valence electrons since it is in Group 2.

66. The correct answer is 4. Since nickel is in the fourth period on the periodic chart, it has four principal energy levels. This gives it four "s" orbitals holding electrons in the ground state.

67. The correct answer is 2. From Table F, the hypochlorite ion has an oxidation number of $^-1$. If we are dealing with nickel (II), then we will need a formula containing two of the hypochlorite ions, which is choice 2 or $Ni(ClO)_2$.

68. The correct answer is 3. The free energy of formation from Table G tells us whether energy was increased or decreased in the formation of each compound from its elements in their standard states. If the value is negative, the compound will sponta-

neously form, and this means the compound is more stable than its separated elements. A larger negative $\Delta G°$ is a more favorable process, hence CO_2 is the most stable.

69. The correct answer is 4. Van der Waals forces are the weak forces that involve a sort of cohesion or sticking together of similar atoms or molecules. It is one of the weakest attractions and is not related to covalent, ionic, or molecule-ion bonds since the inert element krypton does not ionize.

70. The correct answer is 2. Hydrogen bonds occur in polar molecules containing N, O, or F with hydrogen as one of the "poles." All three elements in the question, in combination with hydrogen, do this— H_2O, HF, and NH_3, respectively.

71. The correct answer is 3. The atom with the highest electronegativity would have the greatest ability to attract electrons in a molecule, and that would be nitrogen which sits higher up on the periodic chart than any of the other three and very nearly to the far right.

72. The correct answer is 1. From Table P, we see that Li has the largest covalent radius at 1.23 angstroms, and Li has the configuration in choice 2. Without looking at Table P, we can still arrive at the same answer because atomic size (whatever the term used to measure it) increases down a group and from right to left across a period.

73. The correct answer is 1. Cations, particularly in the transitional metal area of the periodic table, exhibit a color in solution, in the solid phase and in flame tests. Copper is the cation in this compound.

74. The correct answer is 1. Potassium is the only element among those listed that is above strontium on the activity series of metals. Therefore, it is more reactive than strontium.

75. The correct answer is 4. At STP, choices 1, 2, and 3 are, respectively, a gas, a gas, and an amorphous solid with few free electrons. At STP, silver is a metallic solid with plentiful free electrons with which to conduct electricity.

76. The correct answer is 2. If the formula is XO, meaning X and O combine on a 1:1 ratio, then the oxidation number of $^-2$ for O is matched by an oxidation number in X of $^+2$, placing it in Group 2 on the periodic table.

77. The correct answer is 1. Graham's Law states that the least massive gases diffuse the fastest. Helium is the lightest inert gas listed and would diffuse the fastest.

78. The correct answer is 4. One quarter of a mole would contain one quarter of the Avogadro number of particles, which would be $.25 \times (6.02 \times 10^{23}$ particles$) = 1.5 \times 10^{23}$. The tricky part when working with exponents in scientific notation is that it's tempting to take one-quarter of the 10^{23} also, which is not the procedure.

79. The correct answer is 3. The only choice that gives us the correct relationship between volume and the two characteristics given is choice 3. The volume of a gas is inversely proportional to the change in pressure and directly proportional to the temperature change.

80. The correct answer is 4. Freezing point is affected by the number of moles of particles in solution. Choices 1 through 3 will each contribute only 1 mole of particles (in this case, molecules since they will not ionize in water). Choice 4 will ionize into 1 mole of Na^+ ions and 1 mole of OH^- ions, thus making it contribute 2 moles of particles to the solution and having twice the lowering effect as the other choices.

81. The correct answer is 1. If we assume a sample of 100 g of the compound, the figures given would lead to an 85 g sample of silver by weight and 15 g of fluorine by weight. Using the molar masses and these figures, the ratio of particles comes out to 1:1 making the empirical formula AgF.

82. The correct answer is 1. The solubility product $[K_{sp}]$ for silver iodide is less than the K_{sp} for lead carbonate by a little over three orders of magnitude. However, in order to determine which compound is more soluble, we must remember that solubility is defined as the maximum amount of solute ions dissolved in solution: either the molarity of cations or anions, not the

sum of their molarities. So, just looking at which K_{sp} value is the smallest will not always work! For example, in Table M we see that lead chloride $PbCl_2$ will dissolve to make three ions: one Pb and two Cl^- ions. Lead carbonate will only yield two—Pb^{2+} and CO_3^{2-}. The mathematics involved in solving for each molarity is beyond the level of difficulty of this review but fortunately, in *this* problem, we can get the correct answer by comparing only the values of K_{sp} for each compound.

83. The correct answer is 1. The equilibrium reaction given is an endothermic reaction. Increasing the temperature will drive the reaction to the right; adding heat favors the formation of products in an endothermic reaction.

84. The correct answer is 4. Dynamic equilibrium occurs when the rate at which the products are formed in a reaction is the same as the rate at which reactants are formed. It is an "ongoing" equilibrium.

85. The correct answer is 3. In this reaction, both ΔH and ΔG are negative. The negative H indicates that it is exothermic, a class of reactions that tend to proceed on their own. If ΔG is also negative, it indicates that the reaction will proceed spontaneously.

86. The correct answer is 2. The reaction given is an exothermic reaction in which the energy of the reactants equals the energy of the products plus the energy given off by the reaction. Choice 2 satisfies that in the graph. Choice 4 is endothermic and choices 1 and 3 are the reverse of the reaction given.

87. The correct answer is 4. Potassium chloride comes from the neutralization of KOH, a strong base, with HCl, a strong acid. Only choice 4 fits the bill and only strong + strong will be a neutralization reaction.

88. The correct answer is 2. Brönsted-Lowry defines an acid as one capable of donating an H^+ and its conjugate base as the species that receives the H^+. The only pair that acts as a conjugate acid-base pair is $HSO4^-$, the species that donates the H^+, and the SO_4^{2-}, capable of receiving the H^+.

89. The correct answer is 3. The pH is defined as the negative log of the concentration of hydrogen ions in solution also written as "$-\log [H^+]$." The negative log of the concentration of 1×10^{-8} is 8 and that is the pH of a mild base.

90. The correct answer is 4. The product of $(H_3O^+)(OH^-)$ is the same as saying the product of $(H^+)(OH^-)$, or the expression of the total concentration of both ions from dissociated water, which is always 1×10^{-14} at STP (1 atmosphere of pressure and 298°K).

91. Both 1 and 3 are correct. The reaction given is a substitution reaction wherein K^+

replaces H^+ in HNO_3 and H^+ replaces K^+ in KOH. But the reaction is also a neutralization of a strong base KOH with a strong acid HNO_3.

92. The correct answer is 4. Balancing this equation leads to a need for four moles of HCl as its smallest whole-number coefficient.

93. The correct answer is 4. If the electrode potential $E^\circ = E_{red}^\circ - E_{oxid}^\circ$ is > 0, then the material is more likely than hydrogen to be reduced. Its E° will be positive. On the other hand, if the E° is negative (or < 0), then it is less likely than hydrogen to be reduced. Its electrode potential should then be < 0. Only Pb, just below the hydrogen half-cell potential of 0, qualifies for this among the choices given, since its E° is < 0.

94. The correct answer is 2. Combining the E° for the two half-cell reactions, we are looking for the largest number. If the cell potential for the redox reaction is positive, then the reaction is spontaneous. Only choice 2 has a positive E°.

95. The correct answer is 1. The half-reaction for $Mg^\circ \rightarrow Mg^{-2}\ 2e^-$ yields a cell voltage of $+2.36V$. The other half reaction $Zn^{+2} +2e^- \rightarrow Zn^\circ$ yields a cell voltage of $-.76V$. Combining the two, we get $+1.61V$ or choice 1.

96. The correct answer is 1. The flow of anions will be across the salt bridges from right to left, making the flow of electrons follow the path indicated in choice 1, from the Al(s) to the Ni(s).

97. The correct answer is 2. Examining the ratio C:H in the molecule listed, we can see the number of hydrogens is precisely twice that of the carbons plus 2. This would be the choice 2 formula.

98. The correct answer is 1. Isomers are chemical compounds that have the same molecular formula but differ in structure, and that means having the same numbers of each atom in the formula but attached to each other in a different arrangement. The only compound that has six hydrogens, two carbons and one oxygen and that is arranged differently is choice 1. Choice 2 is the exact same molecule (ethanol).

99. The correct answer is 3. The form for a tertiary alcohol is for the functional $-OH$ group to be bonded to a carbon that is bonded to three additional carbons and takes the form R_3–C–OH.

100. The correct answer is 2. Proteins are the only substances on the list that are composed of long chains of monomers, in this case called amino acids. This makes the protein a polymer. The other three are distinct, single units of a particular chemical structure but are not polymers.

101. The correct answer is 3. Glycerol contains a total of three carbon atoms.

102. The correct answer is 1. When a metal undergoes "corrosion," it is almost always taken to mean it is oxidizing. The oxidizing agent is, therefore, being reduced, and we have a case of oxidation-reduction.

103. The correct answer is 3. When we separate a petroleum mixture into its components, we use the process of closed-system heating called distillation and we regulate the temperature in small increments, also known as fractionally. This process has been named fractional distillation.

104. The correct answer is 3. The electrolyte or substance used to promote the production of an electric current by interacting with other parts of the voltaic cell known as the car battery is sulfuric acid.

105. The correct answer is 2. Batteries consist of electrochemical cells that can, using chemicals, generate a flow of electrons. This is also called a voltaic cell wherein the reaction of discharge is called electrochemical and recharge is called electrolytic.

106. The correct answer is 3. Choices 1, 2, and 4 all oxidize quite well in nature. Gold (element Au) does not combine freely with oxygen and so is most always found in the free, or elemental, state.

107. The correct answer is 1. Uranium-238 has a half-life of 4.5×10^9 years and can thus be used to calculate the age of rocks, given the percent of uranium-238 and lead-206 remaining in them at the time of the dating. Cobalt-60 and iodine-131 both have very short half-lives compared to uranium-238. Technetium-99 is a man-made isotope.

108. The correct answer is 1. In a fusion reaction, we would expect two or more substances to combine to form at least one larger particle. Choice 1 seems to do this. Choice 2 is also a possibility—the reactants could fuse to make $^{40}_{19}K$, which then emits a neutron, or the reactants could collide and produce both products at once without fusion occurring. This was an ambiguous question!

109. The correct answer is 4. In a nuclear reactor, only heavy water comes close to being a coolant. Plutonium is a radioactive substance used in certain kinds of reactors, hydrogen is too volatile to be considered, and neutrons are what the heating is all about in a reactor, hardly the stuff of coolants. Heavy water helps in lowering the temperature by being a more dense form of water, a subtance that can absorb large quantities of heat.

110. The correct answer is 3. When we are talking chemical properties, all the isotopes of any given element have the same chemical properties. This is not true if we speak of nuclear matters; the term *isotope* means same element (and therefore the same chemical properties), but not the same nuclear makeup. Chemically, ^{235}U and ^{233}U are identical.

111. The correct answer is 1. The reaction that drives a nuclear reactor is the loss of neutrons from some of the fuel atoms and the subsequent bombarding of other fuel atoms with these neutrons. Reduce the number of neutrons and the reaction slows down or comes under control. The B-Cd control rods slow down the reaction by absorbing neutrons.

112. The correct answer is 1. We're looking for the choice with the set of data that has only one thing varying and that one thing is the surface area. Trials A and B fit these conditions. The variables in Trial A and Trial B are the same except for particle size, which is another way to indicate surface area. Trials D and E are also possible.

113. The correct answer is 4. The fastest reaction would most likely come from the setup with the largest amount of surface area available, the highest temperature, and the highest concentration of particles. Choice 4 or Trial D has the smallest particles (the largest surface area), the highest concentration (2M), and the highest temperature (40°C).

114. The correct answer is 2. The percent of error is calculated by subtracting the accepted value from the experimental value and dividing by the accepted value. In this case, this means $\frac{88-80}{80}$. This becomes $\frac{8}{80}$, which is 10 percent. Note the difference between the two values is positive indicating that the student is 10 percent above the accepted value.

115. The correct answer is 2. The product of the two numbers is 63.8564 cm². The least number of significant figures in the original measurements was three, and so our answer must be reported to no more than 3 significant figures. By rounding the answer off and dropping figures that are not significant, we arrive at 63.9 cm².

116. The correct answer is 3. Ruler A has its smallest markings in whole units, which means we can accurately estimate to tenths on ruler A. Ruler B has its smallest markings in tenths of units, which means we can accurately estimate to hundredths on Ruler B. Choice 3 provides the correct criteria for measuring the metal bar.

Sample Regents Exam 3—August 1996

Part I

Answer all 56 questions in this part. [65]

Directions (1–56): For *each* statement or question, select the word or expression that, of those given, best completes the statement or answers the question. Record your answer on the separate answer sheet in accordance with the directions on the front page of this booklet.

1 At which temperature would glycerol have the highest vapor pressure?

(1) 30°C   (3) 50°C
(2) 40°C   (4) 60°C

2 Given the reaction: $Fe + S \rightarrow FeS + energy$

Which statement about this reaction is true?

(1) It is endothermic.
(2) It is exothermic.
(3) The potential energy of the reactants is lower than the potential energy of the product.
(4) The potential energy of the reactants is the same as the potential energy of the product.

3 When sample X is passed through a filter paper, a white residue, Y, remains on the paper and a clear liquid, Z, passes through. When liquid Z is vaporized, another white residue remains. Sample X is best classified as

(1) an element
(2) a compound
(3) a heterogeneous mixture
(4) a homogeneous mixture

4 What is the total number of calories of heat that must be absorbed to change the temperature of 100 grams of H_2O from 25°C to 30°C?

(1) 100   (3) 2,500
(2) 500   (4) 3,000

5 Which equation represents alpha decay?

(1) $^{116}_{49}In \rightarrow {}^{116}_{50}Sn + X$
(2) $^{234}_{90}Th \rightarrow {}^{234}_{91}Pa + X$
(3) $^{38}_{19}K \rightarrow {}^{38}_{18}Ar + X$
(4) $^{222}_{86}Rn \rightarrow {}^{218}_{84}Po + X$

6 A sample of gas A was stored in a container at a temperature of 50°C and a pressure of 0.50 atmosphere. Compared to a sample of gas B at STP, gas A had a

(1) higher temperature and a lower pressure
(2) higher temperature and a higher pressure
(3) lower temperature and a lower pressure
(4) lower temperature and a higher pressure

7 Which particles are referred to as nucleons?

(1) protons, only
(2) neutrons, only
(3) protons and neutrons
(4) protons and electrons

8 What is the mass number of an atom that contains 19 protons, 19 electrons, and 20 neutrons?

(1) 19   (3) 39
(2) 20   (4) 58

9 Which atom in the ground state has only 3 electrons in the $3p$ sublevel?

(1) phosphorus   (3) argon
(2) potassium   (4) aluminum

10 What is the total number of occupied principal energy levels in a neutral atom of neon in the ground state?

(1) 1   (3) 3
(2) 2   (4) 4

11 Which type of energy is represented in the equation $Na + energy \rightarrow Na^+ + e^-$?

(1) neutralization energy
(2) ionization energy
(3) nuclear energy
(4) formation energy

12 Which particle has approximately the same mass as a proton?

(1) alpha   (3) electron
(2) beta   (4) neutron

13 A radioactive element has a half-life of 2 days. Which fraction represents the amount of an original sample of this element remaining after 6 days?

(1) $\frac{1}{8}$ (3) $\frac{1}{3}$
(2) $\frac{1}{2}$ (4) $\frac{1}{4}$

14 In which compound do the atoms have the greatest difference in electronegativity?

(1) NaBr   (3) KF
(2) $AlCl_3$ (4) LiI

15 Which element would most likely form an ionic bond with chlorine?

(1) O   (3) S
(2) N   (4) K

16 Which formula represents sodium sulfate?

(1) $NaSO_4$ (3) Na_2SO_4
(2) $NaSO_3$ (4) Na_2SO_3

17 The unusually high boiling point of water is due to the

(1) network bonds between the molecules
(2) hydrogen bonds between the molecules
(3) linear structure of the molecules
(4) nonpolar character of the molecules

18 Which electron dot diagram represents H_2?

(1)   H • H   (3)   :H • H:

(2)   H : H   (4)   :H : H:

19 Which is a property of network solids but *not* of molecular solids?

(1) electrical insulators
(2) water soluble
(3) high melting points
(4) high malleability

20 At STP, potassium is classified as

(1) a metallic solid   (3) a network solid
(2) a molecular solid   (4) an ionic solid

21 The elements in the modern Periodic Table are arranged according to their

(1) atomic number   (3) atomic mass
(2) oxidation number   (4) nuclear mass

22 Given the electron configuration of an atom in the ground state:

$$1s^2 2s^2 2p^6 3s^2 3p^4$$

This element is found in the Periodic Table in

(1) Period 4 and Group 16
(2) Period 4 and Group 14
(3) Period 3 and Group 16
(4) Period 3 and Group 14

23 Which element in Group 17 is the most active nonmetal?

(1) Br   (3) Cl
(2) I   (4) F

24 In which group of elements do the atoms gain electrons most readily?

(1) 1   (3) 16
(2) 2   (4) 18

25 What is the gram formula mass of $Na_2CO_3 \cdot 10H_2O$?

(1) 106 g   (3) 266 g
(2) 142 g   (4) 286 g

26 Which solution is the most concentrated?

(1) 0.1 mole of solute dissolved in 400 mL of solvent

(2) 0.2 mole of solute dissolved in 300 mL of solvent

(3) 0.3 mole of solute dissolved in 200 mL of solvent

(4) 0.4 mole of solute dissolved in 100 mL of solvent

27 Which salt has the greatest change in solubility between 30°C and 50°C?

(1) KNO_3 (3) $NaNO_3$
(2) KCl   (4) NaCl

28 The percent by mass of oxygen in $H_2C_2O_4$ is equal to

(1) $\frac{90}{64} \times 100$ (3) $\frac{8}{4} \times 100$
(2) $\frac{64}{90} \times 100$ (4) $\frac{4}{8} \times 100$

29 Given the reaction:

$$C_3H_8(g) + 5O_2(g) \rightarrow 3CO_2(g) + 4H_2O(g)$$

At STP, what is the total number of liters of $CO_2(g)$ produced when 5.0 liters of $C_3H_8(g)$ burns completely?

(1) 1.0   (3) 3.0
(2) 5.0   (4) 15

30 What occurs when a sample of $CO_2(s)$ changes to $CO_2(g)$?

(1) The gas has greater entropy and less order.
(2) The gas has greater entropy and more order.
(3) The gas has less entropy and less order.
(4) The gas has less entropy and more order.

31 Which reaction may be represented by the chemical equilibrium expression $K = \frac{[B]}{[A]}$?

(1) $A(aq) + 2B(aq) \rightleftarrows C(s)$
(2) $2C(s) + A(aq) \rightleftarrows B(aq)$
(3) $2C(s) \rightleftarrows A(aq) + 3B(aq)$
(4) $C(s) + B(aq) \rightleftarrows 2A(aq)$

32 A 1 M solution contains 20 grams of solute in 500 milliliters of solution. What is the mass of 1 mole of the solute?

(1) 10 g   (3) 40 g
(2) 20 g   (4) 80 g

33 The addition of a catalyst to a system at equilibrium will increase the rate of

(1) the forward reaction, only
(2) the reverse reaction, only
(3) both the forward and reverse reactions
(4) neither the forward nor reverse reaction

34 Four aluminum samples are each reacted with separate 1 M copper sulfate solutions under the same conditions of temperature and pressure. Which aluminum sample would react most rapidly?

(1) 1-gram bar of Al
(2) 1 gram of Al ribbon
(3) 1 gram of Al pellets
(4) 1 gram of Al powder

35 According to Reference Table G, the decomposition of which compound is exothermic?

(1) lead (II) oxide   (3) carbon dioxide
(2) nitrogen (II) oxide   (4) sulfur dioxide

36 Based on Reference Table L, which of the following species is the strongest electrolyte?

(1) HF   (3) HNO_3
(2) H_2S (4) HNO_2

37 Based on Reference Table L, which substance is amphoteric (amphiprotic)?

(1) HCl   (3) CH_3COOH
(2) F^- (4) HSO_4^-

38 Which aqueous solution will turn red litmus blue?

(1) $NH_3(aq)$ (3) $CO_2(aq)$
(2) $HNO_3(aq)$ (4) $H_2SO_4(aq)$

39 According to the Arrhenius theory, when a base dissolves in water it produces

(1) H^+ as the only positive ion in solution
(2) NH_4^+ as the only positive ion in solution
(3) OH^- as the only negative ion in solution
(4) CO_3^{2-} as the only negative ion in solution

40 Which compounds are both classified as electrolytes?

(1) NH_4Cl and KCl
(2) $C_6H_{12}O_6$ and CH_3OH
(3) NH_4Cl and $C_6H_{12}O_6$
(4) KCl and CH_3OH

41 Given the reaction at equilibrium:

$$C_2H_3O_2^-(aq) + H_2S(aq) \rightleftarrows$$
$$HS^-(aq) + HC_2H_3O_2(aq)$$

Which pair represents the Brönsted-Lowry bases in this reaction?

(1) $C_2H_3O_2^-(aq)$ and $H_2S(aq)$
(2) $C_2H_3O_2^-(aq)$ and $HS^-(aq)$
(3) $H_2S(aq)$ and $HC_2H_3O_2(aq)$
(4) $HS^-(aq)$ and $HC_2H_3O_2(aq)$

42 Given reactions A and B:

(A) $HCl + H_2O \rightarrow Cl^- + H_3O^+$
(B) $HCl + HS^- \rightarrow Cl^- + H_2S$

In which of the reactions can HCl be classified as a Brönsted-Lowry acid?

(1) A, only
(2) B, only
(3) both A and B
(4) neither A nor B

43 Given the reaction: $Sn^{4+} + 2e^- \rightarrow Sn^{2+}$

This reaction can be classified as

(1) a reduction reaction, because there is a decrease in oxidation number
(2) a reduction reaction, because there is an increase in oxidation number
(3) an oxidation reaction, because there is a decrease in oxidation number
(4) an oxidation reaction, because there is an increase in oxidation number

44 In which compound is the oxidation number of oxygen –1?

(1) CO
(2) CO_2
(3) H_2O
(4) H_2O_2

45 Given the reaction:

$$MnO_2(s) + 4H^+(aq) + 2Fe^{2+}(aq) \rightarrow$$
$$Mn^{2+}(aq) + 2Fe^{3+}(aq) + 2H_2O(\ell)$$

Which species is oxidized?

(1) $H^+(aq)$
(2) $H_2O(\ell)$
(3) $Fe^{2+}(aq)$
(4) $MnO_2(s)$

46 Which half-cell reaction correctly represents oxidation?

(1) $Pb^{2+} + 2e^- \rightarrow Pb$
(2) $Pb + 2e^- \rightarrow Pb^{2+}$
(3) $Pb^{2+} \rightarrow Pb + 2e^-$
(4) $Pb \rightarrow Pb^{2+} + 2e^-$

47 Which equation represents an oxidation-reduction reaction?

(1) $Zn + 2HCl \rightarrow ZnCl_2 + H_2$
(2) $Zn(OH)_2 + 2HCl \rightarrow ZnCl_2 + 2H_2O$
(3) $H_2O + NH_3 \rightarrow NH_4^+ + OH^-$
(4) $H_2O + H_2O \rightarrow H_3O^+ + OH^-$

48 When C_3H_8 burns completely in an excess of oxygen, the products formed are

(1) CO and H_2O
(2) CO_2 and H_2O
(3) CO and H_2
(4) CO_2 and H_2

49 Which formula represents acetic acid?

(1) CH_3OCH_3
(2) CH_3CH_2OH
(3) $HCOOCH_3$
(4) CH_3COOH

50 Which substances are products of a fermentation reaction?

(1) water and carbon dioxide
(2) soap and glycerol
(3) alcohol and carbon dioxide
(4) ester and water

51 A student investigated four different substances in the solid phase. The table below is a record of the characteristics (marked with an X) exhibited by each substance.

Characteristic Tested	Substance A	Substance B	Substance C	Substance D
High Melting Point	X		X	
Low Melting Point		X		X
Soluble in Water	X			X
Insoluble in Water		X	X	
Decomposed under High Heat		X		
Stable under High Heat	X		X	X
Electrolyte	X			X
Nonelectrolyte		X	X	

Which substance has characteristics most like those of an organic compound?

(1) A
(2) B
(3) C
(4) D

52 What type of reaction is represented by the equation below?

$$H-\overset{\overset{\displaystyle H}{|}}{C}=\overset{\overset{\displaystyle H}{|}}{C}-H + H_2 \longrightarrow H-\overset{\overset{\displaystyle H}{|}}{\underset{\underset{\displaystyle H}{|}}{C}}-\overset{\overset{\displaystyle H}{|}}{\underset{\underset{\displaystyle H}{|}}{C}}-H$$

(1) addition
(2) substitution
(3) esterification
(4) fermentation

53 Which structural formula represents a compound that is a member of the alkene series?

(1) $H-\overset{\overset{\displaystyle H}{|}}{\underset{\underset{\displaystyle H}{|}}{C}}-\overset{\overset{\displaystyle H}{|}}{\underset{\underset{\displaystyle H}{|}}{C}}-OH$

(2) $H-\overset{\overset{\displaystyle H}{|}}{\underset{\underset{\displaystyle H}{|}}{C}}=\overset{\overset{\displaystyle H}{|}}{\underset{\underset{\displaystyle H}{|}}{C}}-H$

(3) $H-C\equiv C-H$

(4) $H-\overset{\overset{\displaystyle H}{|}}{\underset{\underset{\displaystyle H}{|}}{C}}-\overset{\overset{\displaystyle H}{|}}{\underset{\underset{\displaystyle H}{|}}{C}}-H$

Note that questions 54 through 56 have only three choices.

54 As electrical energy is converted into heat energy, the total amount of energy in the system

(1) decreases
(2) increases
(3) remains the same

55 In a chemical reaction, as the concentrations of the reacting particles increase, the rate of reaction generally

(1) decreases
(2) increases
(3) remains the same

56 As elements in Group 15 of the Periodic Table are considered in order from top to bottom, the metallic character of each successive element generally

(1) decreases
(2) increases
(3) remains the same

Part II

This part consists of twelve groups, each containing five questions. Each group tests a major area of the course. Choose seven of these twelve groups. Be sure that you answer all five questions in each group chosen. Record the answers to these questions on the separate answer sheet in accordance with the directions on the front page of this booklet. [35]

Group 1 — Matter and Energy

If you choose this group, be sure to answer questions 57–61.

57 The diagrams below represent three 1-liter containers of gas, A, B, and C. Each container is at STP.

A	B	C
He	O_2	CO_2

Which statement correctly compares the number of molecules in the containers?

(1) Container A has the greatest number of molecules.
(2) Container B has the greatest number of molecules.
(3) Container C has the greatest number of molecules.
(4) All three containers have the same number of molecules.

58 An example of a binary compound is

(1) mercury   (3) sodium
(2) ethanol   (4) ammonia

59 A mixture of oxygen, nitrogen, and hydrogen gases exerts a total pressure of 740. mmHg at 0°C. The partial pressure of the oxygen is 200. mmHg and the partial pressure of the nitrogen is 400. mmHg. What is the partial pressure of the hydrogen gas in this mixture?

(1) 140. mmHg   (3) 400. mmHg
(2) 200. mmHg   (4) 740. mmHg

60 All atoms in a given sample of an element contain the same number of

(1) nucleons and electrons
(2) nucleons and neutrons
(3) protons and electrons
(4) protons and neutrons

61 The diagram below represents the uniform heating of a substance that is a solid at Time A.

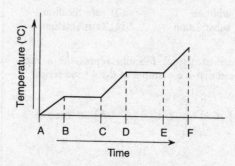

Between which times could the heat of fusion be determined?

(1) A and B   (3) C and D
(2) B and C   (4) E and F

Group 2 — Atomic Structure

If you choose this group, be sure to answer questions 62–66.

62 Which of the following radioisotopes has the shortest half-life?

(1) ^{14}C (3) ^{37}K
(2) ^{3}H (4) ^{32}P

63 What is the total number of sublevels that contain electrons in an atom of zinc in the ground state?

(1) 7   (3) 10
(2) 2   (4) 30

64 In the ground state, atoms of which of the following elements have the highest first ionization energy?

(1) boron   (3) oxygen
(2) carbon   (4) nitrogen

65 Atoms of ^{16}O, ^{17}O, and ^{18}O have the same number of

(1) neutrons, but a different number of protons
(2) protons, but a different number of neutrons
(3) protons, but a different number of electrons
(4) electrons, but a different number of protons

66 Which is the electron configuration of an atom in the excited state?

(1) $1s^1 2s^1$ (3) $1s^2 2s^2 2p^1$
(2) $1s^2 2s^1$ (4) $1s^2 2s^2 2p^2$

Group 3 — Bonding

If you choose this group, be sure to answer questions 67–71.

67 Given the unbalanced equation:

$$Li + N_2 \rightarrow Li_3N$$

When the equation is correctly balanced using smallest whole numbers, the coefficient of the lithium is

(1) 1   (3) 3
(2) 2   (4) 6

68 Which type of bond is formed between the two chlorine atoms in a chlorine molecule?

(1) polar covalent   (3) metallic
(2) nonpolar covalent   (4) ionic

69 In an aqueous solution of $Ca(NO_3)_2$, which kind of attraction exists between the solute and the solvent?

(1) molecule-ion attraction
(2) molecule-molecule attraction
(3) hydrogen bond
(4) van der Waals force

70 Which two compounds contain only polar molecules?

(1) CCl_4 and CH_4 (3) HCl and NH_3
(2) HCl and Cl_2 (4) CO and CO_2

71 When phosphorus and chlorine atoms combine to form a molecule of PCl_3, 6 electrons will be

(1) shared equally   (3) lost
(2) shared unequally   (4) gained

Group 4 — Periodic Table

If you choose this group, be sure to answer questions 72–76.

72 An atom of which element in the ground state has a complete outermost shell?

(1) He   (3) Hg
(2) Be   (4) H

73 Which sequence of elements is arranged in order of decreasing atomic covalent radii?

(1) Al, Si, P   (3) Cl, Br, I
(2) Li, Na, K   (4) N, C, B

74 Which part of the Periodic Table contains elements with the strongest metallic properties?

(1) upper left   (3) lower left
(2) upper right   (4) lower right

75 The elements in Period 3 all have the same number of

(1) valence electrons
(2) orbitals containing electrons
(3) sublevels containing electrons
(4) principal energy levels containing electrons

76 Because of its high reactivity, which element is normally obtained by the electrolysis of its fused salts?

(1) sulfur   (3) argon
(2) lithium   (4) gold

Group 5 — Mathematics of Chemistry

If you choose this group, be sure to answer questions 77–81.

77 What is the molecular formula of a compound with an empirical formula of CH and a molecular mass of 78?

(1) C_6H_6 (3) C_2H_2
(2) C_4H_{10} (4) CH

78 Which gas will diffuse at the fastest rate under the same conditions of temperature and pressure?

(1) O_2 (3) F_2
(2) N_2 (4) H_2

79 What occurs when sugar is added to water?

(1) The freezing point of the water will decrease, and the boiling point will decrease.
(2) The freezing point of the water will decrease, and the boiling point will increase.
(3) The freezing point of the water will increase, and the boiling point will decrease.
(4) The freezing point of the water will increase, and the boiling point will increase.

80 Which gas has a density of 1.54 grams per liter at STP?

(1) H_2S (3) NO
(2) CH_4 (4) CO

81 A gas has a pressure of 300. torr, a temperature of 400. K, and a volume of 50.0 milliliters. What volume will the gas have at a pressure of 150. torr and a temperature of 200. K?

(1) 12.5 mL   (3) 100. mL
(2) 50.0 mL   (4) 200. mL

Group 6 — Kinetics and Equilibrium

If you choose this group, be sure to answer questions 82–86.

82 What will change when a catalyst is added to a chemical reaction?

(1) activation energy
(2) free energy of reaction
(3) potential energy of the reactants
(4) potential energy of the products

83 According to Reference Table *M*, which of the following compounds is most soluble at 1 atmosphere and 298 K?

(1) AgBr   (3) $ZnCO_3$
(2) $CaSO_4$ (4) $PbCrO_4$

84 Which chemical reaction will always be spontaneous?

(1) an exothermic reaction in which entropy decreases
(2) an exothermic reaction in which entropy increases
(3) an endothermic reaction in which entropy decreases
(4) an endothermic reaction in which entropy increases

85 Given the reaction at equilibrium:

$$2SO_2(g) + O_2(g) \rightleftarrows 2SO_3(g) + heat$$

Which change will shift the equilibrium to the right?

(1) decreasing $[SO_2]$
(2) decreasing the pressure
(3) increasing $[O_2]$
(4) increasing the temperature

86 The graph below is a potential energy diagram of a compound which is formed from its elements.

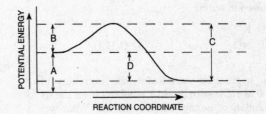

Which interval represents the heat of reaction?

(1) A   (3) C
(2) B   (4) D

Group 7 — Acids and Bases

If you choose this group, be sure to answer questions 87–91.

87 The table below shows the results produced when two drops of phenolphthalein are added to 0.1 M solutions of three salts.

Salt	Resulting Color
$NaNO_3$	colorless
KI	colorless
$NaC_2H_3O_2$	pink

Which ion hydrolyzed when the salt was dissolved in water?

(1) K^+ (3) I^-

(2) NO_3^- (4) $C_2H_3O_2^-$

88 In a titration experiment, 20. milliliters of 1.0 M HCl neutralized 10. milliliters of an NaOH solution of unknown concentration. What was the concentration of the NaOH solution?

(1) 2.5 M   (3) 1.5 M

(2) 2.0 M   (4) 0.50 M

89 What is the hydroxide ion concentration of a solution with a pH of 4?

(1) 1×10^{-4} (3) 1×10^{-10}

(2) 1×10^{-7} (4) 1×10^{-14}

90 Given the net reaction: $H^+ + OH^- \rightarrow H_2O$

This reaction is best described as

(1) neutralization   (3) hydrolysis

(2) reduction   (4) addition

91 What is the conjugate base of OH^-?

(1) H_2O (3) H_3O^+

(2) O^{2-} (4) H^+

Group 8 — Redox and Electrochemistry

If you choose this group, be sure to answer questions 92–96.

92 Which process occurs at the cathode during the electrolysis of fused KCl?

(1) the reduction of K^+ ions
(2) the oxidation of K^+ ions
(3) the reduction of Cl^- ions
(4) the oxidation of Cl^- ions

93 During the electrolysis of water, what volume of oxygen gas is produced in the same amount of time that 40.0 milliliters of hydrogen gas is produced?

(1) 10.0 mL   (3) 40.0 mL

(2) 20.0 mL   (4) 80.0 mL

94 What is the standard reduction potential (E^0) for a Mg(s) half-cell?

(1) +1.19 V   (3) –1.19 V

(2) +2.37 V   (4) –2.37 V

95 Which equation represents the half-cell reaction that occurs at the negative electrode during the electrolysis of fused calcium chloride?

(1) $Ca^{2+} \rightarrow Ca(s) + 2e^-$
(2) $Ca^{2+} + 2e^- \rightarrow Ca(s)$
(3) $2Cl^- + 2e^- \rightarrow Cl_2(g)$
(4) $2Cl^- \rightarrow Cl_2(g) + 2e^-$

96 Which metal will react spontaneously with 1 M HCl at 298 K and 1 atmosphere?

(1) Au   (3) Hg

(2) Cu   (4) Mg

Group 9 — Organic Chemistry

If you choose this group, be sure to answer questions 97–101.

97 The formation of large molecules from small molecules is an example of

(1) polymerization   (3) saponification
(2) decomposition   (4) substitution

98 What type of monohydroxy alcohol is 2-propanol?

(1) primary   (3) tertiary
(2) secondary   (4) dihydroxy

99 Which formula represents the first member of the benzene series?

(1) C_4H_8 (3) C_6H_6
(2) C_5H_{10} (4) C_7H_8

100 Which organic compound is saturated?

(1) ethene   (3) propene
(2) ethyne   (4) propane

101 In the alkane family, each member differs from the preceding member by one carbon atom and two hydrogen atoms. Such a series of hydrocarbons is called

(1) a homologous series
(2) a periodic series
(3) an actinide series
(4) a lanthanide series

Group 10 — Applications of Chemical Principles

If you choose this group, be sure to answer questions 102–106.

102 Which substance is an important source of organic chemical products and fuels?

(1) alcohol   (3) natural gas
(2) benzene   (4) petroleum

103 What kind of reaction occurs during the operation of a nickel-cadmium battery?

(1) a spontaneous redox reaction
(2) a nonspontaneous redox reaction
(3) a reduction reaction, only
(4) an oxidation reaction, only

104 The equation below represents the reaction for a lead-acid battery.

$$Pb + PbO_2 + 2H_2SO_4 \underset{\text{charge}}{\overset{\text{discharge}}{\rightleftharpoons}} 2PbSO_4 + 2H_2O$$

Which species is oxidized during the discharge of the battery?

(1) Pb   (3) $PbSO_4$
(2) PbO_2 (4) H_2SO_4

105 The contact process is used to produce

(1) iron   (3) sulfuric acid
(2) zinc   (4) nitric acid

106 Given the equation:

$$C_{11}H_{24} \xrightarrow[\text{catalyst}]{450°C} C_5H_{10} + C_4H_8 + C_2H_4 + H_2$$

Which type of reaction does this equation represent?

(1) addition   (3) hydrogenation
(2) cracking   (4) substitution

Group 11 — Nuclear Chemistry
If you choose this group, be sure to answer questions 107–111.

107 Which isotope may be used as a tracer to study the way in which an organic reaction takes place?

(1) carbon-12   (3) strontium-88
(2) carbon-14   (4) strontium-90

108 Which fissionable isotope is produced from uranium-238 in a breeder reactor?

(1) lead-206   (3) hydrogen-3
(2) cobalt-60   (4) plutonium-239

109 What is the primary result of a fission reaction?

(1) conversion of mass to energy
(2) conversion of energy to mass
(3) binding together of two heavy nuclei
(4) binding together of two light nuclei

110 Aluminum-27 is bombarded with alpha particles according to the following nuclear equation:

$$^{27}_{13}Al + ^{4}_{2}He \rightarrow X + ^{1}_{0}n$$

The radioactive element represented by X is an isotope of

(1) zinc   (3) sulfur
(2) phosphorus   (4) sodium

111 Which material is used for external shielding in some nuclear reactors?

(1) water   (3) concrete
(2) steel   (4) graphite

Group 12 — Laboratory Activities
If you choose this group, be sure to answer questions 112–116.

112 The diagram below represents a portion of a triple-beam balance.

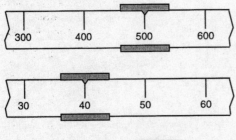

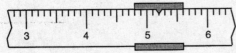

If the beams are in balance with the riders in the positions shown, what is the total mass of the object?

(1) 540.20 g   (3) 545.20 g
(2) 540.52 g   (4) 545.52 g

113 Which piece of laboratory equipment should be used to transport a hot crucible?

(1)

(2)

(3)

(4)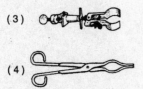

114 An 8.24-gram sample of a hydrated salt is heated until it has a constant mass of 6.20 grams. What was the percent by mass of water contained in the original sample?

(1) 14.1%   (3) 32.9%
(2) 24.8%   (4) 75.2%

115 The table below shows the color of an indicator in specific pH ranges.

Color	pH Range
Red	1–4
Orange	5–6
Green	6–7
Blue	8–10
Violet	11–14

If this indicator is used when titrating an unknown strong base by adding a strong acid, the color of the indicator will change from

(1) blue to green   (3) orange to green
(2) green to blue   (4) green to orange

116 Given the reaction: $A + B \rightarrow AB$

The table below shows student data obtained about the rate of reaction when the concentration of solution A is kept constant and the concentration of solution B is changed by adding H_2O.

Based on the data, the student should conclude

Trial	Volume of Solution A	Volume of Solution B	Volume of H₂O Added	Reaction Time
1	10 mL	10 mL	0 mL	2.8 sec
2	10 mL	5 mL	5 mL	4.9 sec
3	10 mL	3 mL	7 mL	10.4 sec

that the

(1) concentration has no effect on the reaction rate
(2) reaction rate increased when H_2O was added
(3) reaction rate increased as solution B was diluted
(4) reaction rate decreased as solution B was diluted

Sample Regents Exam 3

Answers

1. The correct answer is 4. For all liquids, vapor pressure values increase steadily as the temperature increases. The highest temperature for glycerol would give the highest vapor pressure.

2. The correct answer is 2. Since energy is a byproduct, this reaction would be known as an exothermic reaction. An endothermic reaction would show energy on the left side. The potential energy of the reactants also has to be higher than the products or the reaction won't occur.

3. The correct answer is 3. The fact that ordinary filtering and washing are all that are needed to separate the components indicates that we don't have a situation that requires an extraordinary amount of energy as would be necessary to separate the components of compounds. In addition, since our actions require several separations as opposed to one, we can't guarantee we have a homogenous mixture.

4. The correct answer is 2. The amount of heat required to change 1 gram of water by 1 degree is 1 calorie. Therefore, 100 grams of water raised 5 degrees would require 500 calories.

5. The correct answer is 4. An alpha particle consists of two protons and two neutrons.

Alpha decay of any element should be accompanied by a drop in the atomic number by 2 (the two protons) and a total mass loss of 4 amu's (the two protons and the two neutrons). Answer 4 shows radon-86 decaying to polonium-84 and a drop in mass from 222 to 218.

6. The correct answer is 1. Gas B at STP is at $0°$ C, which is a lower temperature than Gas A. The pressure on Gas B (at STP) is 1 atmosphere, which is a higher pressure than Gas A, which is at 0.5 atmosphere. This condition requires choice 1.

7. The correct answer is 3. Nucleons are the particles that reside in the nucleus and that would be only protons and neutrons.

8. The correct answer is 3. The mass of an atom is primarily the number of nucleons. This would give us nineteen protons and twenty neutrons, the sum of which equals choice 3 only.

9. The correct answer is 1. The only atom with three electrons in the 3p in the ground state is phosphorous, row 3, Group V-A.

10. The correct answer is 2. Being in the second row, a neutral atom of Neon in the ground state has two principal energy levels (completely) occupied: levels 1 and 2.

11. The correct answer is 2. Since we have ionized sodium by the removal of an electron, the energy required to do that would be called the ionization energy of the atom.

12. The correct answer is 4. The neutron is slightly heavier than the proton.

13. The correct answer is 1. Six days constitutes three half-life (two days each) time periods which means three cycles of losing half of the material. That means $\frac{1}{2} \times \frac{1}{2} \times \frac{1}{2}$, which equals $\frac{1}{8}$ of the material remaining.

14. The correct answer is 3. Comparing the electronegativities within the compounds, KF has the greatest difference of 3.2 (F = 4.0 and K = 0.8) and K and F are farthest from each other on the Periodic Table.

15. The correct answer is 4. With potassium's strong tendency to give up its one electron matched with chlorine's strong tendency to take an electron, these two would readily form ions and then bond to each other in an ionic bond.

16. The correct answer is 3. The valence of sodium is 1^+ and the valence of the polyatomic ion sulfate is listed as 2^-. Combining the two to form the compound sodium sulfate so that the net charge is zero gives us the formula found in choice 3 only. All the others do not work with the given valence numbers.

17. The correct answer is 2. The polar nature of the water molecule is such that the attraction of the (+) side (hydrogen) with the (−) side (oxygen on an adjacent molecule)—commonly called hydrogen bonds—creates strong enough associations to result in the boiling point being relatively high among liquids. Choices 3 and 4 are simply erroneous and network bonds would not occur in this type of a substance.

18. The correct answer is 2. Each hydrogen has one electron to share (a total of two between them) so that a Lewis dot diagram would show choice 2 to be the one most accurately to account for the electrons in the bonding of two hydrogens.

19. The correct answer is 3. Network solids, because their bonds exist in all directions, form substances in which the bonds are hard to break; thus, they have high melting points. The multidirectional orientation of the bonds works against malleability, water solubility, and good electrical conductivity.

20. The correct answer is 1. At STP, potassium is neither a molecular solid nor an ionic solid, both of which require electron movement. This is not mentioned and so we must be dealing with the elemental potassium, which exists in a metallic form.

21. The correct answer is 1. The modern periodic table is arranged around the concept

of changing properties due to the difference in the number of protons, which also stands for the atomic number; thus the answer is choice 1. The older tables were arranged around mass and oxidation number was never used as a way to organize the elements.

22. The correct answer is 3. The involvement of three principal energy levels and sixteen electrons makes this element (sulfur) fit choice 3 only. It is on row 3 and in group 16.

23. The correct answer is 4. Fluorine, being at the top of Group 17, has its electrons closer to its nucleus than any of the others in the group. This makes it the most active of the halogens—the most electronegative.

24. The correct answer is 3. Group 18 elements are the inert gases and, therefore, do not take or give electrons. Groups 1 and 2 are named so because they have that many (one and two, respectively) electrons in their outer energy level, meaning they easily give up those electrons. Group 16 elements, therefore are most likely in this list to take up electrons.

25. The correct answer is 4. The mass of all elements, including the ten water molecules attached, total up to 286, or choice 4.

26. The correct answer is 4. Using the formula to determine concentration (mole/Liter of solvent) gives us choice 4 as the most concentrated of the choices.

27. The correct answer is 1. Potassium nitrate has the greatest change in solubility from 30°C to 50°C ($\frac{\sim 48g}{100g}$ of H_2O) according to graph D—its curve has the steepest slope, which is a faster way to find the answer.

28. The correct answer is 2. The total mass of the molecule is 90 and the mass of the oxygen in it is 64 (16×4). When we compare those two numbers, we get an answer of $\frac{64}{90} \times 100$, or choice 2.

29. The correct answer is 4. The molar ratio of propane (C_3H_8) consumed to carbon dioxide (CO_2) produced is 1:3. If 5 liters of propane burn completely, 3 times that, or 15 liters, of carbon dioxide is formed, because for gases the molar and volume ratios are the same.

30. The correct answer is 1. Going from the solid to the gaseous state of any substance increases random, chaotic movement or entropy resulting in less order. When CO_2 goes from solid to gas, the choice that describes this situation best is choice 1. The other choices have either one or both stated incorrectly.

31. The correct answer is 2. The mathematical expression for the equilibrium constant K has product concentrations multiplied together, each raised to the power of its integer or half-integer coefficient in the balanced equation, the entire product divided by reactants following the same

rule, but without any solids or liquids (in the case of a liquid, only if the liquid is the solvent) appearing in the formula.

32. The correct answer is 3. If 20 g of the solute makes a 1M solution with 500 mL of solution (and the formula is 1M = 1 mole/L of solution) then doubling the solution amount, as well as the solute, thus raises the amount of solution to 1 L and raises the top part of the ratio to 1 mole. Since that is 40g, 1 mole of solute equals 40g.

33. The correct answer is 3. Catalysts increase the speed at which a chemical reaction reaches the equilibrium state by lowering the activation energies of both the forward and reverse reactions. Catalysts do nothing to the actual position of equilibrium (and hence do not change the value of K for that reaction). Remembering that at equilibrium the forward and reverse reaction rates have equalized, the only thing a catalyst could do so that it does not affect the position of equilibrium is to speed up both forward and reverse rates, as it always does.

34. The correct answer is 4. The powder form of the reactant will have the most surface area, meaning it will encounter the highest number of collisions of any of the other forms of the substance. This ensures that the reaction will proceed faster than the reactions with the other forms of aluminum.

35. The correct answer is 2. The measure of an exothermic reaction is a $\Delta H < 0$. This means that rather than adding energy to its products, the reaction subtracts it, i.e., releases the energy to the environment. By contrast, an endothermic reaction has a $\Delta H > 0$, i.e., it adds energy to the products, thereby absorbing it from the environment as evidenced by a positive ΔH. This is a table of Formation Energies; therefore, we reverse the sign for decomposition, and doing so makes choice 2 have the only negative ΔH of decompositions. Therefore it is the exothermic choice.

36. The correct answer is 3. With a large K_a, HNO_3 disassociates with the largest number of ions in aqueous solution. This is an ideal setting for being an electrolyte, a good conductor of electricity. Having the largest number of charged particles in solution means this species will be a good electrolyte. All of the other choices have a relatively small K_a—first HNO_2, followed by HF, and the smallest being H_2S.

37. The correct answer is 4. HSO_4^- appears in two places on the chart. Its K_a of 1×10^{-2} as a conjugate acid places it in a good position to donate H^+, and its K_a of "large" as a conjugate base places it in a good position to receive H^+. None of the other choices show this kind of activity according to the chart. This makes HSO_4^- an amphoteric (or amphiprotic, meaning it can both donate and receive H^+) species.

38. The correct answer is 1. An aqueous solution of NH^3 acts as a base and bases turn red litmus to blue. All of the other choices act as acids in aqueous solution.

39. The correct answer is 3. The definition of an Arrhenius's base is satisfied by choice 3. Choice 1, the only other reasonable answer, is the Arrhenius's definition of an acid.

40. The correct answer is 1. Only the substances listed in choice 1 will dissociate in aqueous solution to form ions, which conduct electricity. All the other choices have one or both substances as covalent compounds which will not dissociate in aqueous solution, at least not to form electrolytes.

41. The correct answer is 2. These two substances, being negatively charged, can accept H^+, the definition of a Brönsted-Lowry base. $HC_2H_3O_2$ cannot qualify since it has already accepted the H^+. The same is true of the H_2S.

42. The correct answer is 3. In both reactions A and B, HCl has donated an H^+, satisfying the definition of a Brönsted-Lowry acid.

43. The correct answer is 1. Clearly, the tin ion has gained electrons, which means it has been reduced, resulting in a decrease in the oxidation number from +4 to +2.

44. The correct answer is 4. Since the oxidation number of hydrogen in the metal (first) position in a compound is most always +1, then H_2O_2 is the only compound (total charges = 0) where a +2 for 2 hydrogens can be balanced by a −2 for 2 oxygens; only in this situation does each oxygen have an oxidation number of −1.

45. The correct answer is 3. Only the iron, in solution, has lost an electron when we go from left to right in this reaction and has, therefore, been oxidized. As a reactant, it has an oxidation number of +2, and as a product, it has an oxidation number of +3, indicating it has lost an electron.

46. The correct answer is 4. Placing electrons on the right side of the equation correctly shows the species has lost them (oxidation has occurred). Now we must show the lead oxidation number as reflecting this loss. Lead by itself would be Pb^o, while Pb^{+2} indicates a loss of two electrons, which most closely matches choice 4.

47. The correct answer is 1. The only reaction in which oxidation numbers are changed is reaction 1. While choices 3 and 4 look like the numbers are changed, a closer inspection shows that, while charges are changed on the ions, the oxidation numbers of each element remain the same. Choice 2 is a double replacement reaction where oxidation numbers, again, remain the same.

48. The correct answer is 2. The products of this reaction are CO_2 and H_2O, as well as

approximately 2043 kJ of energy. Hydrogen is not a product because that would be combusted also in the presence of oxygen to form H_2O.

49. The correct answer is 4. The correct way to represent acetic acid is in choice 4. While choice 3 has the same formula, the representing of the organic acid complex as HCOO as shown in choice 3 is incorrect. The COOH in choice 4 is more correct.

50. The correct answer is 3. The incomplete metabolism of a glucose molecule results in the removal of a carbon dioxide molecule and the rearrangement of the remaining complex into an alcohol. The other choices aren't even remotely related to fermentation or are wrong.

51. The correct answer is 2. Organic compounds are typically nonelectrolytes which allows the choice of B or C. Since organic compounds have low melting points and are unstable at high temperatures, only choice 2 is left.

52. The correct answer is 1. By the addition of a hydrogen molecule, the double bond in ethene is transformed with the result being a molecule of ethane. This is an addition reaction. We are not substituting or forming esters, nor are we fermenting anything here.

53. The correct answer is 2. Alkenes are defined as having at least one double bond, and choice 2 is the only structural formula that shows a double bond.

54. The correct answer is 3. The law of conservation of mass and energy dictates that energy is not lost from the system but only converted from one form to the other in a reaction. "The system" in this case can be as large as the universe, so energy would not be reduced or increased but, as previously stated, merely converted with the total amount remaining the same in the system.

55. The correct answer is 2. One of the factors that affects the rate of a chemical reaction is the number of reactant particles available. The more particles, the usually faster the reaction: choice 2.

56. The correct answer is 2. At the top of Group 15, nitrogen and phosphorus are nonmetals, further down Group 15, arsenic and antimony are semimetals and at the bottom of the group, bismuth has metallic properties. The correct answer must be choice number 2.

57. None of the answer choices given are correct. Avogadro's Law—the amount/volume relationship—says that equal volumes of gases under the same conditions contain the same number of particles. But He is not a molecule! Sometimes you must read between the lines and overlook question errors to solve a problem.

58. The correct answer is 4. A binary compound contains two elements and ammonia at NH_3 is the only one on the list that qualifies. Choices 1 and 3 are single ele-

ments and choice 2 is a compound with three elements in it.

59. The correct answer is 1. Dalton's Law of Partial Pressure says that each gas contributes to the total pressure in a mixture of gases. The total pressure in this question is 740 mmHg, with oxygen and nitrogen both contributing for a total of 600 mmHg, leaving 140 mmHg for the remaining gas, hydrogen.

60. The correct answer is 3. Some of the atoms of an element may differ in the number of neutrons they have. This makes them the same atom but different isotopes of that atom. If the question refers to atoms, then only the protons and the electrons will be the same for all of them because different isotopes of an atom are still the same atom.

61. The correct answer is 2. If the substance is a solid at A (and all the way up to B), then at point B, the substance would be changing from the solid state to the liquid state, which is the point at which the heat of fusion could be measured.

62. The correct answer is 3. Table H shows that K-37 has a half life of 1.2 seconds.

63. The correct answer is 1. Zinc, element number 30, has seven sublevels containing electrons in the ground state. They are $1s^2$, $2s^2$, $2p^6$, $3s^2$, $3p^6$, $4s^2$, and $3d^{10}$.

64. The correct answer is 4. In the ground state, nitrogen has one electron in each of the 3p-suborbitals, making it very stable against removal of a first electron. In addition, the electrons in those suborbitals are equally distant from the nucleus. A close second is oxygen, but number 4 is the correct answer.

65. The correct answer is 2. These formulae all represent isotopes of oxygen, and as such, all have the same number of protons (in order to be oxygen, they must) but different masses due to the different number of neutrons in their respective nuclei.

66. The correct answer is 1. This must be the answer because while this atom only has two electrons, they should both be in the 1s suborbital before any go into the 2s under normal conditions. The only explanation for what we see is an atom in the excited state wherein an electron has been pushed up to a higher energy level.

67. The correct answer is 4. Placing a 2 in front of the Li_3N helps us, by inspection, to account for the nitrogen, and that requires us to put a 6 in front of the Li on the left to account for all the lithium.

68. The correct answer is 2. With the mostly equal distribution of the level 3 electrons after covalent bonding of the atoms, no clear separation of charge exists in the chlorine molecule, which creates a nonpolar covalent bond.

69. The correct answer is 1. This is another ambiguous question because of the presence of the nitrogen in the solute. When water dissolves an ionic compound, it is because the attractive forces between the water molecules and the ions in solution produces a lower energy and higher entropy situation than that of an undissolved ionic solid just sitting at the bottom of the water container. This is by definition a molecule-ion attraction. But technically, it is also an attraction with hydrogen bonds, between the H in water and the N in the nitrate ions. So choices 1 and 3 are both correct, with choice 1 being more proper.

70. The correct answer is 3. Both HCl and NH_3 in their formation achieve a definite separation of charge on their respective molecules formed.

71. The correct answer is 2. Covalent bonds share electrons, and only covalent bonds between two atoms of the same element will share those electrons equally. Hence unequal sharing is the answer because each covalent bond will have three electrons, for a total of six. No electrons are lost or gained by the compound in its formation.

72. The correct answer is 1. Helium, the first member of the inert gases, has its outermost shell completed in the ground state. This is the hallmark of the group: complete outer shells.

73. The correct answer is 1. The atoms of the elements in choices 2 and 3, in the order they are listed, are larger and larger in size, which means the electrons are getting farther from the nucleus. This makes any bonds formed weaker, and weaker resulting in the lengths of these bonds being longer and longer. In choice 4, each atom listed has fewer electrons than the previous atom, similarly making for weaker and weaker (longer and longer) bonds. Choice 1 is the only one in which we are adding electrons, making the length of the bonds shorter and shorter (stronger and stronger).

74. The correct answer is 3. As one progresses in the direction of the lower left of the periodic table, one finds increasingly reactive metals. With the outermost electron being farthest from the nucleus, as you travel to the lower left, those atoms give up that electron (e.g., Rb and Cs) quite readily.

75. The correct answer is 4. Orbitals and sublevels describe divisions of the principal energy level and differ among those elements in a row (period). These elements add an electron as you progress across the row, so they vary in the number of valence electrons. The answer is principal energy levels, which are the same for all of the elements all the way across the period.

76. The correct answer is 2. Lithium has the highest reactivity of the elements listed. Argon forms no salts, gold rarely does, and sulfur is a nonmetal.

77. The correct answer is 1. With an empirical ratio of 1:1 and a formula mass of 78, we must search for a molecular formula that reflects these two facts, and C_6H_6 satisfies the numbers.

78. The correct answer is 4. Since mass is a definite property of gases, the lightest one will respond more rapidly to the influences on it. Given equal temperatures, the molecules of hydrogen, being the lightest of the choices, will diffuse the fastest.

79. The correct answer is 2. The addition of a substance to water affects its colligative properties or the depression of the freezing point and the raising of the boiling point. Therefore, the sugar will affect both in the way indicated in choice 2.

80. The correct answer is 1. With a density of 1.54 grams per liter, a mole of H_2S that would occupy 22.4 L would have a mass of approximately 34 grams. Thirty-four grams divided by 22 L would make the density approximately 1.54 grams per liter.

81. The correct answer is 2. The pressure and the temperature changes offset each other and make the new volume identical to the original. The pressure is decreased by a factor of 2, which will increase the volume by 2, making the volume 100 mL at this point. The temperature is reduced by a factor of 2, which reduces the volume by the same factor, bringing it back to a final volume of 50 mL.

82. The correct answer is 1. The purpose of a catalyst is to change the energy needed for a reaction by either raising or lowering the activation energy. The other choices are not possible because the amount of energy in a reaction is set by the materials involved; the catalyst just changes the starting conditions.

83. The correct answer is 3. $CaSO_4$ has the largest K_{sp} among the choices listed. However, as we saw in problem number 82, only if each compound will break up into exactly the same total number of ions can we compare the solubility product constants directly to arrive at our answer. In this problem, all compounds do dissolve into just two total ions, one cation and one anion.

84. The correct answer is 2. The energy given off by an exothermic reaction will help it to be self-sustaining (spontaneous) and will always contribute to the randomness (entropy) of the events surrounding the reaction. From $\Delta G = \Delta H - T\Delta S$ and remembering that T is always positive, a negative ΔH coupled with a positive ΔS will always yield $\Delta G < 0$.

85. The correct answer is 4. Le Châtelier's principle says that in a system at equilibrium, the reaction, if disturbed, will shift in the direction that tends to reduce the effect of the disturbance. Since energy (heat) is written as a product in this reaction, adding heat (increasing the temperature) will drive the reaction to the left, to

use up the extra heat. Decreasing the concentration of any reactant will drive the reaction to the left, to produce more of that reactant. Decreasing the pressure will drive the reaction to the left because there are more reactant gas moles than product gas moles, and the pressure decrease allows for more gases to be produced to bring the pressure back up to its previous value.

86. The correct answer is 4. The difference between the energy level of the reactants and the products is the heat given off as a result of the reaction occurring. B is the activation energy, and C is the total energy.

87. The correct answer is 4. $NaNO_3$ and KI are both salts of strong bases and strong acids and, therefore, will show a neutral reaction to the indicator. $NaC_2H_3O_2$ is a salt of a strong base and a weak acid. The acetate complex will, therefore, accept H+ ions from water, making the solution react to the indicator as a base due to the OH^- ions generated.

88. The correct answer is 2. The volume times the molarity of the acid should equal the volume times the molarity of the base for neutralization to occur in titration. Given the numbers achieved, the concentration of the NaOH must be 2.0M.

89. The correct answer is 3. If the pH of the solution is 4, then the H^+ concentration is 1×10^{-4}, which makes the OH^- concentra-

tion equal to 1×10^{-10} since together, the concentrations must equal 1×10^{-14}. Although the question did not state it, we are to assume that the solvent is H_2O—otherwise, the question is meaningless.

90. The correct answer is 1. The combining of H+ and OH– ions into neutral water makes this a neutralization reaction. Reduction and hydrolysis both would be more like the reverse, if anything, and this is too complex for it to be simple addition of substances.

91. The correct answer is 2. The conjugate base of any species given must be that species minus one proton, H+. Taking away this ion from hydroxide yields the highly reactive oxide conjugate base.

92. The correct answer is 1. The cathode is always where reduction occurs, the electrons coming from the anode through the wire connecting the electrodes, and the ions coming from the solution as they migrate towards the cathode. In this case the only ion that could be reduced would be the cation K^+. Chloride would never take on a second electron to make Cl_2^-.

93. The correct answer is 2. In the electrolysis of water, the production of hydrogen is twice that of oxygen, which gives us the formula H_2O.

94. The correct answer is 4. The standard reduction potential for a Mg(s) half-cell has been measured to be −2.37 V. There is

no need to have to decide on the sign of the number—from table N the standard potentials can be read directly regardless of whether the question says Mg^{2+} or $Mg(S)$.

95. The correct answer is 2. At the negative electrode, the calcium picks up two electrons, is reduced, and is, therefore, deposited as solid calcium. For 1, the + 2e– should be on the left side. The Cl reaction would occur at the positive electrode in choice 4.

96. The correct answer is 4. From Table N, we see that magnesium is the only metal of the four choices whose standard reduction potential is below that of hydrogen. That means that H+ will react spontaneously with Mg metal, oxidizing the metal.

97. The correct answer is 1. The definition of polymerization is the formation of larger and larger molecules from small molecules.

98. The correct answer is 2. 2-propanol is a secondary monohydroxyl alcohol since, as the name indicates, the hydroxyl group is added to the second C-group and not to the end. In order to be a primary, the –OH would have to be added to the end of the molecule.

99. The correct answer is 3. The benzene series starts with a straightforward benzene ring. Hydrogen atoms are attached where a bond is available. This means each

carbon, having three bonds within the ring structure, has one more bond available for hydrogen attachment making the formula that of choice 3.

100. The correct answer is 4. The naming of hydrocarbons with all single (saturated) bonds must always end with "-ane," which makes propane the only choice available. The "-enes" and the "-ynes" are all unsaturated forms.

101. The correct answer is 1. The word *homologous* suggests that substances are related in some way but are not exact copies. Actinide and lanthanide are places on the periodic table that extend the list of atoms and while we can add specific structures to the alkanes, the process is not called a periodic anything.

102. The correct answer is 4. It is well known that petroleum is, in some way, the source for thousands of chemical products and fuels. In fact, the other three choices all come from petroleum.

103. The correct answer is 1. The use of any battery involves a spontaneous reduction-oxidation of the involved chemicals. It must continue to proceed once it has started, so choices 2, 3, and 4 are eliminated.

104. The correct answer is 1. The elemental lead goes from Pb^o to Pb^{+2} on the right side. This is an indication of a loss of electrons or oxidation. The lead in choice 3 stays the same, the Pb in choice 2 is

reduced, and the components of H_2SO_4 are not changed.

105. The correct answer is 3. The process used to make sulfuric acid is known, more fully, as contact catalysis.

106. The correct answer is 2. This equation denotes the high temperature breakup of $C_{11}H_{24}$ into smaller subunits, a process commonly called cracking. There is no substitution nor addition, and there is certainly no addition of hydrogen (also called hydrogenation) to the molecule before it is reacted with a catalyst.

107. The correct answer is 2. Carbon-14 is most commonly used as a radioactive tracer in experiments involving organic reactions. Strontium is, at best, a trace element in living systems.

108. The correct answer is 4. Breeder reactors are designed to change U-238 into plutonium-239.

109. The correct answer is 1. A fission reaction will bombard a fissionable material with free neutrons and in so doing will convert a small amount of mass into energy, mostly for heating water to steam to make electricity in nuclear power plants.

110. The correct answer is 2. The element formed by this reaction will have an atomic number of 15 as noted by the combining of aluminum (number 13) and the two protons from helium, (number 2). This element will be phosphorous-30.

111. The correct answer is 1. The internal mechanism, i.e., directly adjacent to the reaction, for control of the reaction is a series of rods composed of graphite, boron or both. External to this is usually a large pool of water: The correct choice is 1.

112. The correct answer is 3. Adding up the numbers that each pointer indicates, we get 545.20 g. Choices 2 and 4 contain too many significant digits, and choice 1 forgot the 5 on the last scale.

113. The correct answer is 4. The lab equipment used to pick up a hot crucible needs to keep one's fingers as far away from the crucible as possible. Choice 1 is a tweezer-like device for picking up small items, choice 2 is used for picking up and holding test tubes, and choice 3 is a clamp for holding items such as test tubes, flasks, or the like on a ring stand.

114. The correct answer is 2. The difference between the mass before heating and after heating will be the quantity of water driven off by the heating. Dividing this by the mass of the original sample will give the percent of water driven off from (or that was a part of) the original sample. In this case the answer is approximately 24.8 percent.

115. The correct answer is 1. Initially, in the strong base, the best choice indicates a color of violet will be present because strong bases are at high pH (unless the base is present in such small amounts that

it cannot produce enough OH- for a resulting high pH). Titrating with a strong acid will gradually change that toward green, and therefore blue-violet-green should be the color progression. Blue to green is one of the choices—choice 1. All other choices do not fit the strong-acid-into- the-strong-base scenario.

116. The correct answer is 4. The table shows that diluting the concentration of B increased the time of reaction, which is a decrease in the rate of change of the concentrations with time. Hence choice 4 is the only correct statement of this effect.

Sample Regents Exam 4—June 1997

Part I

Answer all 56 questions in this part. [65]

Directions (1–56): For *each* statement or question, select the word or expression that, of those given, best completes the statement or answers the question. Record your answer on the separate answer sheet in accordance with the directions on the front page of this booklet.

1 Which Kelvin temperature is equal to –73°C?

(1) 100 K   (3) 200 K
(2) 173 K   (4) 346 K

2 A substance that is composed only of atoms having the same atomic number is classified as

(1) a compound
(2) an element
(3) a homogeneous mixture
(4) a heterogeneous mixture

3 At which temperature will water boil when the external pressure is 17.5 torr?

(1) 14.5°C   (3) 20°C
(2) 16.5°C   (4) 100°C

4 At which point do a liquid and a solid exist at equilibrium?

(1) sublimation point
(2) vaporization point
(3) boiling point
(4) melting point

5 When 7.00 moles of gas *A* and 3.00 moles of gas *B* are combined, the total pressure exerted by the gas mixture is 760. mmHg. What is the partial pressure exerted by gas *A* in this mixture?

(1) 76.0 mmHg   (3) 532 mmHg
(2) 228 mmHg   (4) 760 mmHg

6 Which radioactive emanations have a charge of 2+?

(1) alpha particles   (3) gamma rays
(2) beta particles   (4) neutrons

7 Which symbols represent atoms that are isotopes of each other?

(1) ^{14}C and ^{14}N (3) ^{131}I and ^{131}I
(2) ^{16}O and ^{18}O (4) ^{222}Rn and ^{222}Ra

8 Which orbital notation correctly represents the outermost principal energy level of a nitrogen atom in the ground state?

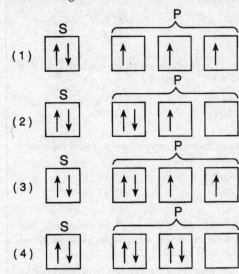

9 The atomic mass of an element is defined as the weighted average mass of that element's

(1) most abundant isotope
(2) least abundant isotope
(3) naturally occurring isotopes
(4) radioactive isotopes

10 When electrons in an atom in an excited state fall to lower energy levels, energy is

(1) absorbed, only
(2) released, only
(3) neither released nor absorbed
(4) both released and absorbed

11 A neutron has approximately the same mass as

(1) an alpha particle   (3) an electron
(2) a beta particle   (4) a proton

12 What is the formula for sodium oxalate?

(1) NaClO

(3) $Na_2C_2O_4$

(2) Na_2O

(4) $NaC_2H_3O_2$

13 Given the unbalanced equation:

$$Al + O_2 \rightarrow Al_2O_3$$

When this equation is completely balanced using smallest whole numbers, what is the sum of the coefficients?

(1) 9

(3) 5

(2) 7

(4) 4

14 One mole of which substance contains a total of 6.02×10^{23} atoms?

(1) Li

(3) O_2

(2) NH_3

(4) CO_2

15 Which formula represents a molecular substance?

(1) CaO

(3) Li_2O

(2) CO

(4) Al_2O_3

16 In an aqueous solution of an ionic salt, the oxygen atom of the water molecule is attracted to the

(1) negative ion of the salt, due to oxygen's partial positive charge

(2) negative ion of the salt, due to oxygen's partial negative charge

(3) positive ion of the salt, due to oxygen's partial positive charge

(4) positive ion of the salt, due to oxygen's partial negative charge

17 What is the empirical formula of the compound whose molecular formula is P_4O_{10}?

(1) PO

(3) P_2O_5

(2) PO_2

(4) P_8O_{20}

18 Which sequence of Group 18 elements demonstrates a gradual *decrease* in the strength of the van der Waals forces?

(1) $Ar(\ell)$, $Kr(\ell)$, $Ne(\ell)$, $Xe(\ell)$

(2) $Kr(\ell)$, $Xe(\ell)$, $Ar(\ell)$, $Ne(\ell)$

(3) $Ne(\ell)$, $Ar(\ell)$, $Kr(\ell)$, $Xe(\ell)$

(4) $Xe(\ell)$, $Kr(\ell)$, $Ar(\ell)$, $Ne(\ell)$

19 In the ground state, atoms of the elements in Group 15 of the Periodic Table all have the same number of

(1) filled principal energy levels

(2) occupied principal energy levels

(3) neutrons in the nucleus

(4) electrons in the valence shell

20 Which elements have the most similar chemical properties?

(1) K and Na

(3) K and Ca

(2) K and Cl

(4) K and S

21 Which three groups of the Periodic Table contain the most elements classified as metalloids (semimetals)?

(1) 1, 2, and 13

(3) 14, 15, and 16

(2) 2, 13, and 14

(4) 16, 17, and 18

22 In which classification is an element placed if the outermost 3 sublevels of its atoms have a ground state electron configuration of $3p^6 3d^5 4s^2$?

(1) alkaline earth metals

(2) transition metals

(3) metalloids (semimetals)

(4) nonmetals

23 A diatomic element with a high first ionization energy would most likely be a

(1) nonmetal with a high electronegativity

(2) nonmetal with a low electronegativity

(3) metal with a high electronegativity

(4) metal with a low electronegativity

24 As the elements in Period 3 are considered from left to right, they tend to

(1) lose electrons more readily and increase in metallic character

(2) lose electrons more readily and increase in nonmetallic character

(3) gain electrons more readily and increase in metallic character

(4) gain electrons more readily and increase in nonmetallic character

25 An atom of an element has 28 innermost electrons and 7 outermost electrons. In which period of the Periodic Table is this element located?

(1) 5   (3) 3
(2) 2   (4) 4

26 Which solution is the most concentrated?

(1) 1 mole of solute dissolved in 1 liter of solution
(2) 2 moles of solute dissolved in 3 liters of solution
(3) 6 moles of solute dissolved in 4 liters of solution
(4) 4 moles of solute dissolved in 8 liters of solution

27 What is the gram formula mass of K_2CO_3?

(1) 138 g   (3) 99 g
(2) 106 g   (4) 67 g

28 What is the total number of atoms contained in 2.00 moles of nickel?

(1) 58.9   (3) 6.02×10^{23}
(2) 118   (4) 1.20×10^{24}

29 Given the reaction at STP:

$$2KClO_3(s) \rightarrow 2KCl(s) + 3O_2(g)$$

What is the total number of liters of $O_2(g)$ produced from the complete decomposition of 0.500 mole of $KClO_3(s)$?

(1) 11.2 L   (3) 44.8 L
(2) 16.8 L   (4) 67.2 L

30 What is the percent by mass of oxygen in magnesium oxide, MgO?

(1) 20%   (3) 50%
(2) 40%   (4) 60%

31 A solution in which the crystallizing rate of the solute equals the dissolving rate of the solute must be

(1) saturated   (3) concentrated
(2) unsaturated   (4) dilute

32 Which statement explains why the speed of some chemical reactions is increased when the surface area of the reactant is increased?

(1) This change increases the density of the reactant particles.
(2) This change increases the concentration of the reactant.
(3) This change exposes more reactant particles to a possible collision.
(4) This change alters the electrical conductivity of the reactant particles.

33 According to Reference Table G, which compound forms exothermically?

(1) hydrogen fluoride   (3) ethene
(2) hydrogen iodide   (4) ethyne

34 The potential energy diagram shown below represents the reaction $A + B \rightarrow AB$.

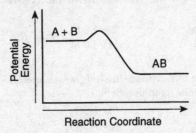

Which statement correctly describes this reaction?

(1) It is endothermic and energy is absorbed.
(2) It is endothermic and energy is released.
(3) It is exothermic and energy is absorbed.
(4) It is exothermic and energy is released.

35 Given the reaction at equilibrium:

$$N_2(g) + 3H_2(g) \rightleftarrows 2NH_3(g)$$

Increasing the concentration of $N_2(g)$ will increase the forward reaction rate due to

(1) a decrease in the number of effective collisions
(2) an increase in the number of effective collisions
(3) a decrease in the activation energy
(4) an increase in the activation energy

36 Based on Reference Table L, which of the following aqueous solutions is the best conductor of electricity?

(1) 0.1 M HF   (3) 0.1 M H_2SO_4

(2) 0.1 M H_2S (4) 0.1 M H_3PO_4

37 Which substance is classified as an Arrhenius base?

(1) HCl   (3) $LiNO_3$

(2) NaOH   (4) $KHCO_3$

38 The conjugate acid of the HS^- ion is

(1) H^+ (3) H_2O

(2) S^{2-} (4) H_2S

39 If 20. milliliters of 1.0 M HCl was used to completely neutralize 40. milliliters of an NaOH solution, what was the molarity of the NaOH solution?

(1) 0.50 M   (3) 1.5 M

(2) 2.0 M   (4) 4.0 M

40 According to Reference Table L, which species is amphoteric (amphiprotic)?

(1) HCl   (3) HSO_4^-

(2) HNO_2 (4) H_2SO_4

41 In the reaction $H_2O + CO_3^{2-} \rightleftarrows OH^- + HCO_3^-$, the two Brönsted-Lowry acids are

(1) H_2O and OH^- (3) CO_3^{2-} and OH^-

(2) H_2O and HCO_3^- (4) CO_3^{2-} and HCO_3^-

42 What happens to reducing agents in chemical reactions?

(1) Reducing agents gain protons.

(2) Reducing agents gain electrons.

(3) Reducing agents are oxidized.

(4) Reducing agents are reduced.

43 What is the oxidation number of carbon in $NaHCO_3$?

(1) +6   (3) −4

(2) +2   (4) +4

44 Which statement correctly describes a redox reaction?

(1) The oxidation half-reaction and the reduction half-reaction occur simultaneously.

(2) The oxidation half-reaction occurs before the reduction half-reaction.

(3) The oxidation half-reaction occurs after the reduction half-reaction.

(4) The oxidation half-reaction occurs spontaneously but the reduction half-reaction does not.

45 Given the redox reaction:

$$Co(s) + PbCl_2(aq) \rightarrow CoCl_2(aq) + Pb(s)$$

Which statement correctly describes the oxidation and reduction that occur?

(1) Co(s) is oxidized and Cl^-(aq) is reduced.

(2) Co(s) is oxidized and Pb^{2+}(aq) is reduced.

(3) Co(s) is reduced and Cl^-(aq) is oxidized.

(4) Co(s) is reduced and Pb^{2+}(aq) is oxidized.

46 Which half-reaction correctly represents reduction?

(1) $Cr^{3+} + 3e^- \rightarrow Cr(s)$

(2) $Cr^{3+} \rightarrow Cr(s) + 3e^-$

(3) $Cr(s) \rightarrow Cr^{3+} + 3e^-$

(4) $Cr(s) + 3e^- \rightarrow Cr^{3+}$

47 Which statement best describes how a salt bridge maintains electrical neutrality in the half-cells of an electrochemical cell?

(1) It prevents the migration of electrons.

(2) It permits the migration of ions.

(3) It permits the two solutions to mix completely.

(4) It prevents the reaction from occurring spontaneously.

48 What is the name of a compound that has the molecular formula C_6H_6?

(1) butane   (3) benzene

(2) butene   (4) butyne

49 The fermentation of $C_6H_{12}O_6$ will produce CO_2 and

(1) $C_3H_5(OH)_3$ (3) $Ca(OH)_2$
(2) C_2H_5OH (4) $Cr(OH)_3$

50 Which is the correct name for the substance below?

(1) ethanol   (3) ethane
(2) ethyne   (4) ethene

51 Which structural formula represents an organic acid?

52 In a molecule of CH_4, the hydrogen atoms are spatially oriented toward the corners of a regular

(1) pyramid   (3) square
(2) tetrahedron   (4) rectangle

Note that questions 53 through 56 have only three choices.

53 Given the reaction at equilibrium:

$$N_2(g) + O_2(g) \rightleftarrows 2NO(g)$$

As the concentration of $N_2(g)$ increases, the concentration of $O_2(g)$ will

(1) decrease
(2) increase
(3) remain the same

54 As the temperature of a sample of a radioactive element decreases, the half-life of the element will

(1) decrease
(2) increase
(3) remain the same

55 As ice cools from 273 K to 263 K, the average kinetic energy of its molecules will

(1) decrease
(2) increase
(3) remain the same

56 As the hydrogen ion concentration of an aqueous solution increases, the hydroxide ion concentration of this solution will

(1) decrease
(2) increase
(3) remain the same

Part II

This part consists of twelve groups, each containing five questions. Each group tests a major area of the course. Choose seven of these twelve groups. Be sure that you answer all five questions in each group chosen. Record the answers to these questions on the separate answer sheet in accordance with the directions on the front page of this booklet. [35]

Group 1 — Matter and Energy

If you choose this group, be sure to answer questions 57–61.

57 The phase change represented by the equation $I_2(s) \rightarrow I_2(g)$ is called

(1) sublimation   (3) melting
(2) condensation   (4) boiling

58 The graph below represents the relationship between temperature and time as heat is added uniformly to a substance, starting when the substance is a solid below its melting point.

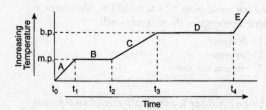

Which portions of the graph represent times when heat is absorbed and potential energy increases while kinetic energy remains constant?

(1) A and B   (3) A and C
(2) B and D   (4) C and D

59 The heat of fusion is defined as the energy required at constant temperature to change 1 unit mass of a

(1) gas to a liquid   (3) solid to a gas
(2) gas to a solid   (4) solid to a liquid

60 Given the equation:

$$2Na + 2H_2O \rightarrow 2NaOH + H_2$$

Which substance in this equation is a binary compound?

(1) Na   (3) H_2O
(2) H_2 (4) NaOH

61 At STP, 1 liter of $O_2(g)$ and 1 liter of Ne(g) have the same

(1) mass
(2) density
(3) number of atoms
(4) number of molecules

Group 2 — Atomic Structure

If you choose this group, be sure to answer questions 62–66.

62 The diagram below represents radiation passing through an electric field.

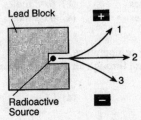

Lead Block

+

1

2

3

Radioactive
Source

−

Which type of emanation is represented by the arrow labeled 2?

(1) alpha particle   (3) positron
(2) beta particle   (4) gamma radiation

63 Which sample will decay *least* over a period of 30 days? [Refer to Reference Table *H*.]

(1) 10 g of Au-198   (3) 10 g of P-32
(2) 10 g of I-131   (4) 10 g of Rn-222

64 A particle has a mass of 1.0 atomic mass unit. What is the approximate mass of this particle in grams?

(1) 1.0 g   (3) 1.7×10^{-24} g
(2) 2.0 g   (4) 6.0×10^{-23} g

65 Which equation represents nuclear disintegration resulting in release of a beta particle?

(1) $^{220}_{87}\text{Fr} + ^{4}_{2}\text{He} \rightarrow ^{224}_{89}\text{Ac}$

(2) $^{239}_{94}\text{Pu} \rightarrow ^{235}_{92}\text{U} + ^{4}_{2}\text{He}$

(3) $^{32}_{15}\text{P} + ^{0}_{-1}\text{e} \rightarrow ^{32}_{14}\text{Si}$

(4) $^{198}_{79}\text{Au} \rightarrow ^{198}_{80}\text{Hg} + ^{0}_{-1}\text{e}$

66 Which electron configuration represents a potassium atom in the excited state?

(1) $1s^2 2s^2 2p^6 3s^2 3p^3$
(2) $1s^2 2s^2 2p^6 3s^1 3p^4$
(3) $1s^2 2s^2 2p^6 3s^2 3p^6 4s^1$
(4) $1s^2 2s^2 2p^6 3s^2 3p^5 4s^2$

Group 3 — Bonding

If you choose this group, be sure to answer questions 67–71.

67 Which type of attraction is directly involved when KCl dissolves in water?

(1) molecule–molecule   (3) molecule–ion
(2) molecule–atom   (4) ion–ion

68 In which compound have electrons been transferred to the oxygen atom?

(1) CO_2 (3) N_2O
(2) NO_2 (4) Na_2O

69 A strontium atom differs from a strontium ion in that the atom has a greater

(1) number of electrons   (3) atomic number
(2) number of protons   (4) mass number

70 Which substance is an example of a network solid?

(1) nitrogen dioxide   (3) carbon dioxide
(2) sulfur dioxide   (4) silicon dioxide

71 Which combination of atoms can form a polar covalent bond?

(1) H and H   (3) N and N
(2) H and Br   (4) Na and Br

Group 4 — Periodic Table

If you choose this group, be sure to answer questions 72–76.

72 Which element has the highest first ionization energy?

(1) sodium   (3) calcium
(2) aluminum   (4) phosphorus

73 Which compound forms a colored aqueous solution?

(1) $CaCl_2$ (3) NaOH
(2) $CrCl_3$ (4) KBr

74 When a metal atom combines with a nonmetal atom, the nonmetal atom will

(1) lose electrons and decrease in size
(2) lose electrons and increase in size
(3) gain electrons and decrease in size
(4) gain electrons and increase in size

75 According to Reference Table *P*, which of the following elements has the smallest covalent radius?

(1) nickel   (3) calcium
(2) cobalt   (4) potassium

76 Which element's ionic radius is smaller than its atomic radius?

(1) neon   (3) sodium
(2) nitrogen   (4) sulfur

Group 5 — Mathematics of Chemistry

If you choose this group, be sure to answer questions 77–81.

77 What is the total number of moles of hydrogen gas contained in 9.03×10^{23} molecules?

(1) 1.50 moles   (3) 6.02 moles
(2) 2.00 moles   (4) 9.03 moles

78 At the same temperature and pressure, which gas will diffuse through air at the fastest rate?

(1) H_2 (3) CO
(2) O_2 (4) CO_2

79 How are the boiling and freezing points of a sample of water affected when a salt is dissolved in the water?

(1) The boiling point decreases and the freezing point decreases.
(2) The boiling point decreases and the freezing point increases.
(3) The boiling point increases and the freezing point decreases.
(4) The boiling point increases and the freezing point increases.

80 A sample of an unknown gas at STP has a density of 0.630 gram per liter. What is the gram molecular mass of this gas?

(1) 2.81 g   (3) 22.4 g
(2) 14.1 g   (4) 63.0 g

81 A compound is 86% carbon and 14% hydrogen by mass. What is the empirical formula for this compound?

(1) CH   (3) CH_3
(2) CH_2 (4) CH_4

Group 6 — Kinetics and Equilibrium

If you choose this group, be sure to answer questions 82–86.

82 In a chemical reaction, a catalyst changes the
(1) potential energy of the products
(2) potential energy of the reactants
(3) heat of reaction
(4) activation energy

83 Which statement describes characteristics of an endothermic reaction?
(1) The sign of ΔH is positive, and the products have less potential energy than the reactants.
(2) The sign of ΔH is positive, and the products have more potential energy than the reactants.
(3) The sign of ΔH is negative, and the products have less potential energy than the reactants.
(4) The sign of ΔH is negative, and the products have more potential energy than the reactants.

84 What is the K_{sp} expression for the salt PbI_2?
(1) $[Pb^{2+}][I^-]^2$
(2) $[Pb^{2+}][2I^-]$
(3) $[Pb^{2+}][I_2]^2$
(4) $[Pb^{2+}][2I^-]^2$

85 Given the equilibrium system:
$$PbCO_3(s) \rightleftarrows Pb^{2+}(aq) + CO_3^{2-}(aq)$$
Which changes occur as $Pb(NO_3)_2(s)$ is added to the system at equilibrium?
(1) The amount of $PbCO_3(s)$ decreases, and the concentration of $CO_3^{2-}(aq)$ decreases.
(2) The amount of $PbCO_3(s)$ decreases, and the concentration of $CO_3^{2-}(aq)$ increases.
(3) The amount of $PbCO_3(s)$ increases, and the concentration of $CO_3^{2-}(aq)$ decreases.
(4) The amount of $PbCO_3(s)$ increases, and the concentration of $CO_3^{2-}(aq)$ increases.

86 A chemical reaction will always occur spontaneously if the reaction has a negative
(1) ΔG
(2) ΔH
(3) ΔS
(4) T

Group 7 — Acids and Bases

If you choose this group, be sure to answer questions 87–91.

87 An acidic solution could have a pH of
(1) 7
(2) 10
(3) 3
(4) 14

88 What is the pH of a 0.00001 molar HCl solution?
(1) 1
(2) 9
(3) 5
(4) 4

89 According to the Brönsted-Lowry theory, an acid is any species that can
(1) donate a proton
(2) donate an electron
(3) accept a proton
(4) accept an electron

90 When the salt Na_2CO_3 undergoes hydrolysis, the resulting solution will be
(1) acidic with a pH less than 7
(2) acidic with a pH greater than 7
(3) basic with a pH less than 7
(4) basic with a pH greater than 7

91 In an aqueous solution, which substance yields hydrogen ions as the only positive ions?
(1) C_2H_5OH
(2) CH_3COOH
(3) KH
(4) KOH

Group 8 — Redox and Electrochemistry

If you choose this group, be sure to answer questions 92–96.

92 In which kind of cell are the redox reactions made to occur by an externally applied electrical current?

(1) galvanic cell
(2) chemical cell
(3) electrochemical cell
(4) electrolytic cell

93 According to Reference Table N, which metal will react spontaneously with Ag^+ ions, but not with Zn^{2+} ions?

(1) Cu   (3) Al
(2) Au   (4) Mg

94 Which atom forms an ion that would migrate toward the cathode in an electrolytic cell?

(1) F   (3) Na
(2) I   (4) Cl

95 Given the equations A, B, C, and D:

(A) $AgNO_3 + NaCl \rightarrow AgCl + NaNO_3$
(B) $Cl_2 + H_2O \rightarrow HClO + HCl$
(C) $CuO + CO \rightarrow CO_2 + Cu$
(D) $NaOH + HCl \rightarrow NaCl + H_2O$

Which two equations represent redox reactions?

(1) A and B (3) C and A
(2) B and C (4) D and B

96 Given the unbalanced equation:

$$\_NO_3^- + 4H^+ + \_Pb \rightarrow$$
$$\_Pb^{2+} + \_NO_2 + 2H_2O$$

What is the coefficient of NO_2 when the equation is correctly balanced?

(1) 1   (3) 3
(2) 2   (4) 4

Group 9 — Organic Chemistry

If you choose this group, be sure to answer questions 97–101.

97 Which polymers occur naturally?

(1) starch and nylon
(2) starch and cellulose
(3) protein and nylon
(4) protein and plastic

98 Which statement explains why the element carbon forms so many compounds?

(1) Carbon atoms combine readily with oxygen.
(2) Carbon atoms have very high electronegativity.
(3) Carbon readily forms ionic bonds with other carbon atoms.
(4) Carbon readily forms covalent bonds with other carbon atoms.

99 Which structural formula represents a primary alcohol?

100 Which compounds are isomers?

(1) 1-propanol and 2-propanol
(2) methanoic acid and ethanoic acid
(3) methanol and methanal
(4) ethane and ethanol

101 Compared to the rate of inorganic reactions, the rate of organic reactions generally is

(1) slower because organic particles are ions
(2) slower because organic particles contain covalent bonds
(3) faster because organic particles are ions
(4) faster because organic particles contain covalent bonds

Group 10 — Applications of Chemical Principles

If you choose this group, be sure to answer questions 102–106.

102 Which products are obtained from the fractional distillation of petroleum?

(1) esters and acids
(2) alcohols and aldehydes
(3) soaps and starches
(4) kerosene and gasoline

103 Given the lead-acid battery reaction:

$$Pb + PbO_2 + 2H_2SO_4 \underset{\text{Charge}}{\overset{\text{Discharge}}{\rightleftharpoons}} 2PbSO_4 + 2H_2O$$

Which species is oxidized during battery discharge?

(1) Pb
(2) PbO_2
(3) SO_4^{2-}
(4) H_2O

104 Given the reaction:

$$ZnO + X + heat \rightarrow Zn + XO$$

Which element, represented by X, is used industrially to reduce the ZnO to Zn?

(1) Cu
(2) C
(3) Sn
(4) Pb

105 Which metal is obtained commercially by the electrolysis of its salt?

(1) Zn
(2) K
(3) Fe
(4) Ag

106 The corrosion of aluminum (Al) is a less serious problem than the corrosion of iron (Fe) because

(1) Al does not oxidize
(2) Fe does not oxidize
(3) Al oxidizes to form a protective layer
(4) Fe oxidizes to form a protective layer

Group 11 — Nuclear Chemistry

If you choose this group, be sure to answer questions 107–111.

107 Fissionable uranium-233, uranium-235, and plutonium-239 are used in a nuclear reactor as

(1) coolants
(2) control rods
(3) moderators
(4) fuels

108 Which reaction illustrates fusion?

(1) $^2_1H + {}^2_1H \rightarrow {}^4_2He$
(2) $^1_0n + {}^{27}_{13}Al \rightarrow {}^{24}_{11}Na + {}^4_2He$
(3) $^{27}_{13}Al + {}^4_2He \rightarrow {}^{30}_{15}P + {}^1_0n$
(4) $^{14}_7N + {}^4_2He \rightarrow {}^1_1H + {}^{17}_8O$

109 An accelerator can *not* be used to speed up

(1) alpha particles
(2) beta particles
(3) protons
(4) neutrons

110 Brain tumors can be located by using an isotope of

(1) carbon-14
(2) iodine-131
(3) technetium-99
(4) uranium-238

111 In the reaction $^9_4Be + X \rightarrow {}^{12}_6C + {}^1_0n$, the X represents

(1) an alpha particle
(2) a beta particle
(3) an electron
(4) a proton

Group 12 — Laboratory Activities
If you choose this group, be sure to answer questions 112–116.

112 Which piece of laboratory equipment should be used to remove a heated crucible from a ring-stand?

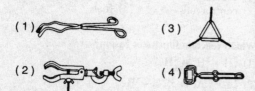

(1)　　　　　　　　　　(3)

(2)　　　　　　　　　　(4)

113 The following set of procedures was used by a student to determine the heat of solution of NaOH.

   (A) Read the original temperature of the water.
   (B) Read the final temperature of the solution.
   (C) Pour the water into a beaker.
   (D) Stir the mixture.
   (E) Add the sodium hydroxide.

What is the correct order of procedures for making this determination?

   (1) $A \rightarrow C \rightarrow E \rightarrow B \rightarrow D$
   (2) $E \rightarrow D \rightarrow C \rightarrow A \rightarrow B$
   (3) $C \rightarrow A \rightarrow E \rightarrow D \rightarrow B$
   (4) $C \rightarrow E \rightarrow D \rightarrow A \rightarrow B$

114 In an experiment, a student found 18.6% by mass of water in a sample of $BaCl_2 \cdot 2H_2O$. The accepted value is 14.8%. What was the student's experimental percent error?

   (1) $\dfrac{3.8}{18.6} \times 100$ 　　　 (3) $\dfrac{14.8}{18.6} \times 100$

   (2) $\dfrac{3.8}{14.8} \times 100$ 　　　 (4) $\dfrac{18.6}{14.8} \times 100$

115 A student obtained the following data in a chemistry laboratory.

Trial	Temperature (°C)	Solubility (grams of KNO_3/100 g of H_2O)
1	25	40
2	32	50
3	43	70
4	48	60

Based on Reference Table D, which of the trials seems to be in error?

   (1) 1 　　　　　　　(3) 3
   (2) 2 　　　　　　　(4) 4

GO RIGHT ON TO THE NEXT PAGE. ⟹

116 A student using a Styrofoam cup as a calorimeter added a piece of metal to distilled water and stirred the mixture as shown in the diagram below. The student's data is shown in the table below.

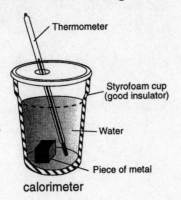

Thermometer

Styrofoam cup
(good insulator)

Water

Piece of metal

calorimeter

DATA TABLE

Mass of H_2O ....50.0 g
Initial temperature of H_2O ....25.0°C
Mass of metal ....20.0 g
Initial temperature of metal..............100.°C
Final temperature of H_2O + metal.....32.0°C

Which statement correctly describes the heat flow in calories? [Ignore heat gained or lost by the calorimeter.]

(1) The water lost 1360 calories of heat and the metal gained 140. calories of heat.
(2) The water lost 350. calories of heat and the metal gained 350. calories of heat.
(3) The water gained 1360 calories of heat and the metal lost 140. calories of heat.
(4) The water gained 350. calories of heat and the metal lost 350. calories of heat.

Sample Regents Exam 4

Answers

1. The correct answer is 3. Each one degree on the Kelvin scale is equivalent to a degree on the Celsius scale; the difference lies in the actual temperature of an object on each of the two scales. On the Kelvin scale, 0° is equivalent to –273° on the Celsius scale and 0° Celsius is the same as +273 Kelvin. In order to calculate the Kelvin temperature equivalent to –73°C, we add 273° which results in a temperature of 200 K.

2. The correct answer is 2. The atomic number of a substance is the number of protons in the nucleus of an atom of a given element. A substance composed only of atoms having the same atomic number would be an element and cannot be a compound. (If it is only atoms with all the same atomic number, it cannot be a compound.) Mixtures, whether homogeneous or heterogeneous, have more than one kind of atom in them.

3. The correct answer is 3. Using the vapor-pressure-versus-temperature chart (at the top of the next column), you will see that 17.5 torr (or mm of mercury) corresponds to a temperature of 20°C. When the external pressure on a sample of water equals 17.5 torr, the sample of water will boil at 20°C.

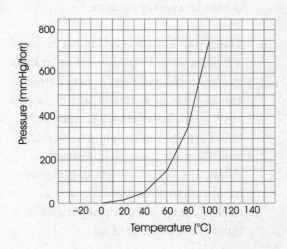

4. The correct answer is 4. The melting point is the point at which the liquid state and the solid state of a substance exist in equilibrium. Choices 2 and 3 each refer to a similar point, but it is the point at which liquid and gas are in equilibrium. Choice 1 is a condition that exists with certain substances that have no liquid phase under certain conditions, such as dry ice (frozen carbon dioxide). Dry ice sublimes from a solid directly to a gas at 1 atm pressure.

5. The correct answer is 3. The total molar volume of the combined substances is 10 moles. Gas A accounts for 70% of the mole fraction in this gas mixture. It will, therefore, according to Dalton's Law of Partial Pressures, account for 70% of the pressure of the gas mixture. Multiplying 70% times a total pressure of 760 mmHg gives us a

partial pressure for gas A of 532 mm Hg. Choice 1 is only one tenth of the total pressure, choice 2 is the partial pressure of gas B, and choice 4 is the total pressure, which cannot be a partial pressure.

6. The correct answer is 1. Gamma rays are not particles and neutrons are neutral, so this leaves choices 1 and 2. Beta particles are known to be electrons, which are negative, which leaves choice 1, alpha particles. These have been found to be essentially the nucleus of a helium atom stripped of electrons. Helium is element number 2, so it has 2 protons and a nuclear charge of 2+. Alpha paricles do indeed have a charge of 2+.

7. The correct answer is 2. In order to qualify as being isotopes of each other, the choices offered must be the same element, which eliminates choices 1 and 4. Choice 3 must also be left out because the formulae presented to us indicate that the choices are identical. This does not define an isotope. Isotopes are similar members of the same element, but with a key difference—the mass. Isotopes of the same element differ in the number of neutrons they contain. Therefore, their masses must be different. The formulae offered in choice 3 have the same masses, namely 131. The formulae offered in choice 2 have different masses, but they are both oxygen; they qualify for our definition of isotopes of each other.

8. The correct answer is 1. Each arrow on the diagram represents an electron with a particular spin. If two electrons are in the same box, theory states that they must have opposite spin. Since nitrogen is element number seven, it has that many protons and, therefore, that many electrons in the ground state. Choices 3 and 4 offer too many electrons in the outermost principal energy levels. (For all diagrams shown, the first energy level, not shown here, contains 2 electrons.) Choices 1 and 2 have the correct number of electrons, but only choice 1 follows Hund's Rule: In the ground state, each orbital is occupied by one electron before any orbital has a second electron. Choice 2 violates this in the p orbital level.

9. The correct answer is 3. We want the atomic mass to represent a typical situation with respect to atoms. Choice 1 excludes the least abundant (naturally occurring) isotopes. Choice 2 excludes the most abundant (naturally occurring) isotopes. Choice 4 excludes all isotopes except the radioactive ones. Choice 3 is the most representative, all inclusive choice.

10. The correct answer is 2. Thermodynamics and the Law of Conservation of Matter and Energy dictate that any energy that excites an electron to a higher orbital must be given back in totality. Choices 1, 3, and 4 are eliminated. When an electron is excited, it absorbs energy, so when it falls back it doesn't absorb, but releases that energy.

11. The correct answer is 4. A neutron is known to be almost exactly like a proton, just a bit heavier. Because it is slightly heavier a free neutron (not bound in a nucleus) will decay spontaneously into a proton (and an electron). By definition, an alpha particle is 2 protons and 2 neutrons (the nucleus of a helium atom) and a beta particle is an electron: Choices 1, 2, and 3 will not work. That leaves choice 4, and it is the right one.

12. The correct answer is 3. All of the formulae presented are for sodium (Na) compounds. The question is which one is the oxalate. C_2O_4 is the formula for an oxalate which makes choice 3 the answer. The ClO formula is a hypochlorite, O is, an oxide, and $C_2H_3O_2$ is an acetate.

13. The correct answer is 1. When balancing the equation for the formation of aluminum oxide, we get the following: $4Al + 3O_2 \rightarrow 2Al_2O_3$. The sum of the coefficients, the numbers in front of the chemical formulae, is 9. All the other choices are incorrect.

14. The correct answer is 1. Choices 2, 3, and 4 all contain more than one atom in their formulae. Therefore, a mole of choice 2 would contain 6.02×10^{23} molecules of NH_3, but each molecule contains 4 atoms, 1 of nitrogen and 3 of hydrogen. Therefore, a mole of NH_3 would contain 4 times 6.02×10^{23} or 24.08×10^{23} atoms. The formula for choice 1 indicates only one atom per particle. A mole of Li, then, would contain only 6.02×10^{23} atoms.

15. The correct answer is 2. Choice 2 is the only one among all four choices in which the compound presented forms covalent bonds. Choices 1, 3, and 4 all are compounds formed by ionic bonds and, therefore, do not qualify for the definition of a molecule. Carbon monoxide, choice 2, is the only compound with a molecular formula.

16. The correct answer is 4. The water molecule is a polar molecule with one side being positive and the other negative. The oxygen side is the more negative of the two sides since it is more electronegative than hydrogen. The oxygen atom of the water molecule will, therefore, be attracted to the positive ion of the salt as it dissolves in water due to the partial negative charge on the oxygen atom.

17. The correct answer is 3. The empirical formula refers to finding the formula with the least number of atoms per compound, which is similar to finding the lowest common denominator of a fraction in math. If the formula can be reduced, then this is done. Both the 4 and the 10 in P_4O_{10} can be further reduced by dividing them both by 2. This, of course, gives us the formula found in choice 3, or P_2O_5. Choices 1 and 2, while reductions, are erroneous; choice 4 is not a reduction, but an expansion.

18. The correct answer is 4. One of the weakest of van der Waals forces, called dispersion forces, is caused by polarizability of the electrons. In general, the fewer the number of electrons, the weaker these forces will be. In addition, the trend toward weaker or stronger dispersion forces, as suggested in this question, ought to be in a sequential fashion. Choices 1 and 2 are to be excluded because they are presented in more or less a random fashion. Choice 3 presents substances in a weaker to stronger progression; neon has fewer electrons than xenon. Choice 4 is the only correct sequence of stronger to weaker forces.

19. The correct answer is 4. In the ground state, that is, as presented on the periodic table, each member of Group 15 is in that group because they have seven valence electrons. Put another way, they all need three electrons to complete their outermost principal energy level. Choices 1 and 2 are similar; the difference is that choice 1 says that the members of Group 15 all have the same number of "filled" principal energy levels, choice 2 says they all have the same number of principal energy levels with "something" in them. This is not true for the same reason choice 3 is not true; as you progress down the periodic chart in Group 15 (or any group for that matter) the nature of the outer principal energy levels does not change, but the number of all the principal energy levels does. Since the atoms are also getting larger as you progress down the column for Group 15 (and again, for any Group) you are also adding neutrons. Choice 4 is the only choice that fits the nature of atoms within any one group.

20. The correct answer is 1. K and Na are elements that reside in the same group, Group 1, on the periodic chart. They will therefore have the same number of valence electrons, making them have the same chemical properties, e.g., they both combine with Cl on a 1-to-1 basis. The other three choices offer element pairs, each of which is in a different Group. This means they must have different numbers of valence electrons and, therefore, different chemical properties.

21. The correct answer is 3. Groups 1 and 2 are firmly metallic elements. Group 13 contains mostly metallic elements, but they become more and more metalloid as you travel down the chart. In the same way, Groups 16, 17, and 18 are firmly nonmetallics. Given the choices in this question, it would appear that choice 3 is the only one that provides the most metalloids, those elements with properties in between those of metals and nonmetals.

22. The correct answer is 2. One might be fooled into picking choice 1 in this question since alkali metals all have their outermost s orbital filled as is the case presented here. However, looking more closely reveals the d orbitals are far from

being filled, not a characteristic of the alkaline earth metals. This is certainly not an example of metalloids nor nonmetals as those elements are characterized by unfilled outermost p orbitals. This most certainly, then, is one of the transition metals, namely manganese.

23. The correct answer is 1. The designation of this element as being "diatomic . . . with a high first ionization energy" indicates that it is either in Group 1 or 17 or N_2 or O_2. The only element in Group 1 that may qualify is hydrogen—in this case representing the metals—but it has a low ionization energy compared to the other choices offered. The halides, nitrogen, and oxygen—representing nonmetals with high electronegativity—are the only other logical choices among those given, making choice 1 the correct answer. In choices 2 and 4, the low electronegativity does not fit with the high first ionization energy indicated in the question.

24. The correct answer is 4. The trend on the periodic chart, when considering elements from left to right in Period 3 (or any other period) is an increase in atomic number, which means they also increase in the number of outer electrons. This means, traveling from left to right on the Periodic Table, we find a tendency to want to gain electrons which is an increase in nonmetallic behavior. Choice 4 is the only one

that fits all the observed behavior of elements as we go from left to right on the Periodic Table.

25. The correct answer is 4. Applying the octet rule to the 28 innermost electrons of this elements gives us 3 energy levels: 2 electrons fill the first, 8 electrons fill the second, and 18 electrons fill the third for a total of 28 innermost electrons. When we now consider those 7 outermost electrons, we are dealing with an additional energy level, which means this element has 4 energy levels which places it in period (or row) four. It is, in fact, element number 35, or bromine, a member of the halide family all of which have 7 outermost electrons.

26. The correct answer is 3. The equation for calculating the concentration of particles in a solution expressed in Molarity is given by the formula M = # of moles of solute (the material being dissolved) divided by liters of solution:

$$M = \frac{\text{\# moles of solution}}{\text{liters of solution}}$$

In applying this formula to all of the answers given, choice 3 yields the largest answer, 1.5M. Choice 1 gives 1M, choice 2 gives 0.67M, and choice 4 gives 0.5M.

27. The correct answer is 1. The gram formula mass (gfm) is the formula mass of a substance expressed in grams. The formula mass is the addition of all the atomic masses for all the constituent elements in the formula as taken from the periodic table. For example, K (potassium) has an atomic mass of 39.098, but the formula indicates 2 atoms of K in the formula, giving us a total of 78.196 as the total mass due to potassium atoms in the formula. Adding in 12 for the one carbon and 48 for the three oxygens, we get 138 g total for the gfm of K_2CO_3.

28. The correct answer is 4. One mole of any substance contains 6.02×10^{23} particles. In the case of nickel, which is monatomic, one mole of nickel would contain that many atoms, i.e., 6.02×10^{23} atoms. Two moles would contain twice that amount or 12.04×10^{23} atoms. Choice 4 has presented that number in the correct scientific notation form, namely one digit before the decimal and all others after the decimal and then adjust the exponent. So, 12.04×10^{23} atoms is the same as 1.204×10^{24} atoms. Choices 1 and 2 are misleading as they are presenting the formula mass of one and two moles respectively. The question asks for the number of atoms, not the formula mass.

29. The correct answer is 2. One mole of gas at STP occupies 22.4 L. Given the reaction in this question, the complete decomposition of 0.500 mole of $KClO_3(s)$ is one-quarter the amount decomposed in the balanced equation. Therefore, instead of producing a total of 67.2 L of O_2 as the balanced equation calls for, the complete decomposition of 0.500 mole of $KClO_3$ will produce one quarter of 67.2 L, or 16.8 L, which is choice 2. Choice 1 is one-sixth the original, choice 3 is two-thirds the original and, as already seen, choice 4 is the original amount.

30. The correct answer is 2. To calculate the percent mass of O in MgO we need to divide the mass of O by the total mass of MgO. Magnesium has a mass of 24.3 and oxygen has a mass of 16. The total, 40.3, divided into 16 gives us a percent by mass figure of O in the compound MgO of 40 percent.

31. The correct answer is 1. Choices 2, 3, and 4 fall short of the equilibrium suggested in the wording of the question. A saturated solution is one in which as one particle solidifies out of solution, theoretically, another particles enters into solution. As the questions says, "the crystallizing rate . . . equals the dissolving rate." A solution may be concentrated, meaning it contains many particles of solute, yet not be near the point of equilibrium referred to in the question. It may also be unsaturated and, therefore, not near the point of equilibrium. In fact, a concentrated solution and a dilute solution may both be unsaturated.

32. The correct answer is 3. When the surface area of the reactant is increased more of the reactant will be exposed to possible collisions. It has nothing to do with the density of the reactant, as choice 1 suggests, nor does it increase the concentration of the reactant as is also suggested in choice 2. Additionally, increasing the surface area of all substances does not increase the electrical conductivity in all substances. Finally, the use of the term "more reactant particles" in choice 3 is correct. Exposing more surface area can come about only by breaking the existing particles up to expose previously unexposed inner areas.

33. The correct answer is 1. Choices 2, 3, and 4, according to Table G, all evidence a positive enthalpy of formation, meaning they absorb energy from the reaction. The Standard Enthalpy of Formation for hydrogen fluoride is a negative number which means its formation releases heat making it the only exothermic reaction of the choices listed. Choice 1 is the only answer that is correct.

34. The correct answer is 4. That energy is released is a certainty: the Potential Energy of reactants is greater than the Potential Energy of the products. The difference can only be accounted for by a release of energy. If it were the other way around, obviously energy would be absorbed. With such a low activation energy and such a difference in Potential Energies,

this must be an exothermic reaction. Choice 4 is the only completely correct answer.

35. The correct answer is 2. Changing the concentration of a reactant does not affect the activation energy of a reaction. Changing the concentration of a reactant will, however, change the number of collisions since they are dependent on the number of reactant particles. In this question we are told that the concentration of N_2 is increased, which means choice 2 being the only correct answer.

36. The correct answer is 3. Referring to Table L reveals that H_2SO_4 has the highest dissociation constant K_a (also known as the ionization constant) of the choices given in this question. This means that in an aqueous solution sulfuric acid has the highest concentration of particles in ionized form. This large number of ions in aqueous solution means sulfuric acid will conduct electricity the best. While H_3PO_4 is next on the list, it is almost two orders of magnitude less ionized than H_2SO_4. HF is even less ionized than phosphoric acid and H_2S has the lowest K_a of the choices offered. Choice 3 is the only correct answer.

37. The correct answer is 2. Arrhenius described bases as donors of hydroxide ions in an aqueous solution. The only choice among those given that will be capable of that is choice 2.

38. The correct answer is 4. A conjugate acid is described as the molecule formed when a base gains a hydrogen ion. When the base HS^- gains a hydrogen ion, it becomes H_2S, capable of losing a hydrogen ion and becoming HS^- again, which is the conjugate base of H_2S. Choice 3 does not even contain sulfur, choice 2 is the conjugate base of HS^- and choice 1 is merely a hydrogen ion.

39. The correct answer is 1. In order to calculate the molarity of a base that is neutralized by a particular volume of an acid with a known molarity, you must know the volume of acid needed to neutralize a given volume of the base. The molarity of the acid times the necessary volume must equal the molarity of the base times the volume neutralized. It appears that half as much acid is needed to neutralize the volume of base given. Applying the $M_a \times V_a = M_b \times V_b$ equation, we find that for this to be true, the molarity of the base must be half that of the acid, making choice 1 the only correct answer.

40. The correct answer is 3. An amphiprotic species is one that can act as an acceptor or a donor of hydrogen ions; that is, it can act as a base and an acid. Examining Table L, we should see, in the acid and the base columns alike, the one choice offered that is amphitropic. It appears that HSO4– is the only one of the four choices offered that fits this condition: it is the conjugate acid of SO_4^{2-} and the conjugate base of H_2SO_4.

41. The correct answer is 2. Both the H_2O and the HCO_3^- in the reaction indicated donate a hydrogen ion. When the reaction proceeds to the right, water donates the H^+ and when the reaction proceeds to the left, the HCO_3^- donates the H^+. Choice 1 is half right in that the water is a donor of H^+, but the OH^- is not. In a like manner, choice 4 is half right, because the HCO_3^- is a donor of H^+, however CO_3^{2-} is not. Choice 3 is completely wrong. Choice 2 satisfies the conditions for correctly identifying the two Brønsted-Lowry acids in this reaction.

42. The correct answer is 3. Oxidation is defined as when a substance loses electrons and reduction as when a substance gains electrons. Lost electrons have to be lost to something. Gained electrons have to be gained by something. A substance that takes the lost electrons is seen as an oxidizing agent. Since it takes lost electrons while acting as an oxidizing agent, this substance is itself reduced. Likewise, any substance that loses electrons is oxidized while acting as a reducing agent for another substance. The only choice that reflects this is choice 3. Choices 2 and 4 are saying the same thing. Choice 1 cannot be correct because redox reactions refer to electron transfers.

43. The correct answer is 4. If sodium, as is usually the case, has an oxidation number of 1^+, then the HCO_3 radical has an oxidation number of 1^-. If hydrogen has its usual 1^+ oxidation number, then remov-

ing the H gives a 2⁻ charge for CO_3 alone. In fact, the CO_3 radical alone is known to have an oxidation number of 2⁻. Since the oxidation number of O is rarely anything but 2⁻, the three oxygens each having an oxidation number of 2⁻ means that in that radical, carbon must have an oxidation number of 4⁺ to account for the excess 2⁻ in the CO_3 radical overall. Choice 4 is the correct choice.

44. The correct answer is 1. Since each choice is referring to the timing of the oxidation phase versus the reduction phase in a redox reaction, the only answer that can be true is choice 1; the reactions must occur simultaneously. Choices 2 and 3 have the reactions NOT occurring at the same time, which cannot be the case. The loss of electrons (oxidation) must occur at the exact moment that those electrons are gained (reduction). Choice 4 is not possible since it has only oxidation occurring and not reduction.

45. The correct answer is 2. In this reaction, Co^0 on the left becomes Co^{2+} on the right, indicating it has been oxidized. Pb^{2+} on the left is reduced by gaining two electrons to become Pb^0. The only choice among the answers that correctly identifies these events in this redox reaction is choice 2. Choices 1 and 3 incorrectly identify Cl as changing its oxidation number, which it does not, and choice 4 contains the correct participants but has the opposite action on them occurring.

46. The correct answer is 1. All reactions proceed to the right in this question. Therefore, choice 2 and choice 4 are erroneous representations since they are incomplete. For example, in choice 2, Cr goes from 3⁺ to 0, which looks like reduction, but then we are told there is still an excess of 3 electrons. Choice 4 is the same, written in reverse. Choice 3 is oxidation where Cr has lost 3 electrons to become 3⁺. Choice 1 is the correct reduction reaction.

47. The correct answer is 2. It does prevent the mixing of the two solutions which makes choice 3 incorrect. However, it does not prevent the migration of electrons critical to the occurrence of the reactions. It permits the ions to migrate, thus ensuring the migration of electrons. Choice 1 is wrong, choice 2 is right. Most importantly, by allowing the migration of ions, it permits the spontaneity of the reaction, and thus, choice 4 is wrong.

48. The correct answer is 3. The prefix *but-* refers to hydrocarbons that contain 4 carbon atoms. The hydrocarbon presented in this question has 6. However, this hydrocarbon with 6 hydrogens attached, one to each carbon as it turns out, is a special hydrocarbon forming a ring structure called a benzene ring. Choice 3 is our only answer. If carbon has its usual oxidation number of 4 when constructing such a ring we see that we must assign alternating single and double bonds to the carbons in the ring. This leaves only one bond open

for each carbon where we can attach a hydrogen, with an oxidation number of 1.

49. The correct answer is 2. In fermentation glucose is incompletely broken down which can occur in plant and animal tissue. In the case presented here, this reaction is occurring in plant tissue and leads to the production of ethyl alcohol, C_2H_5OH. The reaction in totality produces 2 molecules of CO_2 and 2 molecules of ethyl alcohol. Choices 3 and 4 are completely erroneous as they introduce two components, Ca in choice 3 and Cr in choice 4, that weren't there before. The molecule in choice 1 can't be produced from glucose breaking down to yield the molecule in choice 1 and CO_2.

50. The correct answer is 4. The double bond between the two carbons puts this hydrocarbon in the alkene series. Since it has 2 carbons, it would correctly be identified as ethene. Choice 1 is referring to an alcohol that dictates the molecule having oxygen for an OH group, and it clearly does not have O. Choice 2 is a hydrocarbon with triple bonds between the carbons, the alkyne series, and choice 3 is a hydrocarbon with single bonds between the carbons, the alkane series.

51. The correct answer is 3. Organic acids are identified by their characteristic COOH functional group. Generically, they are written R-COOH where R represents any carbon chain or ring. The other choices,

while looking like they might also contain the COOH group, only go so far as having COH at best. In fact, all the other choices have OH as their functional group attached at different parts of the molecule and therefore are all alcohols. The special names of each are as follows: choice 1 is propyl alcohol; choice 2 is isopropyl alcohol (in almost every medicine cabinet); and choice 4 is 1,3-propanediol.

52. The correct answer is 2. Tetra substituted carbon cannot have a planar arrangement of substituents, so choices 3 and 4 are not possible. Choice one is tempting if one conjures up a quick, general view of a pyramid without considering its actual structure. A pyramid has a peak and four corners meaning that any structure we try to equate as analogous must have 6 atoms: carbon at the center of this model and 5 hydrogens at each of the vertices. Methane has only 5 atoms and upon closer inspection, with carbon at the center again, a tetrahedron, with a peak and three corners, fits the bill with a hydrogen at each of the four corners that represent a tetrahedron.

53. The correct answer is 1. The addition of N_2 will push the reaction to the right which would reduce the amount of O_2. It would also reduce the amount of new N_2 that was introduced, until the reaction once again reached equilibrium. Adding NO, which would force the reaction to the left, would increase the two reactants on the left, but this question asks about adding N_2. It

should be clear that the concentration of O_2 would not remain the same. Choices 2 and 3 are incorrect.

54. The correct answer is 3. Temperature has no effect on the rate of decay of a radioactive substance.

55. The correct answer is 1. The appearance of the ice may remain the same with the mere 10° drop in temperature, but the internal forces are changing. Solids have what is called internal energy made up of the vibrations of each atom relative to the atoms directly attached to it. The average internal energy of a solid does relate to its temperature, so choice one is the closest to this idea.

56. The correct answer is 1. The product of the concentrations of H^+ and OH^- ions in aqueous solution is a constant and is the basis for determining pH. Therefore, if the concentration of H^+ ions goes up, the concentration of OH^- will go down. Since the concentrations of the two is a constant the OH^- cannot increase while the H^+ is increasing and, again, they will not remain the same for the same reason; the additional H^+ will bond with the OH^-, lowering the concentration of OH^-.

57. The correct answer is 1. The equation given indicates that there is no liquid phase in this phase change. Sublimation occurs when a substance goes from the solid phase to the gaseous phase with no liquid phase in between. Choice 1 is correct. Choice 2 occurs going from gaseous

to liquid, choice 3 occurs when going from solid to liquid, and choice 4 occurs from liquid to the gaseous phase.

58. The correct answer is 2. An increase in potential energy will be at those times when a substance is heated, but there is no rise in temperature. In addition, the lack of an increase in temperature indicates that kinetic energy is remaining constant as a result of heat being absorbed as potential energy. On a graph such as this, the plateaus or flat places will evidence these conditions. On this graph, that would be the portions labeled B and D or choice 2. Choices 1 and 4 are half right and choice 3 is incorrect.

59. The correct answer is 4. The word fusion refers to the fact that we are dealing with the solid form of a substance. Whether going from solid to liquid or liquid to solid of the same substance under the same conditions, the energy absorbed/released will be identical. The only choice that reflects this is choice 4. Another possible answer not included here could have been liquid to a solid. Choice 1 deals with heat of vaporization and choices 2 and 3 deal with sublimation (see answer to question 57).

60. The correct answer is 3. A binary compound is defined as a compound with only two elements in it which makes choice 3 the only correct answer. Na in choice 1 is only the element sodium and does not qualify for being a compound. In choice 2,

we are presented with a molecule of hydrogen which contains two atoms, but a binary is two elements, not atoms. Finally, choice 4 has three elements and may trick those who think OH is one element; it is not, it is an atom of oxygen and an atom of hydrogen. Along with the atom of Na, choice 4 has three elements.

61. The correct answer is 4. Despite having the same volume, neither will have the same mass as the other since, according to the periodic table, they are different elements with different atomic masses. Choice 1 is incorrect. They will also have different densities for the same reason; therefore, choice 2 is incorrect. However, since a molecule of oxygen contains two atoms, but a "molecule" of neon contains only one atom, they will not contain the same number of atoms. Choice 3 is incorrect. Finally, choice 4 is correct: they will have the same number of molecules. (Note, however, that we do not use the word *molecule* when referring to a substance like Ne, which contains atoms only in the gas phase.)

62. The correct answer is 4. The arrow labeled 2 is unaffected by the electric field and therefore has no charge. Choices 1 and 3 are positive and would be represented by arrow 3 (attracted to negative) and choice 2 is a negative particle and would therefore be represented by arrow 1 (attracted to positive). Gamma radiation is without charge and must be the emanation represented by arrow 2.

63. The correct answer is 3. We have identical masses of each sample according to the answers given. Referring to Table H, Au-198 has a half-life of 2.69 days meaning that after that period of time, we will have 5 g of Au-198 left. I-131 has a half-life of 8.07 days, P-32 has a half-life of 14.3 days and Rn-222 has a half-life of 3.82 days. Clearly, the longest lived that will decay the least over a period of 30 days, will be choice 3, P-32.

64. The correct answer is 3. Using information regarding Avogadro's number of particles, if we assign a gram formula mass (the atomic mass—here given as 1 amu—expressed in grams) then we can say it contains 6.02×10^{23} particles. Dividing 1 g by 6.02×10^{23} particles will give us the weight of one particle, which is 1.7×10^{-24}g. Choices 1 and 2 are grossly incorrect and choice 4 attempts to make it seem simply a matter of the inverse of Avogadro's number. You must perform the operation indicated above and arrive at choice 3 as the correct answer.

65. The correct answer is 4. A beta particle is an electron with a 1^- charge and no mass. Two choices offer that particle in the decay indicated, choices 3 and 4. You can then discount choices 1 and 2 immediately. Choice 3 adds the beta particle to P-32 making it Si-32. The question seeks the release of a beta particle so this will not do. Choice 4, in fact, correctly indicates the release of an electron from Au-198 as the reaction proceeds from left to right.

66. The correct answer is 4. In the ground—or unexcited—state, potassium would have 6 electrons in its 3p orbitals and the configuration would be $1s^2 2s^2 2p^6 3s^2 3p^6 4s^1$. That is the answer offered in choice 3, but that is the ground state, not an excited state. Choice 1 is the configuration for phosphoros P in the ground state, and choice 2 is the configuration for phosphoros in the excited state. These were no doubt chosen as possible answers for those unfamiliar with their chemical symbols. Choice 4 is the correct designation for potassium, K, in the excited state where one 3p electron has been excited to the 4s orbital.

67. The correct answer is 3. When KCl dissolves in water it is dissolving in a substance that is in molecular form. The KCl will dissociate into ions that are pulled apart from each other by the polar nature of the water molecules. The attractions, then, will be K⁺ for the negative side of the water molecule—the O side—and the Cl⁻ will be attracted to the positive side of the molecule—the H side. There is only one source of molecules and one source of ions so choices 1 and 4 are incorrect, and there are no atoms in the attractions, so choice 2 must be considered incorrect also.

68. The correct answer is 4. Carbon and nitrogen will both form covalent bonds with oxygen. Electrons will always be shared. With only one electron in its outermost orbital, sodium, in Na_2O, will likely give up its outer electrons and transfer them to the oxygen atom. Choices 1, 2, and 3 are incorrect. Only choice 4 allows for the transfer of electrons.

69. The correct answer is 1. Whenever we are considering the atomic and ionic form of the same element, the difference will always be electrons. Choice 2 is incorrect since protons do not transfer in forming ions. This also means choice 3 is incorrect since the number of protons is also the atomic number. The mass number is the sum of protons and neutrons in the nucleus, which does not change when forming ions, so choice 4 is incorrect. Choice 1 correctly states that atoms differ from ions of the same element by the number of electrons they each have.

70. The correct answer is 4. At STP, choices 1, 2, and 3 are all gases although they are covalently bonded. They lack one of the key requirements for being a network solid: they must be solid. Silicon dioxide is the only choice offered that is a solid as well as a network of covalently bonded molecules.

71. The correct answer is 2. Despite forming covalent bonds, neither choice 1 nor choice 3 will form polar covalent bonds since they are homonuclear diatomics. Choice 4 will not form a covalent bond; the sodium will transfer its outermost single electron to bromine which needs only one to fill its outermost orbital. Hydrogen, on the other hand, despite operating with

only one outermost electron, will not transfer it to bromine. Hydrogen only has one orbital, the 1s which holds a maximum of only 2 electrons. Therefore, hydrogen will share one of bromine's electrons in a polar (the hydrogen becomes the (+) side and the bromine becomes the (–) side) covalent bond.

72. The correct answer is 4. Traveling across the Periodic Table from left to right one encounters a decreasing tendency to lose electrons, or an increasing affinity for gaining electrons. Known as the first ionization energy, it is the amount of energy needed to strip the first electron from an element. Phosphorous, being the farthest to the right of the choices offered, has the highest first ionization energy. Sodium would be the lowest first ionization energy since it readily gives up electrons. Aluminum and then calcium follow closely in the order.

73. The correct answer is 2. The chloride of chromium, one of the transition metals, forms a colored aqueous solution. All the other alkali or alkaline earth metal salts form white or clear aqueous solutions. Among the other transition metals that form colored aqueous solutions would be Mn, Fe, Co, Ni, and Cu. Choices 1, 3, and 4 are incorrect.

74. The correct answer is 4. A characteristic of nonmetal atoms is that they gain, not lose electrons, so choices 1 and 2 are incorrect.

Of the two choices left number 4 is the correct one as a gain of electrons would tend to increase the size of the atom as it becomes a nonmetal ion.

75. The correct answer is 1. Nickel, with a covalent radius of 1.15 Å, is the smallest covalent radius of the choices offered. Cobalt is 1.16 Å, calcium is 1.74 Å, and potassium is 1.23 Å. Choices 2, 3, and 4 are incorrect. Traveling across the Periodic Table from left to right, we are adding one proton and one electron for each additional atom. The electrons are all added to the same principal energy levels and with the increase of the charge on the nucleus, the effect is to pull the electrons closer, thereby decreasing the size of the atom.

76. The correct answer is 3. It should be noted that choices 1, 2, and 4 are all elements on the right side of the Periodic Table. This should be a clue that the answer is sodium, choice 3, and this is correct. When sodium becomes an ion, it loses occupation of an entire energy level, thus making it smaller. Nitrogen and sulfur, on the other hand, usually add electrons to their outermost energy level when forming compounds, making the ion larger than the atomic form, so choices 2 and 4 are not correct. Choice 1 is also incorrect: Neon does not form ions.

77. The correct answer is 1. One mole of any substance is 6.02×10^{23} particles whether

they be atoms, ions, molecules, electrons, protons, etcetera. If we divide the number of molecules in one mole into the number given we get an answer of 1.50. This is the number of moles that are contained in 9.03×10^{23} molecules of hydrogen gas. Choices 3 and 4 mistakenly use the two key numbers and call them moles and choice 2 is greater than our calculations produced. Choice 1 is the correct answer.

78. The correct answer is 1. Graham's law of effusion states that the rate at which a gas escapes through a tiny hole in a container is inversely proportional to the square root of its formula mass. In other words, the smaller the particle, the faster it will effuse. This has since been shown to be true for rates of diffusion as well. Therefore, the lightest particles will diffuse at the fastest rates and of the choices we are given that would be H_2.

79. The correct answer is 3. Dissolving a salt in water affects the colligative properties such as the boiling and freezing points discussed in this question. Electrolytes (salts) affect these properties more then nonelectrolytes because electrolytes produce multiple particles (ions) when they dissolve. It can be said that the presence of a solute in water pushes the limits according to the number of moles added. By this we mean that the boiling point gets higher (by 0.52°C per mole of particles) and the freezing point gets lower (by 1.86°C per mole of particles). This means choice 3 is the correct answer.

80. The correct answer is 2. Using the equivalences that accompany a discussion of Avogadro's number, we know that a full 22.4 L of any gas at STP contains a mole of particles (6.02×10^{23}) and a gram formula mass of the particles. In this problem, we simply multiply the mass of 1 L of the gas by 22.04 to get the mass of 22.4 L or a mole of the gas. This results in a total mass for one mole of this gas as 14.1 g, which makes choice 2 the right answer.

81. The correct answer is 2. If we assume a total sample weight of 100 g of the compound, that gives us 86 grams of C and 14 grams of H. To calculate the number of moles this would result in, we divide 86 grams by the number of grams in one mole of carbon and that give us 7.16 moles of carbon in the 100 g sample. In a like manner, we find the 100 g sample would yield 14 moles of hydrogen. These figures, 7.16 moles of C and 14 moles of H are in an approximate 1:2 ratio of C:H giving us an empirical formula of CH_2, or choice 2.

82. The correct answer is 4. The role of a catalyst has long been known to be as a non-participant in a reaction. It affects the rate of the reaction without getting involved in it. It cannot affect the heat of the reaction, which is a property based on the nature of the reactants and the products. In a like manner, it cannot affect the potential energy of either the reactant or the products because affecting a change in the products or reactants is something cata-

lysts, both organic (also called enzymes) and inorganic, are known not to do. Choices 1–3 are incorrect as they do not fit the evidence for the action of catalysts.

83. The correct answer is 2. An endothermic reaction is one in which the reactants absorb heat and thus absorbs energy. This is indicated by adding the energy absorbed per mole on the reactant side. When we get to the right side, or product side, of the equation, the energy will be understood to be in the products. This energy is the ΔH indicated in the answer. In addition to ΔH being positive, since energy is absorbed, the products have more energy than the reactants. These are the conditions outlined in choice 2.

84. The correct answer is 1. The K_{sp} for a substance is given by the concentration of the positive ions raised to the power of the number of ions produced times a similar expression for the negative ions. The one choice that reflects this expression is choice 1. Choice 3 includes the concentration of iodine molecules, choice 2 places the 2 as a coefficient instead of as an exponent, and choice 4 also contains the 2 as a coefficient for I^-.

85. The correct answer is 3. Adding $Pb(NO_3)_2$ to the solution at equilibrium will provide more Pb^{2+} ions that can then combine with available CO_3^{2-} ions. This will lower the concentration of CO_3^{2-} as it produces more $PbCO_3$. This is, of course, choice 3. Choice 1 identifies an incorrect decrease

in $PbCO_3$. Choice 2 has both constituents incorrectly changing. Choice 4 has an incorrect increase in the CO_3^{2-} ion.

86. The correct answer is 1. ΔG or the Gibbs free energy of any reaction is given by the equation $\Delta G = \Delta H - T\Delta S$, where T is the temperature, ΔH is the enthalpy change (meaning the heat change in the system) and ΔS is the entropy change (meaning the decrease in order in the system). Although either ΔH or $-T\Delta S$ may be negative, it is their sum being negative that is required for spontaneity. This is choice 1. All the other choices are merely a list of the components in the equation.

87. The correct answer is 3. Acids are defined as having a pH below 7 at 25°C which means choice 3 is the one we want. Choices 2 and 4 indicate a pH above 7, which is in the range of bases (14 being a very strong base). Choice 7 is the point of neutral pH at 25°C, and, therefore, not associated with an acid. (Actually, for temperatures below 25°C, pH7 *could* be acid—the question needs to state temperature to avoid ambiguity.)

88. The correct answer is 3. The pH is defined as the negative log of the concentration of hydrogen ions in a solution. The concentration given can also be written as 1×10^{-5} M. When we do this, we can see that the negative log of that figure, also written merely as 10^{-5}, results in a pH of 5. Choice 3 is the correct answer.

89. The correct answer is 1. Brønsted-Lowry acids are defined as any species that can donate a proton. Of course the proton is a hydrogen ion. Choice 1 appears to be what we want. Choice 3 is incorrect because that defines a Brønsted-Lowry base.

90. The correct answer is 4. There are a variety of salts formed from the action of an acid and a base. These resulting salts may show significant acid/base activity depending on the species of acids and bases from which they formed. Na_2CO_3 is formed from a weak acid, H_2CO_3, and a strong base, NaOH. When it dissociates in aqueous solution, it will create basic solution with a pH greater than 7. Choices 1 through 3 are all, in some way, incorrect.

91. The correct answer is 2. In aqueous solution, ethyl alcohol, C_2H_5OH, will not dissociate into any available ions. KH will decompose (violently) in water to form KOH and H_2 gas. Potassium hydroxide will dissociate, but into K^+ and OH^- ions only. Acetic acid, CH_3COOH, will dissociate into H^+ and $CH_3CO_2^-$ ions making hydrogen ions available as the only positive ions.

92. The correct answer is 4. An electrochemical cell is defined as any device that converts chemical energy into electrical energy by the nature of the reactants. A galvanic (or voltaic) cell is just such a device and could also be called a chemical cell although that is not as complete a

description as a voltaic cell. These all depend on spontaneous reactions within the cell. An electrolytic cell, as the name suggests, needs an externally applied electrical current to work. Choices 1 through 3 describe basically the same thing, whereas choice 4 is the correct answer.

93. The correct answer is 1. Silver is above copper on Table N of Standard Electrode Potentials and therefore will react with copper, but zinc is below copper, which means copper will not react with zinc. Choice 2 is incorrect since gold is far above silver and will not react with it. Choices 3 and 4 will also not work as they are farther down than even zinc.

94. The correct answer is 3. The cathode part of an electrolytic cell is the negative electrode where reduction takes place and electrons are consumed making it attractive to positive particles. The only atom given among the choices that would form a positive ion is choice 3, sodium. All of the other choices are halides and they form negative ions. They would migrate toward the anode.

95. The correct answer is 2. Redox is the oxidation of substances (loss of electrons) accompanied by the simultaneous reduction of other substances (gain of electrons). Evidence of this in a reaction is that oxidation numbers will change from one side of the equation to the other. This is not the case with reaction A, where the oxidation

numbers of each substance remains the same on both sides. The same is true of reaction D. In reaction B, however, our first clue is that chlorine goes from the elemental form to an ionic form, meaning it is changed. In fact, the Cl is reduced in HCl and oxidized in HClO. Similarly, copper in reaction C is reduced by gaining electrons and the carbon is oxidized with the loss of 2 electrons when going from left to right. Choice 2 is the answer.

96. The correct answer is 2. When the equation is correctly balanced it provides for the loss of two electrons from Pb to oxidize it so the nitrogen in NO_3^- may be reduced to the nitrogen in NO_2. Doing so requires a 2 in front of the NO_3^- and the NO_2. The coefficient of NO_2 would, therefore, be a 2, which is choice 2.

97. The correct answer is 2. Polymers are known as long chains of individually distinct but bonded together units known as monomers and can be produced synthetically or in nature. Two of the most widespread kinds of polymers produced in nature are starch and cellulose, which is choice 2. Protein is another natural polymer, but in all the choices given with protein, it is coupled with a synthetic polymer. Choice 1 couples starch with a synthetic, and so cannot be the answer.

98. The correct answer is 4. Carbon needs to do much more than just form bonds with oxygen readily; that would produce a very

limited variety of molecules. Choice 1 is incorrect. Carbon atoms also do not have a very high electronegativity, so choice 2 is out. Carbon atoms generally do not form ionic bonds—where one atom gives and one atom takes electrons—with other atoms. Carbon shares electrons readily with other carbon atoms producing an infinite number of starting molecules from which countless others can be manufactured, therefore choice 3 is incorrect.

99. The correct answer is 3. Choice 1, with its characteristic RCHO is an aldehyde, namely propanal. Choice 2 evidences the COOH of an organic acid and is known as propanoic acid. Choice 4 is a secondary alcohol with the characteristic 2 R-groups attached to the C-OH. Choice 3 then is the primary alcohol with one R-group attached to the C-OH.

100. The correct answer is 1. Isomers are defined as having the same molecular formula, but a different structural formula. Choice 2 indicates two different molecular formulas entirely: methanoic acid is HCOOH, whereas ethanoic is CH_3COOH. This is incorrect. In the same way, choice 3 presents an alcohol, methanol, with a methyl base and an aldehyde, methanal, with a methyl base. However, their molecular formulas are once again not alike: methanol is CH_3OH and methanal is CH_2O or HCHO. Similarly, choice 4 presents the same incorrect solution, ethane is a hydrocarbon and ethanol is an alco-

hol. Choice 1 is the only one that presents identical molecular formulas with different structural formulas.

101. The correct answer is 2. The formation and breakup of ionic bonds occurs much more rapidly than is characteristic of covalent bonds. Consequently, the correct answer is choice 2. Organic compounds contain many covalent bonds but they do not proceed faster as choice 4 incorrectly points out. It has already been stated that organic compounds contain mostly covalent bonds, not ionic, which makes choices 1 and 3 both incorrect.

102. The correct answer is 4. Petroleum is composed mostly of alkanes from continuous chains to branched chains. The separation of these from crude oil into their constituent parts, known as cracking, yields mostly kerosene and gasoline. Petroleum does not contain large enough amounts of oxygen to help form the other compounds listed such as acids, esters, alcohols, starches, etcetera. Choice 4 is the only correct answer.

103. The correct answer is 1. On the left of the equation is lead in its elemental state. As the battery is discharged, the reaction proceeds from left to right and lead loses 2 electrons to become Pb^{2+} in the compound $PbSO_4$. Oxidation is the loss of electrons, so choice 1 is correct. Choices 3 and 4 are incorrect as these species are unchanged. The PB^{+4} is PbO_2 was reduced.

104. The correct answer is 2. As in the production of several metals from their oxide form, carbon is used to "draw" off the oxygen from the zinc in a single replacement reaction as is given in this question. None of the three metals would be used as given in choices 1, 3, or 4 since the activity series would come into play and we might even form alloys rather then drawing off pure zinc. Choice 2 is the only correct answer.

105. The correct answer is 2. Choices 1, 3, and 4 all refer to metals that can be precipitated out of an aqueous solution or released through electrolysis of an aqueous solution. Potassium, choice 2, reacts violently with water so a simple precipitation in an aqueous solution or electrolysis having to do with water are both out of the question. Therefore, potassium must be produced by the electrolysis of its molten salt. Choice 2 is the correct one produced by this process. The other three may also be produced this way, but at a far greater cost. With potassium, we have no choice.

106. The correct answer is 3. The "corrosion" of aluminum does, in fact produce a protective layer wherein the particles are so closely associated that it prevents further oxygen from attacking the aluminum. Iron does not have this capability. Both metals oxidize, which makes choices 1 and 2 incorrect. Additionally, iron does not form a protective coating, so choice 4 is incorrect.

107. The correct answer is 4. All three substances are the fuels that provide energy in a nuclear

reactor. Far from being coolants, they provide the heat to create the super-heated steam that drives the turbines. Additionally, they are not designed to absorb energy as control rods or moderators are in the reactor core. Choices 1–3 are all incorrect.

108. The correct answer is 1. Only reaction 1 outlines a reaction in which all the reactants end up in one product. Two heavy hydrogen atoms, or deuteriums, are fused to make an atom of helium. Choices 3 and 4 could be fusion reactions where a "compound" nucleus, formed by the fusing of the two reactants, "evaporates" (releases) the neutron in choice 3 or the proton in choice 4. However, choice 1 is still the best option: light hydrogen atoms combining to make helium.

109. The correct answer is 4. A particle accelerator makes use of electromagnetic fields to cause the particles to move faster and faster. It makes use of the knowledge that charged particles will respond to magnetic fields and if positioned correctly, we can make the charged particles move close to the speed of light. Neutrons are neutral, electrically, and so will not respond to a magnetic field electrically induced or not. Choice 4 is the correct answer.

110. The correct answer is 3. This substance is readily taken up by certain tissues in the body, in particular, the more active tissues in a cancer such as a brain tumor. Carbon-14 and Uranium-238 are far too dangerous to be used in this area as they will persist for thousands of years. Iodine is not part of the biochemistry of brain tumors and would be useless. Once the technetium is taken up by the brain tumor, certain imaging equipment can be used to locate the tumor after which time the isotope decays quickly.

111. The correct answer is 1. The difference in mass from the left to the right side of the equation is 4 and reflects a difference of that many AMU's in mass. The difference between atomic numbers of the two substances is 2 which represents protons. Those two numbers match exactly a helium nucleus, which is also known as an alpha particle, with a mass of 4 and 2 protons. Choice 1 is the correct answer.

112. The correct answer is 1. Choice 1 is a picture of the proper tongs to be used on such a small article as a crucible. Choice 2 is a clamp used on a ring stand and wouldn't be used to pick something up. Choice 3 is a heating triangle used in conjunction with a ring stand to set containers on while heating them. It is also used to position funnels when pouring things. Finally, choice 4 represents the tongs used to hold test tubes.

113. The correct answer is 3. The sequence is as follows: pour water into beaker (C), read original temperature (A), add the NaOH (E), stir the mixture (D), read the final temperature (B); this is reflected in choice 3 only.

114. The correct answer is 2. The correct way to calculate percent of error is in choice 2. The accepted value is subtracted from the experimental which will give an accurate difference. If the experimental value is under the accepted value, the answer will be a negative indicating the experimental value was lower than expected. Then the result is divided by the accepted value and turned into a percent by multiplying it times 100.

115. The correct answer is 4. The solubility increases as the temperature increases, but in trial 4 the solubility is decreased compared to trial 3. From Trial 1 to Trial 2 there was an increase of 7 degrees for 10 g of KNO_3 solubility. From Trial 2 to Trial 3 there is an increase of 11 degrees per 10 g of KNO_3 solubility. But from Trial 3 to Trial 4, there is an increase of 5 degrees but a decrease of 10 g of KNO_3 solubility. Choice 4 is the correct answer.

116. The correct answer is 4. Water absorbed a total of 7 degrees for its 50 g of mass, which means it absorbed a total of 350 calories. The gain in energy to the water must have come from the metal and choice 4 is the only accurate representation of that conclusion.

Sample Regents Exam 5—August 1997

Part I

Answer all 56 questions in this part. [65]

Directions (1–56): For *each* statement or question, select the word or expression that, of those given, best completes the statement or answers the question. Record your answer on the separate answer sheet in accordance with the directions on the front page of this booklet.

1 Which phase change represents sublimation?

(1) $H_2O(\ell) \rightarrow H_2O(s)$ (3) $I_2(s) \rightarrow I_2(g)$
(2) $H_2O(\ell) \rightarrow H_2O(g)$ (4) $I_2(s) \rightarrow I_2(\ell)$

2 At STP, which substance has a crystalline structure?

(1) Ne   (3) Hg
(2) Zn   (4) He

3 As a solid is heated, its temperature increases from 10°C to 25°C, remains at 25°C for 5 minutes, and then increases to beyond 45°C. Based on this information, what conclusion can be drawn about the substance?

(1) Its melting point is 45°C.
(2) Its boiling point is 45°C.
(3) Its melting point is 25°C.
(4) Its boiling point is 25°C.

4 At a constant pressure, how does the volume of 1 mole of an ideal gas vary?

(1) directly with the Kelvin temperature
(2) indirectly with the Kelvin temperature
(3) directly with the mass of the gas
(4) indirectly with the mass of the gas

5 Gas samples A, B, and C are contained in a system at STP. The partial pressure of sample A is 380 torr and the partial pressure of sample B is 190 torr. What is the partial pressure of sample C?

(1) 760 torr   (3) 380 torr
(2) 570 torr   (4) 190 torr

6 In an atom of lithium in the ground state, what is the total number of orbitals that contain only 1 electron?

(1) 1   (3) 3
(2) 2   (4) 4

7 An atom of $^{40}_{18}Ar$ has a nucleus that contains a total of

(1) 18 electrons   (3) 18 neutrons
(2) 18 protons   (4) 18 nucleons

8 Atoms of which element have the highest first ionization energy?

(1) calcium   (3) potassium
(2) sodium   (4) magnesium

9 Given the nuclear equation:

$$^{232}_{90}Th \rightarrow \, ^{228}_{88}Ra + X$$

The letter X in the equation represents

(1) an alpha particle   (3) a gamma ray
(2) a beta particle   (4) a neutron

10 What is the total number of electrons in an atom of $^{19}_{9}F$?

(1) 9   (3) 19
(2) 10   (4) 28

11 Which kind of nuclear radiation has high energy and no mass?

(1) alpha   (3) gamma
(2) beta   (4) neutron

12 What is the electronegativity value for an element whose atoms in the ground state have an electron configuration of $1s^2 2s^2 2p^6 3s^2 3p^6 4s^1$?

(1) 0.8   (3) 100
(2) 0.9   (4) 119

13 Which kind of compound generally results when nonmetal atoms chemically combine with metal atoms?

(1) network   (3) molecular
(2) ionic   (4) metallic

14 Which is the empirical formula of a compound?

(1) K_2O_2 (3) Al
(2) O_2 (4) Al_2O_3

15 What is the total number of moles of hydrogen in 1 mole of $(NH_4)_2HPO_4$?

(1) 5   (3) 8
(2) 7   (4) 9

16 The bonds in all network solids are

(1) covalent   (3) metallic
(2) ionic   (4) nonpolar

17 What is the correct name of Fe_2O_3?

(1) iron (I) oxide   (3) iron (III) oxide
(2) iron (II) oxide   (4) iron (V) oxide

18 In which reaction are the products at a lower potential energy than the reactants?

(1) $KNO_3(s) + 8.3\ kcal \xrightarrow{H_2O} K^+(aq) + NO_3^-(aq)$

(2) $2C(s) + 2H_2(g) + 12.5\ kcal \xrightarrow{H_2O} C_2H_4(g)$

(3) $NH_4NO_3(s) + 6.1\ kcal \xrightarrow{H_2O} NH_4^+(aq) + NO_3^-(aq)$

(4) $CH_4(g) + 2O_2(g) \longrightarrow CO_2(g) + 2H_2O(l) + 212.8\ kcal$

19 Which element is a noble gas?

(1) antimony   (3) gold
(2) krypton   (4) francium

20 Which element is a metalloid (semimetal)?

(1) Mg   (3) Cr
(2) Si   (4) Ar

21 Which element in Group 15 has the greatest metallic character?

(1) nitrogen   (3) antimony
(2) phosphorus   (4) bismuth

22 Which nonmetal is the most reactive?

(1) fluorine   (3) bromine
(2) chlorine   (4) iodine

23 Which electron configuration represents a transition element?

(1) $1s^2 2s^2 2p^5$ (3) $[Ar]3d^5 4s^2$
(2) $[Ne]3s^2$ (4) $[Ar]3d^{10}4s^2 4p^6$

24 Which element has atoms with the largest covalent radius?

(1) Rb   (3) Sr
(2) Cs   (4) Ba

25 How does the size of an aluminum atom change when it becomes an ion with a charge of +3?

(1) It becomes smaller by losing 3 electrons.
(2) It becomes smaller by gaining 3 electrons.
(3) It becomes larger by losing 3 electrons.
(4) It becomes larger by gaining 3 electrons.

26 At STP, which gas sample has a volume of 11.2 liters?

(1) 1.00 mole of CO_2
(2) 0.750 mole of NH_3
(3) 0.500 mole of CO_2
(4) 0.250 mole of NH_3

27 What is the gram molecular mass of 1 mole of $C_3H_5(OH)_3$?

(1) 48 g   (3) 74 g
(2) 58 g   (4) 92 g

28 Given the reaction:

$$2KClO_3(s) \rightarrow 2KCl(s) + 3O_2(g)$$

What is the total number of moles of $KClO_3(s)$ needed to produce 6 moles of $O_2(g)$?

(1) 1   (3) 3
(2) 2   (4) 4

29 In an aqueous solution of potassium chloride, the solute is

(1) Cl   (3) KCl
(2) K   (4) H_2O

30 Given the reaction at STP:

$$C_3H_8(g) + 5O_2(g) \rightarrow 3CO_2(g) + 4H_2O(g)$$

What is the total volume of $H_2O(g)$ formed when 2.5 liters of $O_2(g)$ is completely reacted?

(1) 5.0 L   (3) 2.5 L
(2) 2.0 L   (4) 4.0 L

31 Equilibrium between dissolved and undissolved solute exists in a solution that is

(1) saturated
(2) supersaturated
(3) dilute and unsaturated
(4) concentrated and unsaturated

32 The energy needed to start a chemical reaction is called

(1) potential energy   (3) activation energy
(2) kinetic energy   (4) ionization energy

33 Given the potential energy diagram:

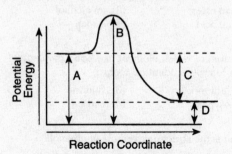

Reaction Coordinate

Which lettered interval represents the potential energy of the activated complex?

(1) A   (3) C
(2) B   (4) D

34 As the temperature increases from 0°C to 25°C, the amount of NH_3 that can be dissolved in 100 grams of water

(1) decreases by 10 grams
(2) decreases by 40 grams
(3) increases by 10 grams
(4) increases by 40 grams

35 Based on Reference Table L, which of the following is the strongest Brönsted acid?

(1) H_2SO_4 (3) HSO_4^-
(2) H_3PO_4 (4) HPO_4^{2-}

36 According to the Arrhenius theory, when a base is dissolved in water it produces a solution containing only one kind of negative ion. What is the name of this negative ion?

(1) hydrogen carbonate ion
(2) hydrogen sulfate ion
(3) hydride ion
(4) hydroxide ion

37 Based on Reference Table L, which 0.1 M aqueous solution is the best conductor of electricity?

(1) HI   (3) H_2S
(2) HNO_2 (4) H_3PO_4

38 What is the molarity of an HNO_3 solution if 50.0 milliliters of 0.50 M LiOH is required to exactly neutralize 100. milliliters of the HNO_3 solution?

(1) 1.5 M   (3) 0.50 M
(2) 2.0 M   (4) 0.25 M

39 Given the reaction:

$$HI(g) + H_2O(\ell) \rightleftarrows H_3O^+(aq) + I^-(aq)$$

Which species represents the Brönsted-Lowry base in the forward reaction?

(1) HI(g)   (3) $H_3O^+(aq)$
(2) $H_2O(\ell)$ (4) $I^-(aq)$

40 What is the pH of a 0.01 M solution of HNO_3?

(1) 1   (3) 13
(2) 2   (4) 14

41 According to Reference Table L, which species can act only as a Brönsted base?

(1) H_2SO_4 (3) NH_3
(2) HSO_4^- (4) NH_2^-

42 The diagram below represents a chemical cell.

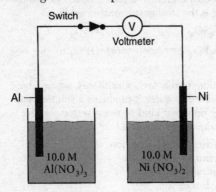

In order for the cell to operate, it should be provided with

(1) a cathode
(2) an anode
(3) a salt bridge
(4) an external path for electrons

43 In a chemical cell, electrical energy will be produced when

(1) only oxidation occurs
(2) only reduction occurs
(3) both oxidation and reduction occur
(4) neither oxidation nor reduction occurs

44 Which oxidation number change could occur during an oxidation half-reaction?

(1) +1 to –1   (3) +3 to +1
(2) –2 to –3   (4) +2 to +3

45 Which half-reaction correctly represents reduction?

(1) $Al(s) \rightarrow Al^{3+}(aq) + 3e^-$
(2) $H_2(g) + 2e^- \rightarrow 2H^+(aq)$
(3) $I_2(s) \rightarrow 2I^-(aq) + 2e^-$
(4) $Cu^{2+}(aq) + 2e^- \rightarrow Cu(s)$

46 What is the sum of the oxidation numbers of the atoms in the compound CO_2?

(1) 0   (3) –4
(2) –2   (4) +4

47 Given the reaction:
$$2Fe^{3+} + Sn^{2+} \rightarrow 2Fe^{2+} + Sn^{4+}$$
Which species is the oxidizing agent?

(1) Fe^{3+} (3) Fe^{2+}
(2) Sn^{2+} (4) Sn^{4+}

48 Which compound has the molecular formula C_5H_{12}?

(1) butane
(2) pentane
(3) 2,2-dimethyl butane
(4) 2,2-dimethyl pentane

49 In which compound does a double covalent bond exist between two carbon atoms?

(1) C_2H_2 (3) C_3H_8
(2) C_2H_4 (4) C_4H_{10}

50 What is a product of both fermentation reactions and saponification reactions?

(1) an ester   (3) an alcohol
(2) an acid   (4) a soap

51 An atom of which element can bond covalently with four other identical atoms?

(1) lithium   (3) fluorine
(2) oxygen   (4) carbon

52 What is the structural formula of ethanol?

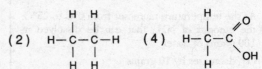

Note that questions 53 through 56 have only three choices.

53 As a catalyst is added to a system in equilibrium, the amount of products formed

(1) decreases
(2) increases
(3) remains the same

54 Different masses of copper and iron have the same temperature. Compared to the average kinetic energy of the copper atoms, the average kinetic energy of the iron atoms is

(1) less
(2) greater
(3) the same

55 As an electron in a hydrogen atom moves from the second principal energy level to the first principal energy level, the energy of the atom

(1) decreases
(2) increases
(3) remains the same

56 As the pressure of a gaseous mixture at equilibrium increases at constant temperature, the equilibrium constant

(1) decreases
(2) increases
(3) remains the same

Part II

This part consists of twelve groups, each containing five questions. Each group tests a major area of the course. Choose seven of these twelve groups. Be sure that you answer all five questions in each group chosen. Record the answers to these questions on the separate answer sheet in accordance with the directions on the front page of this booklet. [35]

Group 1 — Matter and Energy

If you choose this group, be sure to answer questions 57–61.

57 What is the total number of calories of heat absorbed by 65.0 grams of water when the temperature of the water is raised from 25.0°C to 40.0°C?

  (1) 15.0 cal   (3) 975 cal
  (2) 25.0 cal   (4) 1630 cal

58 Which material is a substance?

  (1) air   (3) fire
  (2) water   (4) earth

59 Given the reaction: $A + B \rightleftarrows C + D +$ heat

Which statement best describes this reaction?

  (1) The forward reaction is exothermic, and the reverse reaction is always exothermic.
  (2) The forward reaction is exothermic, and the reverse reaction is always endothermic.
  (3) The forward reaction is exothermic, and the reverse reaction can be either exothermic or endothermic.
  (4) The forward reaction is endothermic, and the reverse reaction can be either endothermic or exothermic.

60 At a pressure of 1 atmosphere, what is the temperature of a mixture of steam and water at equilibrium?

  (1) 100°C   (3) 273°C
  (2) 212°C   (4) 373°C

61 A sample of gas has a volume of 12 liters at 0°C and 380 torr. What will be its volume when the pressure is changed to 760 torr at constant temperature?

  (1) 24 L   (3) 12 L
  (2) 18 L   (4) 6.0 L

Group 2 — Atomic Structure

If you choose this group, be sure to answer questions 62–66.

62 The average isotopic mass of chlorine is 35.5. Which mixture of isotopes (shown as percents) produces this average mass?

  (1) 50% ^{12}C and 50% ^{13}C
  (2) 50% ^{35}Cl and 50% ^{37}Cl
  (3) 75% ^{35}Cl and 25% ^{37}Cl
  (4) 75% ^{12}C and 25% ^{13}C

63 Which emanation is attracted toward a negatively charged electrode?

  (1) alpha particle   (3) gamma ray
  (2) beta particle   (4) neutron

64 What is the total number of protons and neutrons in the nuclide $^{80}_{35}Br$?

  (1) 35   (3) 80
  (2) 45   (4) 115

65 What is the total number of completely filled principal energy levels in an atom of argon in the ground state?

  (1) 1   (3) 3
  (2) 2   (4) 4

66 The atomic mass of an atom is measured in atomic mass units. This unit is based on

  (1) ^{1}H (3) ^{16}O
  (2) ^{14}N (4) ^{12}C

Group 3 — Bonding

If you choose this group, be sure to answer questions 67–71.

67 Which substance has the highest normal melting point?

  (1) CH_4 (3) C_3H_8

  (2) C_2H_6 (4) C_4H_{10}

68 Which molecule contains a nonpolar covalent bond?

  (1) I_2 (3) H_2O

  (2) NH_3 (4) CO

69 Which type of bond is formed between the carbon and oxygen atoms in a CO_2 molecule?

  (1) nonpolar covalent   (3) ionic

  (2) polar covalent   (4) electrovalent

70 Given the reaction:

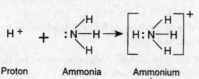

Proton   Ammonia   Ammonium ion

Which type of bond is formed between the proton (H^+) and the ammonia molecule?

  (1) ionic   (3) coordinate covalent

  (2) network   (4) nonpolar covalent

71 Which diagram best illustrates the hydration of sodium ions in an aqueous solution? [The diagrams are not drawn to scale.]

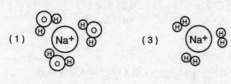

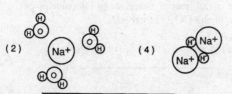

Group 4 — Periodic Table

If you choose this group, be sure to answer questions 72–76.

72 Which is a common characteristic of the elements Rb, Te, I, and Xe in the ground state?

  (1) They have the same number of valence electrons.

  (2) They have similar chemical properties.

  (3) They have electrons occupying the same number of principal energy levels.

  (4) They have completely filled principal energy levels.

73 Which property is generally characteristic of metallic elements?

  (1) low electrical conductivity

  (2) high heat conductivity

  (3) existence as brittle solids

  (4) existence as molecular solids

74 Which element is a nonmetallic liquid at room temperature?

  (1) hydrogen   (3) mercury

  (2) oxygen   (4) bromine

75 Which group in the Periodic Table contains an element that can form a blue sulfate compound?

  (1) 1   (3) 11

  (2) 2   (4) 17

76 In which section of the Periodic Table are the most active metals located?

  (1) upper right corner

  (2) lower right corner

  (3) upper left corner

  (4) lower left corner

Group 5 — Mathematics of Chemistry

If you choose this group, be sure to answer questions 77–81.

77 When 20.0 grams of a substance is completely melted at its melting point, 820. calories is absorbed. What is the heat of fusion of this substance?

(1) 41.0 cal/g   (3) 840. cal/g
(2) 800. cal/g   (4) 16400 cal/g

78 Under the same conditions of temperature and pressure, which gas will diffuse at the *slowest* rate?

(1) He   (3) Ar
(2) Ne   (4) Rn

79 How does the presence of a nonvolatile dissolved solute affect the freezing point and boiling point of pure water?

(1) It lowers the freezing point and lowers the boiling point.
(2) It lowers the freezing point and raises the boiling point.
(3) It raises the freezing point and lowers the boiling point.
(4) It raises the freezing point and raises the boiling point.

80 Under which conditions will the volume of a given sample of a gas decrease?

(1) decreased pressure and decreased temperature
(2) decreased pressure and increased temperature
(3) increased pressure and decreased temperature
(4) increased pressure and increased temperature

81 A compound contains 57% sulfur and 43% oxygen by mass. What is the empirical formula of this compound?

(1) SO   (3) SO_3
(2) SO_2 (4) S_2O_3

Group 6 — Kinetics and Equilibrium

If you choose this group, be sure to answer questions 82–86.

82 According to Reference Table G, which substance will form spontaneously?

(1) CO(g)   (3) C_2H_2(g)
(2) NO(g)   (4) C_2H_4(g)

83 Given the reaction at STP and at equilibrium:

$$H_2(g) + Cl_2(g) \rightleftarrows 2HCl(g)$$

Which change will result in an increase in the concentration of Cl_2(g)?

(1) decreasing the pressure of the system
(2) decreasing the concentration of HCl(g)
(3) increasing the concentration of H_2(g)
(4) increasing the concentration of HCl(g)

84 Given the reaction at STP and at equilibrium:

$$AgI(s) \rightleftarrows Ag^+(aq) + I^-(aq)$$

What will occur when $AgNO_3$(s) is added to the equilibrium mixture?

(1) The amount of AgI(s) will decrease, and the amount of I^-(aq) will decrease.
(2) The amount of AgI(s) will decrease, and the amount of I^-(aq) will increase.
(3) The amount of AgI(s) will increase, and the amount of I^-(aq) will decrease.
(4) The amount of AgI(s) will increase, and the amount of I^-(aq) will increase.

85 Based on Reference Table M, which compound is most soluble in water?

(1) $PbCO_3$ (3) $CaSO_4$
(2) $ZnCO_3$ (4) $BaSO_4$

86 Given the equation:

$$2CO(g) + O_2(g) \rightarrow 2CO_2(g) + 135.4 \text{ kcal}$$

What is the heat of reaction, in kilocalories per mole, of the CO_2(g) formed?

(1) +67.7   (3) –67.7
(2) +135.4   (4) –135.4

Group 7 — Acids and Bases

If you choose this group, be sure to answer questions 87–91.

87 According to Reference Table L, the Br^- ion is classified as a

(1) strong conjugate base
(2) strong conjugate acid
(3) weak conjugate base
(4) weak conjugate acid

88 An aqueous solution of which substance will turn red litmus paper blue?

(1) H_2SO_4
(2) HCl
(3) C_2H_5OH
(4) KOH

89 When the pH of a solution is 8, what is the OH^- ion concentration in moles per liter?

(1) 1×10^{-6}
(2) 1×10^{-7}
(3) 1×10^{-8}
(4) 1×10^{-14}

90 Given the reaction:

$$HSO_4^-(aq) + NH_3(g) \rightleftarrows NH_4^+(aq) + SO_4^{2-}(aq)$$

Which statement best describes the action of $NH_3(g)$ in the reaction?

(1) It acts as a base, because it is a proton acceptor.
(2) It acts as a base, because it is a proton donor.
(3) It acts as an acid, because it is a proton acceptor.
(4) It acts as an acid, because it is a proton donor.

91 According to Reference Table L, which is an amphoteric (amphiprotic) substance?

(1) HI
(2) H_2S
(3) $H_2PO_4^-$
(4) NO_3^-

Group 8 — Redox and Electrochemistry
If you choose this group, be sure to answer questions 92–96.

92 Which half-reaction is the arbitrary standard used in the measurement of the electrode potentials listed in Reference Table N?

(1) $8H^+ + MnO_4^- + 5e^- \rightarrow Mn^{2+} + 4H_2O$

(2) $4H^+ + O_2(g) + 4e^- \rightarrow 2H_2O$

(3) $2H^+ + 2e^- \rightarrow H_2(g)$

(4) $2H_2O + 2e^- \rightarrow 2OH^- + H_2(g)$

93 Given the reaction:

$$Zn(s) + 2Ag^+(aq) \rightarrow Zn^{2+}(aq) + 2Ag(s)$$

The net potential (E^0) for the reduction half-reaction is

(1) +0.76 V (3) +0.80 V

(2) –0.76 V (4) –0.80 V

94 Given the reaction:

$$Ni(s) + 2Fe^{3+}(aq) \rightarrow Ni^{2+}(aq) + 2Fe^{2+}(aq)$$

What is the net potential (E^0) for the overall reaction?

(1) –1.03 V (3) –0.51 V

(2) +1.03 V (4) +0.51 V

95 When an electrochemical cell is operating, it is

(1) approaching equilibrium

(2) approaching maximum E^0

(3) undergoing oxidation, only

(4) undergoing reduction, only

96 The diagram below shows a spoon that will be electroplated with nickel metal.

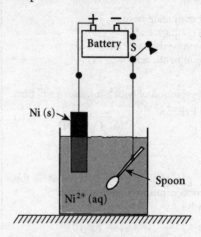

What will occur when switch S is closed?

(1) The spoon will lose mass, and the Ni(s) will be reduced.

(2) The spoon will lose mass, and the Ni(s) will be oxidized.

(3) The spoon will gain mass, and the Ni(s) will be reduced.

(4) The spoon will gain mass, and the Ni(s) will be oxidized.

Group 9 — Organic Chemistry

If you choose this group, be sure to answer questions 97–101.

97 Which structural formula represents a mono-hydroxy alcohol?

(1)

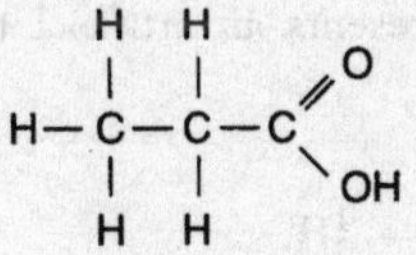

```
      H  H
      |  |    //O
  H—C—C—C
      |  |    \OH
      H  H
```

(2)

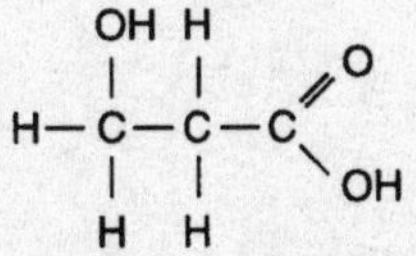

```
     OH  H
      |  |    //O
  H—C—C—C
      |  |    \OH
      H  H
```

(3)

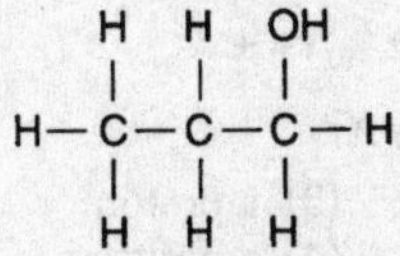

```
      H  H  OH
      |  |  |
  H—C—C—C—H
      |  |  |
      H  H  H
```

(4)

```
     OH  H  OH
      |  |  |
  H—C—C—C—H
      |  |  |
      H  H  H
```

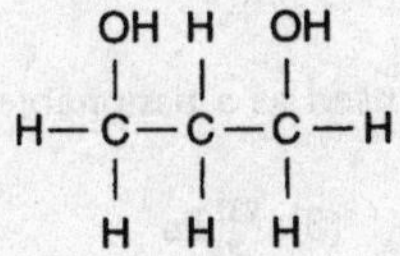

98 Which general formula represents an organic acid?

(1) R—OH   (3) R_1—O—R_2

(2) R—CHO   (4) R—COOH

99 During condensation polymerization, two monomers may be joined by the removal of a molecule of

(1) carbon dioxide   (3) oxygen

(2) hydrogen   (4) water

100 Which organic compound is a weak electrolyte?

(1) acetic acid

(2) carbon tetrachloride

(3) pentane

(4) benzene

101 What is the total number of pairs of electrons shared between the two adjacent carbon atoms in an ethyne molecule?

(1) 1   (3) 3

(2) 2   (4) 4

Group 10 — Applications of Chemical Principles

If you choose this group, be sure to answer questions 102–106.

102 Which process is used to separate a mixture of hydrocarbons with different boiling points?

(1) cracking
(2) oxidation
(3) fractional distillation
(4) dehydration synthesis

103 The chemical reaction that causes corrosion of metals in contact with water and oxygen is

(1) a substitution reaction
(2) an addition reaction
(3) a neutralization and ionization reaction
(4) a reduction and oxidation reaction

104 In the contact process, sulfide ores such as iron pyrites are burned primarily to produce

(1) O_2 (3) H_2S
(2) SO_2 (4) H_2O

105 Given the reaction at equilibrium:

$$N_2(g) + 3H_2(g) \rightleftarrows 2NH_3(g) + \text{heat}$$

At constant temperature, which changes would produce a greater yield of $NH_3(g)$?

(1) decreasing the pressure and decreasing the concentration of $N_2(g)$
(2) decreasing the pressure and increasing the concentration of $N_2(g)$
(3) increasing the pressure and decreasing the concentration of $N_2(g)$
(4) increasing the pressure and increasing the concentration of $N_2(g)$

106 The reaction below is the probable reaction for the nickel-cadmium battery.

$$2NiOOH + Cd + 2H_2O \underset{\text{Charge}}{\overset{\text{Discharge}}{\rightleftarrows}} 2NiO(OH)_2 + Cd(OH)_2$$

During discharge, the reducing agent is

(1) Cd   (3) Ni^{3+}
(2) H_2O (4) Ni^{2+}

Group 11 — Nuclear Chemistry

If you choose this group, be sure to answer questions 107–111.

107 Which equation represents an artificial transmutation?

(1) $^{16}_{7}N \rightarrow ^{16}_{8}O + ^{0}_{-1}e$

(2) $^{14}_{7}N + ^{4}_{2}He \rightarrow ^{17}_{8}O + ^{1}_{1}H$

(3) $^{37}_{19}K \rightarrow ^{37}_{18}Ar + ^{0}_{+1}e$

(4) $^{42}_{19}K \rightarrow ^{42}_{20}Ca + ^{0}_{-1}e$

108 Given the nuclear reaction:

$$^{234}_{90}Th \rightarrow ^{234}_{91}Pa + X$$

What is represented by X?

(1) an alpha particle   (3) a proton
(2) a beta particle   (4) a positron

109 Which isotope can be used as a fissionable fuel in a nuclear reactor?

(1) $^{32}_{15}P$ (3) $^{231}_{91}Pa$

(2) $^{206}_{82}Pb$ (4) $^{239}_{94}Pu$

110 Which particle can be accelerated by an electric field?

(1) a proton   (3) a helium atom
(2) a neutron   (4) a hydrogen atom

111 Which substance is used as a coolant in a fission reactor?

(1) $B(s)$ (3) $H_2(g)$
(2) $Cd(s)$ (4) $Na(\ell)$

Group 12 — Laboratory Activities

If you choose this group, be sure to answer questions 112–116.

112 The diagram below shows NaOH(aq) being added to HCl(aq). A few drops of phenolphthalein were added to the flask before the titration was started.

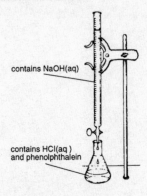

contains NaOH(aq)

contains HCl(aq) and phenolphthalein

The endpoint in this titration is reached when the solution in the flask appears

(1) pink   (3) blue
(2) colorless   (4) yellow

113 Which laboratory glassware is shown in the diagram below?

(1) Florence flask   (3) distilling flask
(2) Erlenmeyer flask   (4) volumetric flask

114 A student determines that the gram formula mass of AgO is 128.40 grams. If the accepted value is 123.87 grams, what is the student's percent error?

(1) 0.366%   (3) 3.80%
(2) 3.66%   (4) 4.53%

115 A student tested the solubility of a salt at different temperatures and then used Reference Table *D* to identify the salt. The student's data table appears below.

Temperature (°C)	g of salt per 10 g of water
30	1.2
50	2.2
62	3.0
76	4.0

What is the identity of the salt?

(1) potassium nitrate
(2) sodium chloride
(3) potassium chlorate
(4) ammonium chloride

116 Which mass measurement contains a total of three significant figures?

(1) 22.0 g   (3) 220 g
(2) 22.00 g   (4) 2200 g

Sample Regents Exam 5

Answers

1. The correct answer is 3. The phase change known as sublimation involves a change from the solid phase directly to the gaseous phase with no liquid phase in between. From the equations given, choice 3 appears to do that. Choices 1 and 2 are phase changes of water, both of which contain the liquid phase; choice 1 is loss of energy and indicates the solidification of water and choice 2 indicates the gain of energy as water vaporizes. Choice 4 is not sublimation, since it involves a liquid phase; this reaction may be possible, but does not occur at STP.

2. The correct answer is 2. At standard temperature (0°C) and pressure (1 atm) neon and helium are gases which makes choices 1 and 4 incorrect. At STP, mercury is a liquid —it is the silvery column used in many standard thermometers that measure temperature. Thus, choice 3 cannot be correct. Zinc, which is a solid at STP, then, must be the substance with a crystalline structure at STP.

3. The correct answer is 3. Since we are starting from a solid, the only phase changes that can occur are melting and sublimation. That means, choices 2 and 4 must be excluded as they are referring to the boiling point. Sublimation is not a possible answer, so the phase change must be melting. Since the temperature of the substance remains at 25°C for some time and then begins to rise beyond 45°C, we can assume the substance is melting at 25°C, so its melting point is 25°C, not 45°C. The leveling off of the temperature as the solid becomes liquid—a similar leveling off also occurs at the boiling point of a substance—occurs as the molecules absorb energy to break free of the solid structure and become liquid.

4. The correct answer is 1. If the pressure in a gas is held constant, the volume varies directly with the Kelvin temperature; if the temperature doubles, the volume doubles. As we add energy to the particles, as in doubling the temperature, they move faster, but in order to hold constant pressure, the gas takes up more space, thereby the particles move twice as fast, but have to go twice as far to collide, so the pressure remains the same. The mass of the gas has little to do with this relationship and a simple demonstration of blowing a balloon up and then placing it in the freezer for several hours will demonstrate that choice 2 is incorrect.

5. The correct answer is 4. We must know the total pressure in order to answer this question and the key to that is that the conditions are at STP. That means the

total pressure is 760 mmHg or 760 torr. If we add up the partial pressure of gases A and B and then subtract that from 760, according to Dalton's Law of Partial Pressure, this will equal the partial pressure of gas C. The answer is 190 torr, which is choice 4. Choice 1 is, of course, SP. Choice 2 is the sum of the partial pressures of gases A and B, a dangerous choice presented to us. Choice 3 is the partial pressure of one of the gases by itself.

6. The correct answer is 1. "The ground state" means that the atom of lithium has all its electrons and they are in their lowest energy configuration. As such, lithium, with only three electrons (we know this because it says we have an atom of lithium, and an atom of lithium, element #3, has three electrons) in the ground state follows the rule of placing two of the three in principal energy level or orbital 1 leaving one electron to be placed in the second orbital. Therefore, while lithium contains two orbitals, only one contains a single electron. Choice 2 is deceiving if the question is incorrectly read. Lithium is element #3 and so choice 3 might also be incorrectly chosen for the same reason.

7. The correct answer is 2. The configuration given is the standard presentation of the number of subatomic particles in an atom. The upper left number, in this case 40, is the number of nucleons, namely protons and neutrons; just how many of each may not be known unless we look at the other number, the lower left number. This is the number of protons in the nucleus. Therefore, we have 18 protons in the nucleus of Argon and 22 neutrons. Since we are talking about the nucleus, choice 1 can be immediately discarded and one sees the only choice that is correct is choice 2.

8. The correct answer is 4. The first ionization energy—the amount of energy needed to remove the first valence electron from an atom—increases as we go from left to right across the Periodic Table. In doing so, we encounter atoms that want to gain electrons, not give them away, so it is increasingly harder to remove electrons as we go from left to right. As we look at the Periodic Table, we see magnesium as the right-most and closer to the top of the table of the choices offered and thus the correct answer.

9. The correct answer is 1. In order to determine the identity of X in the equation, we must determine what has changed (lost or gained) in the equation between reactants and products. This is most easily done by taking the difference between the numbers given for the two elements in the equation. The mass number of Th is 232 and the mass number of Ra is 228, or a difference of 4 AMU. The atomic number of Th is 90 and the atomic number of Ra is 88, or a difference of 2, which would identify X as having an atomic number (as well as the number of protons) of 2 with a mass of 4 AMU. The Periodic Table reveals this

as relating to helium. Since there is no indication of electrons, we can assume this is a nucleus of a helium atom—the choices given in the question help here—which is an alpha particle or choice 1. Note that it is not a helium atom, as that would need to include the electrons.

10. The correct answer is 1. We are told this is an atom of fluorine, so the number of electrons will be the same as the number of protons. The number on the lower left of the symbol for the element indicates the atomic number, which indicates the number of protons in an atom, which in the case of fluorine presented here is 9. This means, the fluorine in this question has 9 electrons as well.

11. The correct answer is 3. An alpha particle contains 4 nucleons and is the most "sluggish" of the particles indicated here. The next, a beta particle, is a high speed electron, but still with comparatively little energy. A neutron, being larger than a beta particle, can release more energy on impact. The only choice which has no mass, however, is the gamma ray. Note that gammas do not have to be high energy—an alpha, beta, or neutron can easily carry more energy, depending on the nuclear process involved.

12. The correct answer is 1. The atom indicated in this question is the element #19 in its ground state (with 19 electrons) or potassium. Table K reveals its electronega-

tivity to be 0.8. Caution must be advised here as 100 is potassium's first ionization energy, not it's electronegativity as this question asks for. The electronegativity of 119 could mistakenly be read as the ionization energy above potassium on Table K, as could the electronegativity 0.9. These two are for sodium.

13. The correct answer is 2. The combination of a metal with a nonmetal usually results in the transfer of electrons to form ions. The bond, then, would be an ionic bond. Network and molecular bonds are, of course, covalent, and the metallic bond is exclusive of the presence of a nonmetal.

14. The correct answer is 4. Our definition of a compound is two or more elements chemically combined. Chemical combination is usually indicated by placing the symbols, and any subscripts needed, next to each other with no spaces. Initially, we note that choice 3 is only one element and so is discarded as an answer. Additionally, *empirical formula* means that, like a fraction can be, the formula for the compound can be reduced to its lowest whole number terms. Choices 1 and 2 can be reduced further and so are not our answers. Choice 4 is reduced as far as it can be reduced in whole number terms and so is the correct answer.

15. The correct answer is 4. The number of moles of any element in a mole of compound can be found by adding up the

number of that element's atoms in the compound. For example, keeping close record of the subscripts in the compound given, we find 9 atoms of hydrogen; 4 in each NH_4, but there are 2 such NH_4 particles which gives 8 hydrogens, and 1 hydrogen in the HPO_4 part, giving a total of 9 moles of hydrogen in 1 mole of the compound.

16. The correct answer is 1. The intricate bonding we find in a network is always covalent. Ionic bonds are relatively simple and dominated by electrostatic forces. Nonpolar bonds would mitigate against any intricacies between particles thus bonded and metallic bonding is more a result of the free movement of excess electrons which also belies any intricate, networklike bonds.

17. The correct answer is 3. In order to name the correct form of iron that we have in the compound presented, we have to see how it bonds. The compound is formed with oxygen that generally has an oxidation number of 2–. If 3 oxygens balance 2 irons, then the iron in this compound must have an oxidation number of 3+ and, therefore, it is the iron (III) oxide name we seek. Choice 2 would be the closest erroneous choice we might make, if we had little knowledge of correct bonding of these two elements.

18. The correct answer is 4. Inspecting the options offered carefully, it will be noted

that all of the choices, except number 4, have the energy added in on the left side. In choices 1, 2, and 3, this means the energy is incorporated into the product which will result in the products having more energy than the reactants. In choice number 4, the energy is on the right side, which means the reactants will produce the products plus 21.8 kcal of energy.

19. The correct answer is 2. Noble gases are in Group 18 on the Periodic Table. They react with no other element under ordinary circumstances. Inspection of that column on the Periodic Table indicates that, of the choices we are given, number 2 is a noble—or inert—gas. Of the other choices, gold, for example rarely combines with other elements, but that is not for the same reason that noble gases do not combine with other elements.

20. The correct answer is 2. Metalloids sit between the metals and the nonmetals on the Periodic Table and have specific properties. Among the choices given, silicon is the best candidate for being a metalloid. Magnesium is a definite metal as is chromium, a little farther along the Periodic Table to the right of magnesium but having definite metallic properties. Argon is an inert gas.

21. The correct answer is 4. Group 15 is a group with nonmetals appearing toward the top of the group; nitrogen would be the most nonmetallic. The furthest from

the top, then, in the group would be the most metallic. The Periodic Table reveals bismuth to be in this position. The next most like a metal would be antimony, the two being used in metal alloys frequently. Choice 4, however, is the most correct answer.

22. The correct answer is 1. Among the choices given, the most reactive will be the one with valence electrons sitting closest to the nucleus. This is fluorine. As we go down the group, we find the valence electrons farther and farther away from the nucleus, in addition to which the presence of larger numbers of inner electrons creates a shielding effect on those valence electrons. Fluorine has no such effect and, so, is the most reactive among the choices given.

23. The correct answer is 3. Alkali metals will have the outer s- and p-orbitals incomplete. Nonmetals will tend to have just the p-orbital incomplete. Transition metals have a combination of those as well as some occupation of d-orbitals. Inspection of the answers reveals that choice 3 is the most likely candidate for this answer. Choice 1 is fluorine, a nonmetal. Choice 2 is magnesium, a metal. Choice 4 is krypton, an inert gas in Group 18. Choice 3 is #27, cobalt, our sought-after transition element.

24. The correct answer is 2. Table P indicates that the largest covalent radius among the choices offered is cesium, at 2.35 Ångstrom units, the atom farthest to the

left and toward the bottom of the table. Cesium rarely shares electrons and strongly prefers to bond ionically, thus its covalent radius is large. The smallest is strontium, farthest to the right and top of the table, of the choices offered.

25. The correct answer is 1. The charge of +3 indicates that the aluminum is going to lose 3 electrons. In that period, the third period, that is an entire principal energy level. These two facts combined are found in choice 1, our correct answer. The other choices have a mix of errors in size and loss/gain of electrons.

26. The correct answer is 3. At STP, 1 mole of any ideal gas will occupy 22.4 L. At STP, a volume of 11.2 L of any ideal gas is one half the volume expected for 1 mole of that gas. This would, then, represent 0.5 moles of the gas, which is choice 3.

27. The correct answer is 4. The gram molecular mass will be found by adding up the masses as found on the Periodic Table for the correct number of atoms represented in the formula and assigning that number to grams of mass. In the molecule in question, we have 3 carbons for a mass of 36 g; 8 hydrogens (5 from the CH_5 and 3 from inside the parentheses) totaling another 8 g; 3 oxygens from inside the parentheses gives an additional 48 g. In all we have a total of 92 AMUs for the weight of a molecule which gives us a gram molecular mass of 92 g.

28. The correct answer is 4. The reaction indicates 2 moles of $KClO_3(s)$ are consumed to produce 3 moles of $O_2(g)$ on the right side of the equation. In order to produce twice that amount of oxygen, we need twice the amount of $KClO_3$. So to produce 6 moles of O_2, we need 4 moles of $KClO_3$.

29. The correct answer is 3. Aqueous solution refers to the fact that we are putting something into water and the water will act the part of a solvent. We put solutes into solvents (*Memory device:* sol-U-te goes into sol-V-ent, i.e., in the alphabet, "U" comes before "V") therefore, if we are putting KCl into water to make an aqueous solution, the entire KCl acts as the solute. Care must be taken to note that the question is not asking for ions that might make one select either choice 1 or 2. In fact, that kind of thinking would really cause one to wrestle between choices 1 and 2 since the two together, and only together, must be the right answer. Therefore, choice 3 can be the only right answer.

30. The correct answer is 2. Reacting 2.5 L of O_2 in this reaction effectively indicates we are cutting the entire reaction in half. If the full 5 L of O_2 produces 4 L of H_2O as indicated in the balanced equation, then only 2 L of H_2O would be produced if we reacted 2.5 L of O_2 completely. Choice 2 is the right answer.

31. The correct answer is 1. Equilibrium as stated here between dissolved and undis-

solved particles in solution means that we are right at the boundary of an equal number of particles crystallized as are being dissolved. This point is known as the point of saturation and we have here a saturated solution. Anything less, no matter how concentrated, would be unsaturated. Anything more than that would be supersaturated.

32. The correct answer is 3. Potential energy and kinetic energy appear in a number of instances in the discussion of energies involved in chemical reactions. However, activation energy, as can easily be seen by the terminology, is the energy needed to "activate" or start a reaction, regardless of the PE or KE. Ionization energy is the energy required to produce ions from atoms or molecules, an altogether different series of events.

33. The correct answer is 2. The activated complex is the reactants elevated to their level of activation, which will be seen to be the peak indicated by B. A indicates the potential energy in the reactants before activation. D indicates the potential energy of the products after the reaction occurs, and C is the difference between A and D that is released in this exothermic reaction.

34. The correct answer is 2. From Table D, we can see that the curve for NH_3 begins with water at 0°C able to dissolve about 90g of NH_3 in 100g of water (0.1 L). Following this curve over to 25°C, we see that now

only 50g of NH_3 dissolves in 100g of water. The difference, then, is about 40 grams between the two and is a decrease in solubility, not an increase.

35. The correct answer is 1. A Brønsted-Lowry acid is one that donates H^+ ions. Of the choices given, the strongest acid listed on the chart (which runs from strongest at the top to weakest at the bottom) is H_2SO_4, sulfuric acid, with a strength listed merely as "large." HPO_4^{2-} is the lowest on the chart, almost at the very bottom.

36. The correct answer is 4. An Arrhenius base is defined as an OH^- donor (unlike a Brønsted-Lowery base, which is a H^+ acceptor). Bases dissolved in water, then, will produce OH^- ions as the negative ion. Not all bases will have HCO^{3-} or HSO_4^- ions, and a hydride ion is the hydrogen part of a binary compound.

37. The correct answer is 1. According to Table L, HI is indicated to dissociate with a "very large" K_a. In fact, it is on the top of the list. The next closest is H_3PO_4 at a, no doubt, significantly lower K_a of almost 1×10^{-2}. HNO_2 has an even lower K_a with H_2S almost 7 orders of magnitude farther down the list. HI, then, would produce the most ions with which to conduct electricity.

38. The correct answer is 4. The equation $M_a \times V_a = M_b \times V_b$ gives us the means for answering this question where M = molarity and V = volume and "a" and "b" stand

for acid and base, respectively. Placing the values in the equation, we get the result of $M_a = 50.0$ mL $\times 0.50$ M/100 mL. The answer is a molarity of 0.25 M for the acid HNO_3.

39. The correct answer is 2. Brønsted-Lowry acids donate H^+ in chemical reactions. HI donates its H^+ to H_2O, so HI is the Brønsted-Lowry acid and H_2O must be the Brønsted-Lowry base.

40. The correct answer is 2. The molarity of the solution allows us to find the negative log of the H^+ concentration, which is the pH. Changing 0.01 to scientific notation gives us 10^{-2} for the concentration of H^+. The negative log of 10^{-2} is +2 which is then the pH. Choices 3 and 4 indicate far smaller concentrations than we are given here, and 1 misses the concentration by a decimal place.

41. The correct answer is 4. Brønsted-Lowry acid is defined as one that donates a H^+. As we look at Table L, the species least likely to donate a H^+ is NH_2^- (NH_3 donated an H^+ to become NH_2^-). Compared to NH_2^-, all the other choices have a fairly large Ka in aqueous solution. NH_2^-, then, prefers to accept H^+ rather than receive it. In other words, the last line of the table with NH_2^- rarely proceeds to the right.

42. The correct answer is 3. The voltaic or galvanic cell pictured here has all the elements in place to work except an internal

means by which the ions (and therefore electrons that make it work) can migrate. In order to achieve this end, a salt bridge must be placed between the two solutions. This will allow ions to migrate completing the flow of electrons.

43. The correct answer is 3. Although we separate the reactions in a chemical cell into constituent half-reactions, namely oxidation and reduction, the cell will not work unless they both occur simultaneously. In fact the two reactions, wherever they occur, must work simultaneously. Choice 3 is the only correct answer.

44. The correct answer is 4. Oxidation is the loss of electrons that provides a free electron with which to reduce another species in the reaction. The loss of this electron will change an oxidation number to make it positive or as is the case here, more positive. Choices 1 through 3 all make the situation more negative. Only choice 4 represents loss of an electron.

45. The correct answer is 4. Reduction is the accepting of electrons so we will be looking for a neutral to become negative, a positive to become less so, or a negative to become more so. Choice 1 is oxidation where 3 electrons are released from Al. Choices 2 and 3 are not charge balanced, an error. Only choice 4 indicates the receiving of electrons with the oxidation number becoming more negative, Cu going from 2+ to 0.

46. The correct answer is 1. The sum of all atoms' oxidation numbers is the total charge on the molecule, in this case 0 for neutral CO_2.

47. The correct answer is 1. Oxidation is the loss of electrons and the oxidizing agent is the one that receives these "lost" electrons. This means the oxidizing agent is the one reduced. In this reaction, Sn appears to lose 2 electrons, meaning the iron is the oxidizing agent in this reaction. The equation balances by having 2 Fe(III) receiving the electrons to become 2 Fe(II).

48. The correct answer is 2. C_5H_{12} follows the formula C_nH_{2n+2} where n = the number of carbon atoms. This is found to be true in the class of hydrocarbons known as the alkanes. Since the prefix *penta-* signifies 5 carbons, this compound must be pentane. Choices 3 and 4 have six and seven carbons, respectively.

49. The correct answer is 2. A double bond between carbons in the hydrocarbons indicates the alkenes and follows the formula C_nH_{2n}, where n = the number of carbon atoms. Of the compounds presented here, choice two follows that exact formula and, with the two carbon base, is the alkene known as ethene.

50. The correct answer is 3. Alcohols are the product of both fermentation, the incomplete metabolism of plant tissue rich in glucose, and saponification, wherein fats

or oils are hydrolyzed with hot, aqueous NaOH as in the making of soap. It would be misleading to say that soap was the product of both reactions. Esters and acids are not products of either of the reactions.

51. The correct answer is 4. The property referred to here is, of course, a unique ability of carbon. To be able to do this with the other choices, oxygen would have to bond with four other oxygens (the question says identical atoms), lithium with 4 other lithiums and fluorine with 4 other fluorines. Carbon, as has been noted, is unique.

52. The correct answer is 1. Ethanol is a two-carbon alcohol. Organic compounds known as alcohols contain an OH group. Choice 2 is discarded for the lack of an OH, as is choice 3. Choice 4, while looking like it has an OH, has, in reality the carboxylic acid group signified by the COOH.

53. The correct answer is 3. The trick here is that the system has achieved equilibrium. The addition here of a catalyst will do nothing since the reaction has reached its end point, namely equilibrium. Only the addition of reactants or products will change the reaction until it reaches a new equilibrium.

54. The correct answer is 3. If the samples are at the same temperature, the law of Kinetic Molecular Motion for gases says that the average kinetic energy of their particles is the same. We do not know the phase that the copper and iron names are in (solid, liquid or gas), but this is not needed—for solids, and liquids, temperature is a measure of the average internal energy just as for gases and their kinetic energies. The same temperature must mean that the two samples contain the same average energy per atom.

55. The correct answer is 1. The normal position of an electron in hydrogen (which possesses only one electron normally) is in the first principal energy level. If it is falling back to that level from the second level, that means it absorbed energy to get up to the second level and is then going to release energy in falling back. If the electron is in the second level, the atom absorbed energy, so in the release of that energy as the electron falls back, the atom will then have less energy.

56. The correct answer is 3. The key to the wording in this question is the indication that the temperature remains constant. K_{eg} depends on only temperature, so if the temperature remains constant, K_{eg} does not change.

57. The correct answer is 3. A calorie is defined as the amount of energy needed to raise the temperature of one gram of water by one degree Celsius. In this problem, the amount of heat absorbed is calculated by taking the mass of the water into consideration and the total change in temperature.

Multiplying 65g times a temperature change of 15°C gives us 975 total calories absorbed by the water sample.

58. The correct answer is 2. A substance would be defined as one particular material having a measurable volume and mass. In the case of this question, fire is more the combustion of a variety of materials and cannot be pinned down to a particular volume or mass. Air is a complex mixture of material as is earth. Water is the one item that is merely one thing, and has a measurable volume and mass.

59. The correct answer is 2. This reaction to the right indicates that, from a set of reactants, we have the formation of products as well as energy being given off. When viewed to the left, the energy is added in with the reactants on the right and is absorbed by the products on the left. Choice 2 satisfies these facts and correctly names the forward reaction as exothermic, since energy is a byproduct of that reaction. In addition, the reaction to the left is endothermic as energy is added in on the reactant side and must be absorbed by the products on the left.

60. The correct answer is 1. At a standard pressure of 1 atmosphere, the vaporization point of water is 100°C. This is the point at which liquid and gaseous water are in equilibrium, that is they exist simultaneously as a mixture. 373°C is misleading, making us think of 100°C as 373 K, but the answer says 373°C. Similarly, choice 2 uses the Fahrenheit number for the boiling point of water but with the °C label.

61. The correct answer is 4. If the temperature is held constant the relationship between volume and pressure in a gas is an inverse one. In this instance, the pressure is increased and we want to know the effect on the volume when the temperature is held at 0°C. The pressure is specifically doubled in this question, so the volume will be cut in half (the inverse of the doubling of the pressure) from 12 L to 6 L, or choice 4.

62. The correct answer is 3. At first, we can discard choices 1 and 4 since they deal with carbon (element symbol C, not Cl as chlorine is). We can make a fairly accurate guess if we note that the result of the mathematical operations that need to be done, with 75 percent of the Cl as Cl-35, will be closer to 35 than 37. This would mean choice 3 is the answer. If we do the math, however, we would say that Cl-35 is 75 percent of the average isotope mass and Cl-37 is 25 percent. Cl-35 would weight the total with 26.25 and Cl-37 would weight it 9.25 for a total of 35.5 indicating that choice 3 is indeed the answer.

63. The correct answer is 1. Particles that emanate from the nucleus of an atom, as those listed do, and that are attracted to a negatively charged electrode must be positive. An alpha particle—choice 1—is the

nucleus of a helium atom that contains 2 protons and 2 neutrons. Thus, this emanation would be positive and attracted to a negative electrode.

64. The correct answer is 3. The numbers given need explanation. The top number, 80 in this example, is the number of nucleons in an atom, specifically the number of protons and neutrons. The bottom number, 35 in this example, is the number of protons, also called the atomic number. The total number of protons and neutrons, then, in Br-35 indicated here, is 80.

65. The correct answer is 2. Argon is in the third row of the Periodic Table. In the ground state, then, it has 2 completely filled principal energy levels (1 and 2) and, since it is also in the inert gases column and is element number 18 it has a partially filled third level (s and p filled, d empty). We place 2 electrons in the first principal energy level, filling it and leaving 16 electrons yet to account for. In the second principal energy level, we place 8 electrons filling it up and leaving 8 electrons yet to be accounted for. The third principal energy level holds the final 8 electrons, but requires 18 to be filled.

66. The correct answer is 4. It would seem that the system would be based on the unit mass element on the Periodic Table, or hydrogen. In fact, scientists agreed on carbon-12 as the standard for measuring atomic mass units (AMU) for a variety of

reasons, not the least being its abundance in living tissue and its covalent nature. This means the mass of every element is compared to or relative to the agreed upon mass of carbon. For example, hydrogen's mass would then be seen as 1/12 that of carbon-12.

67. The correct answer is 4. The list of alkanes given increases by one carbon when we look from choice 1 to choice 4. This increase of C in the constituents causes each increasingly larger molecules to have larger and larger van der Waals forces binding them. This means C_4H_{10} will have the highest melting point ($-138.4°C$) as well as the highest boiling point ($-0.5°C$).

68. The correct answer is 1. When we refer to our chart of electronegativity values, Table K, we see that an iodine (I_2) molecule, with both components being iodine meaning they both have the same electronegativity, has an electronegativity difference of 0. Atoms with differences of less than 0.4 form nonpolar covalent bonds. Atoms with a difference of between 0.4 and 2.1 will form polar covalent bonds and anything greater than an electronegativity difference of 2.1 would have bonds categorized as ionic.

69. The correct answer is 2. Carbon and oxygen have electronegativity differences of approximately 1, which means the bond formed between them is a polar covalent bond. The principal reason would be that

oxygen has more protons than carbon but the same number of principal energy levels. Because the attractive forces acting on the bonding electrons are not equal, the electrons will not be shared equally, thus creating the conditions for polar covalent bonds.

70. The correct answer is 3. When one of the atoms in a polyatomic ion, as is the case here, provides both electrons that form a covalent bond, it is called a coordinate covalent bond. In this case the bond is formed between a hydrogen ion and two unpaired electrons on the nitrogen atom. Once formed, this kind of a bond is indistinguishable from the other covalent bonds in the ammonia cation.

71. The correct answer is 2. We discard choices 3 and 4 immediately as they do not illustrate an aqueous solution; water must be present. Between choices 1 and 2, we must decide on the electrically correct orientation for the particles shown. It is known that the oxygen side of the water molecule is the negative side and the hydrogen side of the water molecule is the positive side. The diagrams correctly show the sodium ions as positively charged, which means only choice 2 will work in illustrating the hydration of sodium in an aqueous solution.

72. The correct answer is 3. The elements listed exist in the fifth row of the Periodic Table and thus share the same number of principal energy levels. Starting with Rb in the left-most position and concluding with Xe in the right-most position, these elements fill those five energy levels to varying degrees until we get to xenon, which has them all filled with the number of electrons that follow the octet rule. Choice 3 is the correct answer.

73. The correct answer is 2. Metals are neither ionic nor covalent as elements alone (as opposed to being in combination with other elements), and so choices 3 and 4 can be ignored. Metals with their free electrons that traverse the network have a high degree of electrical conductivity. In addition, they have a high heat conductivity, again owing to the nature of their network.

74. The correct answer is 4. Hydrogen and oxygen are gases at room temperature, so it doesn't matter whether or not they are nonmetallic. The diversion here is the use of mercury as a choice because it is known that it is a liquid at room temperature, a very shiny liquid, indicating its metallic nature. Bromine is also a liquid at room temperature and is the nonmetal we seek to answer this question.

75. The correct answer is 3. Elements in Group 17 do not normally form sulfates, let alone blue ones, and the elements in Groups 1 and 2 typically will form white or transparent sulfates, as in the case of potassium sulfate and magnesium sulfate,

respectively. A glance at Group 11 reveals the presence of copper whose sulfate has a blue coloration to it.

76. The correct answer is 4. The most active metals are in the lower left section of the Periodic Table. The shielding effect on the elements, as we go down the left side of the Periodic Table increases which makes the loss of outer electrons an extremely easy event to occur, and, in fact, does. In addition, further proof is in their electronegativities, the lowest on the Table.

77. The correct answer is 1. If the amount of energy needed to melt 20 grams of a substance is 820 calories, then the heat of fusion for this substance must be 820cals/20g or 41 calories/g of mass. This is not only the energy absorbed at melting point, but is also the energy released upon freezing, which is still called the heat of fusion.

78. The correct answer is 4. Graham's Law of Effusion—the movement of a gas through a small opening—applies also to diffusion. The lighter the particle, the farther it will move over a measured period of time under the random influence of Brownian motion ambient temperature. The slowest particle in this case, then, would be the gas with the largest mass, which is radon.

79. The correct answer is 2. The presence of nonvolatile dissolved substances in water means that we are talking about colligative properties, namely the change in the boiling point and the freezing point. To be more specific, the presence of just such a solute raises the boiling point and lowers the freezing point; choice 2.

80. The correct answer is 3. In studying the gas laws, the three components in this question—namely volume, temperature, and pressure—all interact. Volume and temperature are in a direct relationship with each other, meaning that whatever one does the other does too. If we want to know under what conditions the volume of a gas decreases, we would look for a temperature decline. Choice 1 and 3 are possible, but only one is right, namely choice 3. The reason this answer works is that it has the other correct component, namely that pressure increases. Volume and pressure are in an inverse relationship, an increase in pressure bringing about a decrease in the volume of the gas in question. Considering all these together, choice 3 is the correct answer.

81. The correct answer is 4. The empirical formula is the mathematical ratio relationship between constituents in the lowest possible form. For example, water could have a formula of $H_{18}O_9$, but we reduce it to H_2O. Knowing the percent composition as we do in this question, we can use the molar mass to complete the rate of S to O. Thus, 100g of a compound would contain 57g of S atoms or 1.8 moles. The remaining 43g is oxygen atoms or 2.7 moles. The

ratio 1.8 : 2.7 is, in whole numbers 2:3, corresponding to answer 4.

82. The correct answer is 1. Table G indicates the free energy of formation for the four compounds listed as possible answers. Choices 2, 3, and 4 all have a positive free energy of formation. The formation of these substances tends toward order and/or a higher energy state. Choice 1, CO, has the only negative free energy of formation, indicating that its formation should be spontaneous.

83. The correct answer is 4. What we are looking for is a choice that drives the reaction to the left, which will favor the formation of $Cl_2(g)$. Adding $HCl(g)$ to the reaction will drive it to the left since Le Châtelier's principles hold that one of the factors affecting the rate of a reaction will be increasing the concentration of particles. Adding $HCl(g)$ will drive the reaction to the left, thus increasing the $Cl_2(g)$.

84. The correct answer is 3. $AgNO_3$ added to the reaction in aqueous solution will add Ag^+ ions and NO_3^- ions. This will make more Ag^+ ions available to bind with I^- since the reaction driven to the left favors the formation of AgI if there are available Ag^+ ions to do this.

85. The correct answer is 3. Table M presents the solubility constants of the four substances at 1 atm and 25°C. Because each compound in the four choices will break up into just one cation and one anion, we are able to simply compare K_{sp} values and the largest K_{sp} will identify the most soluble compound. $CaSO_4$ has the largest K_{sp} of the four choices listed, being a full 4 orders of magnitude larger than the next closest compound. Careful use of the chart indicates an order based, not on K_{sp}, but on the alphabet.

86. The correct answer is 3. This reaction produces an additional 135.4 kcal of energy when it forms CO_2 from the reaction of CO and O_2. The change in energy in the reactants is a release of energy which shows up as a positive on the right, or product side. This would be a negative on the reactant side. The loss of energy to the system for each mole of CO_2 formed would be half of the energy indicated—the reaction that forms 2 moles of CO_2 releases 135.4 kcal, we want one mole of CO_2 formed—which would be—67.7 kcal.

87. The correct answer is 3. Whatever the Br^- is, it will be weak in being it. The "it" must be a weak conjugate base. Conjugate acids are defined as the particle formed when a base gains a H^+. Br^- gains the H^+ as the reaction proceeds to the left, which makes it the base. The particle formed from this union is an acid, so that acid, HBr is the conjugate acid of Br^-.

88. The correct answer is 4. Red litmus turns blue in the presence of a base. Choices 1 and 2 are clearly acids and will not do the trick.

Choice 3 looks like a base, but upon closer inspection, we see it is an organic alcohol, which is not basic. Choice 4 is the strong base that turns red litmus paper to blue.

89. The correct answer is 1. The pH of a substance is defined as the negative logarithm of the H^+ concentration. In this question, a substance with pH of 8 would have a concentration of 1×10^{-8} or choice 3. The concentration of OH^- is determined from $[H^+]$ and the ionization constant for water, $K_w = 10^{-14}$ moles^2/liter^2 (at 25°C) = $[H^+][HO^-]$. Thus, $[OH^-] = 10^{-14}/10^{-8} = 1 \times 10^{-6}$ moles/liter.

90. The correct answer is 1. The substance NH3(g) in this reaction appears to have accepted an H^+ ion. According to the Brønsted-Lowry definition of a base is that it is an H^+ acceptor, which $NH_3(g)$ qualifies for in this reaction. It is a base due to its acceptance of an H^+.

91. The correct answer is 3. A substance that can act as both an acid and a base is said to be amphoteric. Looking at Table L, we see one-third of the way down the chart that $H_2PO_4^-$ can accept an H^+ to become H_3PO_4. Further down, we see $H_2PO_4^-$ donating an H^+ to become HPO_4^{2-}. Brønsted-Lowry theory says this is both an acid and a base and such species were later defined as amphoteric.

92. The correct answer is 3. If we look at Table N, we look for the value of E^o equivalent to zero. This indicates neither a net gain nor a net loss of energy and this is the standard to which we compare all others. The reaction given in choice 3 satisfies these conditions and is the arbitrary standard used in measuring electrode potentials.

93. The correct answer is 3. The reduction half-reaction in the full reaction given is $2Ag^+(aq) \rightarrow 2Ag(s)$. Reduction is the gain of electrons, which this half-reaction indicates is happening. Looking at Table N for the E^o of the reaction, we see a net potential of +0.80 volts as the answer for silver ions gaining an electron to become elemental silver.

94. The correct answer is 2. Separating this reaction into its half-reactions and then adding the two figures is the way to approach this problem. The first half reaction we will choose will be the oxidation of Ni which is found in reverse on Table N as $Ni^{2+} \rightarrow Ni(s)$. The electrode potential for this reaction, a reduction, is –0.26, so we take the opposite, or +0.26. Now looking at the oxidation half-reaction, we get an electrode potential of +0.77 for $Fe^{3+} + e^-$ $\rightarrow Fe^{2+}$. Adding the two together, we get a net potential of +1.03 V.

95. The correct answer is 1. We must discard choices 3 and 4 outright because the half-reactions cannot occur separately without the other. For the purposes of analyzing a system, we may conceptually separate them, but to actually do so is not possible. Choice 2 tries to mislead by using the standard cell potential E^0, a special case which does not apply to most cell systems. Given the definition of an electrochemical

cell, it operates when there is a balance between the redox reactions and approaches equilibrium over time.

96. The correct answer is 4. When the switch is closed, the spoon will gain mass by attracting Ni^{2+} out of solution at the negative electrode. This will create a need for electrons so that the system will remain at equilibrium between the two reactions. This means that $Ni(s)$ will lose electrons, becoming oxidized and completing the system circuit.

97. The correct answer is 3. Alcohols contain a group with a hydrogen atom and an oxygen atom that is called a hydroxyl and looks like this: OH. It looks like all of the molecules pictured have at least one, but we are looking for the molecule with only one. Choice 1, upon closer inspection, has a COOH group, not the desired OH group. Choices 2 and 4 each have more than one OH group and, looking closely at choice 3, we see that it does, indeed, have only one OH, making it the sought-after monohydroxy alcohol.

98. The correct answer is 4. Organic acids have the group COOH attached to their basic (or R) group. Choice 4 is the only one that qualifies for this definition.

99. The correct answer is 4. Condensation occurs when, for example, water is removed from the atmosphere. We see it on glasses of iced drinks in humid weather. Therefore, polymerization (the building of a larger molecule from smaller, monomer, units) that involves condensation will occur with the removal of a water molecule. We see it in the formation of such compounds as carbohydrates (a disaccharide from two monosaccharides) or proteins (two amino acids joining to form a peptide bond).

100. The correct answer is 1. We are looking for a compound that ionizes and does so weakly, i.e., poorly dissociates. Acetic acid has a K_a of 10^{-4} indicating a poor tendency to ionize. The other choices, in fact, do not ionize, and therefore are actually nonelectrolytes.

101. The correct answer is 3. The hydrocarbons known as -*ynes* have triple bonds between carbons somewhere in the molecule. This means that the carbons share 6 electrons, 2 shared electrons in each bond. The question asks for pairs of electrons shared, which, of course, would be 3 pairs for 6 electrons.

102. The correct answer is 3. All four of the choices can be used to isolate or separate materials, only one by the method asked for in the question: by boiling point. When we distill a mixture, we heat it to a vapor, then cool the vapor and allow it to collect. Since each substance has a discreet boiling point, as the temperature holds steady, one of the components of the mixture must be vaporizing. Once this component is collected to completion, the

temperature will rise until the next vapor-ization point is reached, and so on. This is called fractional distillation.

103. The correct answer is 4. As soon as oxygen is indicated, we know that the donation of electrons to the oxygen is possible since it prefers an oxidation number of 2–. While oxygen is receiving electrons (acting as an oxidizing agent while itself being reduced), some other substance must be donating the electrons and, most likely, forming the oxide of that metal when it combines with the reduced oxygen. This clearly is a redox reaction where both occur simultaneously.

104. The correct answer is 2. The burning of sulfide ores, in the presence of O_2, always produces SO_2 and reduces iron to the solid form (in this case). The purpose is to take the S from the sulfide ore and produce the solid form of the ore in question as the free element for use as a much stronger substance than the sulfide form.

105. The correct answer is 4. Since we have all gases in this reaction, we can apply Le Châtelier's principle that dictates a change in a reaction that involves gases if we change the concentration of the reactants and the pressure. An increase in pressure causes a change in the equilibrium to the side with fewer moles of gas, in this case, favoring the formation of NH_3. Addition of N_2 to the reaction would also favor a shift to the right, thus forming more NH_3. Choice 4 is the correct answer.

106. The correct answer is 1. (There is a mis-print in the Regents Exam. The correct nickel species on the right hand side should be $2Ni(OH)_2$. The equation shown in the exam is unbalanced. However, given the right equation, the correct answer would be 1.) As we look at the reaction, we note that Cd is oxidized upon discharge of the battery. Any substance that is oxidized (donates electrons) is the agent for the reduction of some other sub-stance. Cd is the reducing agent.

107. The correct answer is 2. Choices 1, 3, and 4 all involve one substance on the left with no indication of another material or energy. These, then, must be natural transformations that occur on their own, just as we see them. The reaction in choice 2 takes two substances that, under normal circumstances, do not combine—a check on the energy involved would show this—and so must be the artificial transforma-tion.

108. The correct answer is 2. When Th-234 decays to Pa-234, there appears to be a gain of a proton as the atomic number of Pa is one more than that of Th. No outside addi-tion is given, so the process must be inter-nal to the reaction. In fact, in beta decay, an atom loses an electron from an excited neutron, changing it into a proton as the electron escapes the atom. Particle X must be an electron with negligible mass and a charge of –1. There is no change in mass number from Th to Pa confirming this.

109. The correct answer is 4. Plutonium 239 is the isotope used as a fissionable fuel in a nuclear reactor. The other choices either do not undergo fission or decay with a loss of less than an efficient (economical) amount of energy compared to Pu-239.

110. The correct answer is 1. An electric field will have a magnetic field associated with it as well as a positive and a negative direction of the field. A charged particle, then, will be affected by the field and a proton is the only particle on the list that satisfies this condition. A helium nucleus (an alpha particle) would also be affected, but we are given a helium atom. The other choices are, likewise, neutral.

111. The correct answer is 4. Sodium, with a melting point of 97.81°C but a boiling point of 882.9°C, is an ideal substance to absorb significant amounts of energy before it boils. Choice 4 is the answer.

112. The correct answer is 1. If we are titrating an acid with phenolphthalein in it, the starting solution will be clear. Phenolphthalein turns pink in the presence of a base and NaOH is a base. As the solution nears the endpoint (equilibrium with respect to the neutralization of the acid) the solution will turn pink with the next drop of NaOH.

113. The correct answer is 2. The laboratory glassware shown is an Erlenmeyer flask with its characteristic triangular shape allowing for the mixture of substances with a very small exit point (unlike beakers).

114. The correct answer is 2. Taking the difference between the accepted value and the experimental value, dividing this figure by the accepted value and multiplying by 100 gives us the percent difference between the two values, which in this case is 3.66 percent.

115. The correct answer is 3. Using Table D, the salt that matches the data most closely at the temperature indicated is potassium chlorate. The figures indicated here are tested in 10g of water while the chart is constructed from data in 100g of water dictating that we multiply the student's data by 10 in order to be able to locate them on the chart as $KClO_3$.

116. The correct answer is 1. In choices 3 and 4 the zeroes are holding places and are deemed not significant. In choices 1 and 2 the zeroes are indicated as part of the measurement as they involve places to the right of the decimal. Choice 2, then, has four significant figures, and choice 1 has the sought after number of 3 significant figures.

Subject Index

Acids, 107–109
    Arrhenius definition, 107
    Brønsted-Lowry, 107
    equilibrium constant K_a, 109
Activation energy, 97
Alpha decay, 62
Anode, 117
Atom, 57–62
Atomic
    mass, 59
    mass number, 58–59
    number, 58
    orbital, 60–61
    radii, 80–81
Aufbau principle, 61
Avogadro's Hypothesis, 51

Bases, 107-109
    Arrhenius definition, 108
    Brønsted-Lowry, 108
Beta decay, 62
Bohr model of atom, 60
Boiling point, 51
    normal, 51
Boyle's Law, 50
Bunsen Burner, 140

Calorimetry, 92
Cathode, 117
Charles' Law, 50–51
Chemical
    bonds, 70–72
        covalent bonds, 70–71
        hydrogen bonds, 72
        ionic bonds, 70
        energy, 69–70

equations, 74
    formulae, 72–73
Chemistry, definition, 47
Colligative properties, 91–92
Compound, 48
Conjugate acid-base pair, 109

Dalton's Law, 51
Dilution, rules, 142

Electrochemical cells
    Daniell, 118
    electrolytic, 117
    galvanic/voltaic, 117
    half-cell, 116
Electrolyte, 107
Electron, 58–62
    configurations, 61
    valence, 61
Electronegativity, 70
Element, 47–48
Energy, 48–49,101
    activation, 97
    chemical, 69–70
    nuclear, 133–134
Entropy, 101
Equilibrium, 99
    chemical, 99–100
    constant, 100–101,109
    phase, 99
    solution, 99

Filter paper, 142
Fission, 133–134
Funnel, 142
Fusion, 134

Gamma decay, 63
Gibb's free energy, 101
Graham's Law, 92
Gram atomic mass, 89
Gram molecular mass, 89
Groups, 80–82

Half-life, 63
Half-reactions, 116
Handling chemicals, 143–144
Heat
    of fusion, 50, 94
    of reaction, 97
    of vaporization, 51, 92
Hund's rule, 61
Hydrocarbons, 124–125
Hydrogen bonding, 72

Ion, 61
Ionization energy, 62
Isomer (molecular), 123
Isotope, 59

K_a, 109
K_w, 109
Kinetic Molecular Theory of
    gases, 50
Kinetics, 97–99

Le Châtelier's Principle, 99–100

Melting point (normal), 52
Metalloids, 81
Metals, definition, 81
Mixture, 48
Molality, 91

How Did We Do? Grade Us.

Thank you for choosing a Kaplan book. Your comments and suggestions are very useful to us. Please answer the following questions to assist us in our continued development of high-quality resources to meet your needs.

The Kaplan book I read was: _____

My name is: _____

My address is: _____

_____

My e-mail address is: _____

What overall grade would you give this book?　Ⓐ　Ⓑ　Ⓒ　Ⓓ　Ⓕ

How relevant was the information to your goals?　Ⓐ　Ⓑ　Ⓒ　Ⓓ　Ⓕ

How comprehensive was the information in this book?　Ⓐ　Ⓑ　Ⓒ　Ⓓ　Ⓕ

How accurate was the information in this book?　Ⓐ　Ⓑ　Ⓒ　Ⓓ　Ⓕ

How easy was the book to use?　Ⓐ　Ⓑ　Ⓒ　Ⓓ　Ⓕ

How appealing was the book's design?　Ⓐ　Ⓑ　Ⓒ　Ⓓ　Ⓕ

What were the book's strong points? _____

How could this book be improved? _____

Is there anything that we left out that you wanted to know more about?

Would you recommend this book to others?　☐ YES　　　☐ NO

Other comments: _____

_____

_____

Do we have permission to quote you?　☐ YES　　　☐ NO

Thank you for your help. Please tear out this page and mail it to:

Dave Chipps, Managing Editor
Kaplan Educational Centers
888 Seventh Avenue
New York, NY 10106

Or, you can answer these questions online at www.kaplan.com/talkback.

Thanks!

SIXTY · YEARS · OF
KAPLAN
60
BUILDING · FUTURES

About

Educational Centers

Kaplan Educational Centers is one of the nation's leading providers of education and career services. Kaplan is a wholly owned subsidiary of The Washington Post Company.

TEST PREPARATION & ADMISSIONS

Kaplan's nationally recognized test prep courses cover more than 20 standardized tests, including secondary school, college and graduate school entrance exams and foreign language and professional licensing exams. In addition, Kaplan offers private tutoring and comprehensive, one-to-one admissions and application advice for students applying to college and graduate programs. Kaplan also provides information and guidance on the financial aid process. Students can enroll in online test prep courses and admissions consulting services at www.kaptest.com

SCORE! EDUCATIONAL CENTERS

SCORE! after-school learning centers help K-9 students build confidence, academic and goal-setting skills in a motivating, sports-oriented environment. Its cutting-edge, interactive curriculum continually assesses and adapts to each child's academic needs and learning style. Enthusiastic Academic Coaches serve as positive role models, creating a high-energy atmosphere where learning is exciting and fun. *SCORE!* Prep provides in-home, one-on-one tutoring for high school academic subjects and standardized tests. www.eSCORE.com provides customized online educational resources and services for parents and kids ages 0 to 18. eSCORE.com creates a deep, evolving profile for each child based on his or her age, interests and skills. Parents can access personalized information and resources designed to help their children realize their full potential.

KAPLAN LEARNING SERVICES

Kaplan Learning Services provides customized assessment, education and professional development programs to K-12 schools and universities.

KAPLAN INTERNATIONAL PROGRAMS

Kaplan services international students and professionals in the U.S. through a series of intensive English language and test preparation programs. These programs are offered campus-based centers across the USA. Kaplan offers specialized services including housing, placement at top American universities, fellowship management, academic monitoring and reporting, and financial administration.

KAPLAN PUBLISHING

Kaplan Publishing produces books and software. Kaplan Books, a joint imprint with Simon & Schuster, publishes titles in test preparation, admissions, education, career development and life skills; Kaplan and Newsweek jointly publish guides on getting into college, finding the right career, and helping your child succeed in school. Through an alliance with Knowledge Adventure, Kaplan publishes educational software for the K-12 retail and school markets.

KAPLAN PROFESSIONAL

Kaplan Professional provides assessment, training, and certification services for corporate clients and individuals seeking to advance their careers. Member units include Dearborn, a leading supplier of licensing training and continuing education for securities, real estate, and insurance professionals; Perfect Access/CRN, which delivers software education and consultation for law firms and businesses; and Kaplan Professional Call Center Services, a total provider of services for the call center industry.

DISTANCE LEARNING DIVISION

Kaplan's distance learning programs include Concord School of Law, the nation's first online law school; and Kaplan College, a leading provider of degree and certificate programs in criminal justice and paralegal studies.

COMMUNITY OUTREACH

Kaplan provides educational career resources to thousands of financially disadvantaged students annually, working closely with educational institutions, not-for-profit groups, government agencies and other grass roots organizations on a variety of national and local support programs. Kaplan enriches local communities by employing high school, college and graduate students, creating valuable work experiences for vast numbers of young people each year.

BRASSRING

BrassRing Inc., headquartered in New York and San Mateo, CA, is the first network that combines recruiting, career development and hiring management services to serve employers and employees at every step. Through its units BrassRing.com and HireSystems, BrassRing provides an array of on- and off-line resources that help employers simplify and accelerate the hiring process, and help individuals to build skills and find a better job. Kaplan is BrassRing's majority shareholder.

KAPLAN®

Want more information about our services, products, or the nearest Kaplan center?

1 **Call our nationwide toll-free numbers:**

1-800-KAP-TEST for information on our courses, private tutoring and admissions consulting
1-800-KAP-ITEM for information on our books and software
1-888-KAP-LOAN * for information on student loans

2 **Connect with us in cyberspace:**

On AOL, keyword: "Kaplan"
On the World Wide Web, go to:
www.kaplan.com
www.kaptest.com
www.eSCORE.com
www.dearborn.com
www.BrassRing.com
www.concord.kaplan.edu
www.kaplancollege.com
Via e-mail: info@kaplan.com

3 **Write to:**

Kaplan Educational Centers
888 Seventh Avenue
New York, NY 10106